The Birth of the
Japanese Labor Movement

Takano Fusatarō. *(Courtesy of Iwanami Shoten)*

The Birth of the Japanese Labor Movement

TAKANO FUSATARŌ AND THE RŌDŌ KUMIAI KISEIKAI

Stephen E. Marsland

University of Hawaii Press • Honolulu

94 93 92 91 90 89   5 4 3 2 1

Library of Congress Cataloging-in-Publication Data

Marsland, Stephen E., 1955–
 The birth of the Japanese labor movement : Takano Fusatarō and the
Rōdō Kumiai Kiseikai / Stephen E. Marsland.
  p. cm.
 Bibliography: p.
 Includes index.
 ISBN 0-8248-1167-4
 1. Trade-unions—Japan—History. 2. Rōdō Kumiai Kiseikai—
History. 3. Takano, Fusatarō, 1868–1904. 4. Trade-unions—Japan—
Officials and employees—Biography. I. Title.
HD6832.M338 1989   88–21622
331.88'0952—dc19   CIP

CONTENTS

PREFACE

This work has two purposes. The first is to chronicle the birth of the Japanese labor movement, which until now has received only a few scant pages in other works. The second is to document early union structures, constitutions, and ideology for those who wish to compare the early Japanese labor movement to that of other countries. Many books that deal only briefly with this period contain errors and inconsistencies, or omit notes to explain sources. Access to *Labor World,* the labor newspaper of the period, and other documents recently compiled by the Tokyo University Committee on Labor Movement Documents enabled me to resolve many of these problems. I am deeply indebted to this committee, whose careful research made this book possible.

Throughout the book I have given Japanese family names first, which seems most natural to me. I have used the Hepburn system at the publisher's recommendation even though I prefer the system developed by Eleanor Harz Jorden, which I feel more closely parallels how the Japanese write in *hiragana.*

Labor World had both English and Japanese sections in each issue. A typical issue was ten pages, nine in Japanese and one in English. From the perspective of an English reader, the Japanese title, *Rōdō Sekai,* appeared on the last page. The English title, *Labor World,* appeared on the first page. Issues were numbered in Japanese sequentially from one to one hundred. The English title page carried a numbering system of volumes and numbers. Thus the issue numbered 67 in Japanese was volume three, number one in English. Pagination started from the Japanese title page, except that the English title page was unnumbered.

To avoid confusion, I have used the English title, *Labor World,* but followed the Japanese numbering system. Thus the English title page in a ten-page issue would be page ten. Quotations are from the English section except where I have indicated "my translation."

I owe a great deal to many individuals who helped in the creation of this work. I began work on this manuscript during my junior year abroad at Keio University while a student at the New York State School of Industrial and Labor Relations at Cornell University. Professors at both schools, as well as scholars and staff at the Japan Institute of Labour to which I was attached that year, guided and assisted my studies. Professor Emeritus Alice Cook directed my research from Cornell, while in Japan Professor Komatsu Ryūji of Keio took me under his wing and fueled my interest in the Meiji-period labor movement. I am indebted to Professors John P. Windmuller, Gerd Korman, and Walter Galenson at Cornell, who fostered my love of history, economics, and comparative industrial relations. In Japan Professors Sumiya Mikio, Ōkōchi Kazuo, Iida Kanae, Ōshima Kiyoshi, and Umetani Shun'-ichirō all took time to clarify various aspects of Japanese labor history.

Hirota Osamu and Yamamoto Hisao at the Japan Institute of Labour went out of their way to make me feel at home and introduce me to scholars in the field. Professor Earl Kinmonth was kind enough to evaluate and direct editing of the manuscript while I was at Cornell, and Professors Solomon Levine and Robert Cole offered much encouragement while I was rewriting the manuscript. My parents, Bill and Amy Marsland, did an excellent final editing. The best support a man could ask for was given by my wife Yaeko, who strongly encouraged me to finish rewriting the manuscript.

Early Japanese labor history fascinates me because it represents an early convergence of Japanese and American ideas. The founder of the Japanese labor movement traveled to the United States and studied American unions for years. He became an organizer for the American Federation of Labor and wrote many articles for the *Federationist. Labor World's* English section reflects this close association, as does the fact that many of the original source documents are in English. The blend of Japanese and American labor ideologies created at that time, which continues to have a major impact today, is an example of how international cultural exchange can produce a result that is greater than the sum of the parts. I fervently pray that today's deeper contacts between Japan and the United States will foster creativity, mutual respect, and appreciation between the people of these two great nations, following the example of the labor leaders of the 1890s.

The Birth of the
Japanese Labor Movement

1

THE SETTING

On the morning of January 3, 1868, troops under the command of Saigō Takamori of the Satsuma feudal domain seized the imperial palace gates in Kyoto. A council of those favorable to the coup approved a decree stripping the ruling dictator—the shogun—of his lands and office. In place of the shogun, the Emperor Meiji was returned to power. It was this event that inspired the name the Meiji Restoration and marked the end of the feudal dictatorship that had governed Japan since 1603.

With the change of government came changes in policies. The feudal dictatorship had tried to shut Japan off from intercourse with foreigners and spurned foreign technology. The new government sought out foreign contact and foreign technology in an effort to modernize the country. As Japan became more open to new ideas and modern technology, sweeping changes began to take place.

It was in this rapidly changing and evolving situation that Japan began to develop modern labor organizations and a labor movement. The environment of the early labor movement must be understood to appreciate how and why the unions appeared when and where they did. Many factors—politics and government, the legal framework, the structure of industry and employment, the labor market, labor relations and conditions of labor in the period —influenced work stoppages and labor organizations.

Even as Japan changed rapidly, certain aspects of Japanese culture and tradition remained unchanged. Labor relations, even as they evolved, still relied strongly on hierarchical traditions such as the fictional parent-child relationships established between superior and inferior, senior and junior, or master craftsman and apprentice. These relationships formed the basis of the *oyakata* ("parent") or labor boss system, which dominated heavy industry and mining. Labor relations for the women workers in textiles depended on the "learning to be a woman" tradition *(jochū mina-rai)* whereby poor peasant girls worked in wealthier households as servants for several years and then returned home to be married. As Japan industrialized, these traditional relationships between people within households became the basis for relationships between workers and managers.

Another tradition unchanged by modernization was the strong desire for harmony within the Japanese culture. This made industrial disputes such as strikes and lockouts unacceptable and kept the level of physical violence low when they occurred. It also forced managers and union leaders to resign their positions if their differences caused a strike, much as feudal officials had to resign or commit ritual suicide if their actions caused dishonor or inconvenience to the government or society.

This combination of strong continuing traditions with rapid changes in industry and society caused Japan to evolve a union movement very different from the West's. The first Japanese unionists sought to include all workers at a particular workplace regardless of trade, age, or skill level. This inclusive structure was in direct contrast to the narrowly defined craft-based unions in the West during early industrialization, which, disregarding workplace, sought to group together all those in a single highly-skilled trade excluding apprentices, the unskilled, and coworkers in different trades. The inclusive shop-based structure of the Japanese system became the basis for Japan's company-based unionism of today.

The ideology and strategies of the early labor leaders, as they tried to blend new ideas and traditional values within Japan's authoritarian political structure, created divisions in the labor movement. One ideological faction favored discussion and cooperation with management, avoided strikes and political issues, and tried to win higher wages through improved productivity. These were the moderates who favored harmony between labor and capital. The other major faction favored confrontation with management, thrived on political issues, and embraced the strike weapon. These were the left-wing socialists. This ideological rift between moderates and militant socialists has never healed and continues today.

The early leaders of the Japanese labor movement had studied labor and social problems for years in the United States before returning to Japan to organize the workers. In fact, the top leader of the Japanese labor movement was an official organizer for the American Federation of Labor. The Japanese labor leaders applied their knowledge and experience of American unions to the Japanese situation, and strove to reconcile the ideologies and tactics of successful American unions with the traditions, ideologies, and political situation in Japan. This integration of ideologies and tactics has been a major factor influencing the development of Japan's labor movement throughout its history. The movement's appeal to the workers, its challenge to authoritarian government, its internal rifts, and its eventual growth to the second-largest labor movement in the free world were all decisively influenced by the decisions and compromises made by the first Japanese unionists.

Politics and Government

No factors are more important for an understanding of Japan's early labor movement than the political climate and the structure of government. The period 1868–1900 was characterized by the gradual consolidation of power within the ruling oligarchy and government bureaucracy of Japan. Although there was increasing pressure for the introduction of democratic institutions of government and participation in government from those outside the oligarchy, the oligarchs who had overthrown the feudal government grew stronger and more dominant, making the government bureaucracy more entrenched. The oligarchs ruled through control of the cabinet that advised the emperor, and also indirectly through the bureaucracy. The oligarchs undercut their opposition by gradually defining a Japanese government structure possessing a full set of democratic institutions but in which real power was reserved for the cabinet and government bureaucracy in the name of the emperor.

The key leaders of the forces that overthrew the Tokugawa shogunate in the name of Emperor Meiji in 1868 governed Japan for a generation afterward. Four feudal provinces had led the revolt, and their leaders formed a Council of State to advise the emperor and direct the government bureaucracy. The oligarchs did not always see eye to eye, and over the next thirty years some left the government over key issues, thus forming an opposition group. Opposition leaders initially embraced military rebellion, but when this was crushed focused on the absence of representative institutions in government and the lack of human rights. By forming political parties to mobilize popular support, the opposition leaders hoped to return to power.

Initially, the oligarchs in power sought to maintain their position by suppressing the opposition. As this ceased to be effective due to the growing size of the opposition, they changed tactics, adopting the form but not the substance of democratic government. Finally, when this was insufficient, they chose to coopt the opposition. Throughout this process, however, control of the government and the country gradually came to be focused in the cabinet and the government bureaucracy as the status quo of oligarchic control was maintained.

The first opposition to the central government materialized soon after the Restoration. At that time, Japan's government had made several diplomatic overtures to Korea. When these overtures were rebuffed, several leaders in the oligarchy favored chastising Korea with an expeditionary force. Other oligarchs felt that this was foolhardy when Japan was already involved in disputes with Russia over Karafuto (Sakhalin) and with China over Formosa. Those who favored peace succeeded in convincing the emperor, so the pro-war oligarchs, who were primarily from the feudal provinces of Tosa and Hizen, resigned from the government in 1873. This left the leaders of Satsuma and Chōshū, the remaining provinces prominent in the Meiji Restoration, in control. The key leader of the oligarchy was Ōkubo Toshimichi (of Satsuma) while the key opposition leader was Itagaki Taisuke (of Tosa).[1]

Itagaki immediately set about establishing political groups that clamored for popular rights and representative government. These political groups were made up of samurai who agreed with Itagaki's view that the government was being conducted exclusively at the whim of government officials and was not really in the hands of the emperor and the people. Itagaki strongly favored imperial rule, but he felt that a popularly elected government would be better able to advise the emperor, recommend legislation, and hear grievances because of its intimate contact with the people of Japan.[2]

By 1875 the administration, led by Ōkubo Toshimichi, was in a precarious political and financial situation. The resignation of the Tosa and Hizen oligarchs in 1873 and the subsequent political opposition by Itagaki had weakened the government. Furthermore, another important leader of Chōshū had recently resigned his position in opposition to the expedition to conquer Formosa. The remaining oligarchs were also beset by the financial burden of paying rice stipends to the samurai, a practice continued from the Tokugawa period. Ōkubo decided to concede to some of Itagaki's demands if Itagaki would join the oligarchy. In return, Itagaki was to support the government's new policy of requiring the samurai to exchange their stipends for government bonds by 1876. By requiring this exchange the oligarchs hoped to eliminate the constant financial drain of the stipends.[3]

No sooner had the government enlisted Itagaki's support and required the samurai to exchange stipends for bonds than Itagaki resigned over the lack of real government reform and the failure to chastise Korea for its insolence to Japan. Opposition to the administration grew rapidly, particularly among the samurai. Since the government was printing money to finance the budget deficit, thus causing inflation, the bonds the samurai had just received were being rapidly devalued. In 1877 Saigō Takamori of Satsuma led a military revolt against the oligarchs.[4]

The Japanese Army, composed primarily of commoners, crushed the rebellion, but political opposition led by Itagaki Taisuke remained strong. In 1878 Ōkubo was assassinated by a zealot who favored human rights and representative government. Two years later, 114 delegates of Itagaki's party, representing 87,000 party members throughout Japan, met in Tokyo. The remaining oligarchs, Itō Hirobumi of Chōshū and Ōkuma Shigenobu of Hizen, agreed that the popular rights movement was growing and that the safest way to contain it would be to set up a government with representative bodies, but they disagreed over how to do this. Ōkuma favored representative government on the British model, while Itō favored the more centralized German model. The Ōkuma-Itō rift resulted in Ōkuma's ouster from the oligarchy in 1881. Itō and his supporters announced that a constitution would be established for Japan in 1890. Ōkuma, meanwhile, formed a new antigovernment party.[5]

The following years witnessed major changes in preparation for the constitution. In 1884 five orders of nobility were created so that a House of Peers could be established. In 1885 the Council of State was replaced with a cabinet consisting of ten ministers, with Itō as the first premier. The government throttled opposition parties with a series of edicts and laws, and finally forced them to dissolve pending the promulgation of the constitution. In 1889 the constitution was presented to the people in the name of the emperor.[6]

The constitution, modeled on Germany's, established the first national assembly—the Diet—composed of an appointive House of Peers and an elective House of Representatives. All males over the age of twenty-five who paid taxes of at least fifteen yen per year were eligible to vote (except for priests, teachers of religion, active servicemen, and the insane). Of the Japanese population of 40 million people, about 450,000 were eligible to vote. The largest group of voters were the landowners, followed by the prosperous ex-samurai, who constituted about one-third of the electorate.[7]

The constitution stated that every law required the approval of the majority in each house of the Diet. However, cabinet ministers directly advised the emperor and were not responsible to the Diet, and any law passed by the Diet required the approval of a minister of state. Thus, Diet initiatives could be blocked by the cabinet, but the Diet could also block cabinet initiatives. The emperor's power was well-nigh absolute, and this was the cabinet's advantage over the Diet: if the Diet blocked the cabinet, the intervention of the emperor could assure that cabinet policies would be carried out. Amendments to the constitution could only be proposed by the emperor, but required a two-thirds' majority in each house of the Diet for approval.[8]

The constitution not only upheld the absolute sovereignty of the throne (behind which worked the oligarchy), but also placed the cabinet and the House of Peers effectively outside of any popular control. Popular government through the House of Representatives could serve, at best, as an obstructionist force. Accordingly, the first Diets brought the oligarchs and the leaders of the popular parties into direct confrontation.

Since the oligarchs did not have their own party (because of the government's "transcendental" policy, the cabinet considered itself above and not related to party politics), Itagaki's and Ōkuma's parties commanded a majority in the House of Representatives. They immediately passed a budget reducing government spending by 10 percent, thus attacking the bureaucracy. The government responded initially with physical intimidation of party representatives. When this failed, the government bribed enough representatives to back a compromise budget that reduced the proposed cuts.[9]

When the second Diet cut the budget again the next year, the oligarchs responded by dissolving it and calling another election. Despite government strong-arm tactics that resulted in 25 deaths and 388 injuries, the popular parties won another majority in the lower house of the Diet because the government refused to engage in party politics and run government candidates in the election. In response to government violence, the third Diet launched a drive to impeach the government. The cabinet ignored this and adjourned the House for seven days. Upon its return the third Diet again cut the budget.[10]

The fourth Diet, convened in November 1892, marked the fundamental test between the lower house of the Diet and the cabinet. After cabinet opposition frustrated a move to cut naval appropriations, the popular parties presented the emperor with a memorial bearing 146 signatures supporting the impeachment of the cabinet. The emperor responded by decreasing his household allowance and administrative salaries to fund the naval program, which effectively undercut the impeachment effort by making the liberal parties seem petty and unpatriotic.[11]

The next two Diets had to be dissolved over foreign policy conflicts, and in 1894 the Sino-Japanese War broke out. During the war, the political parties and the Diet remained calm, but unity between the two popular parties, one led by Itagaki, and the other by Ōkuma, began to dissolve under years of government pressure and inducement. After the war, the Itagaki party moved into tacit alliance with the Itō faction among the oligarchs in return for a cabinet post and a role in the government. This saved the Itō cabinet from another impeachment vote in 1895. Itagaki adamantly opposed admitting Ōkuma to the cabinet when Itō tried to form a national unity cabinet encompassing both popular parties. The entire Itō cabinet resigned over this in 1896, to be followed by one dominated by the Matsukata faction of the oligarchy supported by Ōkuma, who received a cabinet post. When Matsukata failed to honor his other commitments to Ōkuma, Ōkuma resigned and brought down the cabinet in November 1897.[12]

While the popular leaders and the oligarchs confronted each other, the government bureaucracy and the military were becoming ever more firmly entrenched. For example, after 1895 the ministers of war and of the navy were selected from the top two ranks of officers on active duty in the respective services. Also, the civil service regulations were tightened to make party infiltration by means of any patronage program difficult. In this way, effective control of government policy and action became increasingly concentrated in the bureaucracy and the military.[13]

The Legal Framework

The entire framework of Japanese law with respect to human rights and popular movements in the period 1868–1890 represented an effort by the ruling oligarchy and bureaucracy to control and restrict any freedoms that could constitute a challenge to their power. The oligarchy severely limited freedom of the press, freedom of assembly, and other rights deemed essential to democracy. After 1890 the newly promulgated constitution preserved oligarchic control and administrative autonomy by making the oligarchs and bureaucracy responsible only to the emperor. The constitution furthermore limited and restricted human rights and representative government to such an extent that there was no effective check to oligarchic power. While the Diet after 1890 was able to overturn the most extreme provisions of government oppression, the structure of censorship and control of the right of assembly continued unabated.

Censorship was a useful tool for the oligarchs, and they lost no time in using it. In 1868, with the restoration of the emperor, secret publications were prohibited and all manuscripts had to be reviewed and approved by the Department of Education prior to publication. In 1869, 1872, and 1875 these regulations were tightened to provide punitive provisions and prohibit publications making false statements, publicizing state secrets, expressing religious views, or opposing existing laws. Thereafter, despite revision by the Diet in 1893 dropping prior review requirements, the censorship ability of the government remained intact through powers to forbid publication and to confiscate forbidden books and original printing blocks.[14]

The oligarchy also tightly censored newspapers after the clamor for popular rights began. Newspaper regulations from 1873 forbade criticism of the government—officials, policies, or laws. The regulations also banned advocation or adoption of foreign laws or religious doctrines. Punitive provisions were included in the law. Censorship was further tightened in 1875 and 1876 with new regulations requiring government approval of all periodicals and making both the editor-in-chief and author personally responsible for any violation of the censorship laws. The libel law was rewritten to make any damage to reputation libelous and subject to prosecution. Under these provisions, over two hundred writers were punished between 1875 and 1880.[15]

The oligarchs issued more decrees in 1883 to quell an increasingly antigovernment press. Under these decrees a security deposit was required to publish a newspaper. In cases where a newspaper was suppressed by the government, all publications by the owner or publisher of the suppressed newspaper would be prohibited by the government. The Home Minister could also prohibit publication and seize a newspaper's printing equipment if he deemed its articles prejudicial to public peace and order.[16]

In 1887 most of the 1883 provisions were removed as the oligarchy prepared to present the constitution to the people. In 1897 the Diet removed the last remaining provision of the 1883 law, which allowed the Home Minister to suppress publications at his whim. However, the basic censorship provisions of the 1873, 1875, and 1876 laws remained in place, allowing the government sufficient latitude to dominate and restrict public debate.[17]

Public assembly was also suppressed by the oligarchy. After the abortive rebellion by Saigō Takamori in 1877, it became clear that military opposition to the government was impossible, and those who opposed the government's policies turned to mass meetings and public speechmaking. To control this, regulations were put in place in 1878 and 1880 requiring prior police approval for public political meetings or speeches. Police attended the meetings to disband them if they inflamed public opinion or disturbed the peace. Similar restrictions applied to meetings of political associations. Military men, teachers, students, apprentices, and police officers were forbidden to attend meetings of a political nature or become members of political associations. Political groups could not advertise meetings, proselytize, communicate with other political groups, or hold open-air meetings.[18]

The government further restricted the right to assembly with new regulations in 1882, 1887, 1890, and 1892. Organizers were required to notify the police prior to forming new political groups, and the government could ban speakers from discussing politics for a year. Political parties could not form branches, and the Home Minister could ban any meeting he felt was prejudicial to public peace. Further, police could expel at their discretion any potential violator of the peace from a 7.5-mile radius of the imperial palace and any imperial resort. This was used to keep Tokyo clear of political activists. No woman, foreigner, or underage male could join a political association. The law provided for up to three years' imprisonment for violation.[19]

The popular parties managed to repeal some of the most oppressive of these police measures after 1892, when government interference in Diet elections reached its peak and began to wane. In 1893 the Diet allowed branch political organizations to be created, and in 1898 the police lost the power to expel people from areas near the imperial palace and resorts. But the key elements of oppression and restriction of the right to assemble remained intact.[20]

The preindustrial character of the Japanese economy was reflected in the tardy regulation of labor. Labor organizations were not legally restricted until 1900, and conditions of labor were not regulated until the provisions of Japan's first factory act, passed in 1911, came into effect in 1916. Several efforts to pass legislation to regulate conditions of labor took place in the period 1868–1900. These were the proposed Statute of Laborers and Apprentices, and the Mines Statute.

The Ministry of Agriculture and Commerce began to collect data in 1881 to prepare laws regulating workers and factories. The ministry finished investigations in 1883, and at the encouragement of a Tokyo commercial and industrial association drew up a draft Statute of Laborers and a draft Statute of Apprentices. The Statute of Laborers proposed limiting child and female labor, establishing a savings system to assist workers, and clarifying the duties of the worker and the rights of employers. The Statute of Apprentices proposed similar clarification of duties, as well as legislation regarding runaway apprentices and a certificate system verifying the completion of apprenticeship. These statutes were modeled on the Elizabethan statutes of the same name.[21]

Several years of discussion between government officials and businessmen followed, and by 1887 the bills had been combined into one statute. Discussion had led to the addition of several new provisions, including arbitration by chambers of commerce in case of industrial disputes between workers and employers, Sundays and holidays off for underage workers, prohibition of child labor under ten years of age except for apprentices, and limitation of labor to six hours a day for those under fourteen and ten hours a day for those under seventeen. This law was never enacted since no consensus could be obtained between the government and business leaders about whether government regulation was appropriate. Many industrialists and bureaucrats favored laissez-faire or viewed the modern enterprise as a reflection of the traditional Japanese family, where the father, or employer, had absolute power.[22]

The Mines Statute was the ministry's next effort at regulating conditions of labor. The Mines Statute was an effort to revise and improve the Japanese Mines Law, whose inadequacies had been made clear by the Takashima mine scandal in 1888. Government officials saw the Mines Statute as a national extension of local ordinances that by 1890 regulated factories to provide safety for residents living near them. Yet the provisions for protection of labor were novel: regulation of miners' safety and mine sanitation, limitation of child and female labor in the mines, restriction of the work day to twelve hours, elimination of the truck system, and workmen's compensation. It was indeed progressive legislation for the times.[23]

The Mines Statute went into effect in 1892, but without its provisions for the protection of labor. Despite attempts by government officials to increase the scope of state control, Japanese capitalists and laissez-faire bureaucrats had sufficient political power to block government intervention in the area of management rights. The industrial work force was still very small, and Japanese society did not yet regard labor conditions and industrial-safety issues as important. It was only natural that Japanese labor organizations and labor conditions should have gone unregulated at this time.[24]

The Structure of Industry and Employment

The structure of Japanese industry in 1868–1900 was determined by the Japanese government's efforts to solve two key problems— one military, and one financial. The military problem was the threat of colonization or conquest by the much stronger Western powers. In order to prevent this, the Japanese government sought to achieve self-sufficiency in weapons manufacture and to build up a rail and telegraph network to allow rapid troop movements and communication without relying on sea transport, which could be blocked by superior foreign naval strength.

The financial problem was a chronic trade deficit and shortage of foreign exchange as Western goods flooded into Japan after 1868. Not only did the Japanese government need to import weapons, technology, and transportation and communications equipment, but the Japanese people preferred the cheap, comfortable cotton cloth of Western manufacture to the coarse, expensive Japanese cotton goods. To pay for these imports, the Japanese government needed to boost exports, and do it quickly.

Japan had agricultural and natural products in high demand in the West—raw silk and tea, as well as reserves of coal, silver, copper, and gold. So the Japanese government adopted a two-pronged trade strategy: first, to increase exports by increasing the value of Japanese raw material exports (raw silk to silk thread, ore to refined precious metals, etc.), and second, to cut imports and dependency on foreign supply by boosting domestic output of key imported goods (cotton and cotton cloth, heavy machinery, weapons, and ships). This "added value to exports plus import substitution" strategy resulted in a large and increasing proportion of Japanese industrial output and employment being focused on four key sectors in the period 1868–1900: silk-reeling, cotton-spinning, heavy industry (shipbuilding, iron and steel, and weapons manufacture), and metals mining and processing. By 1886 over half of

Japanese industrial employment was in these sectors, and by 1897 this proportion had increased to nearly 70 percent (see table 1).

While the Japanese government had long had a monopoly on mining and had started the first cotton mills, by 1880 budget pressures combined with operating losses had convinced the government to sell state-owned enterprises to the private sector. The government sold its cotton mills and many mines and other enterprises from 1880 onward, and worked to subsidize or support private business. In response to these policies industrial output grew rapidly after 1880 while infrastructure was greatly expanded.

Silk-reeling exports grew eightfold between 1875 and 1895, while industry was so thoroughly modernized that machine-reeled silk went from 7 percent to 68 percent of silk exports. Precious metal and coal output increased tenfold from 1874 to 1897. Domestic-built shipping tonnage rose fivefold between 1893 and 1900 alone. Cotton-spinning grew fastest, by nearly one hundred times to one million spindles between 1872 and 1897. Cotton-spinning also modernized rapidly, with 72 percent of spindles being of the high-output ring type in 1892 versus only 8 percent in 1874.[25]

Along with rapid growth and modernization, the scale of firms and individual factories increased dramatically. For example, in

Table 1. Industrial Employment in Japan, 1886–1897 (thousands of persons)

	1886	1888	1892	1897
Silk-Reeling	51 (25%)	76 (33%)	69 (21%)	105 (24%)
Cotton-Spinning	2 (1%)	8 (3%)	29 (9%)	42 (10%)
Heavy Industry	14 (7%)	13 (6%)	16 (5%)	32 (7%)
Metals Mining	35 (17%)	40 (17%)	106 (33%)	120 (28%)
Other[a]	105 (51%)	94 (41%)	104 (32%)	136 (31%)
Total Industry	207 (100%)	231 (100%)	324 (100%)	435 (100%)

Sources: Sumiya Mikio, *Nihon Rōdō Undō Shi* [Japanese labor movement history] (Tokyo, 1966), 9; Hyōdō Tsutomu, *Nihon ni Okeru Rōshi Kankei no Tenkai* [The development of labor relations in Japan] (Tokyo, 1971), 90; Sung Jae Kō, *Stages of Industrial Development in Asia* (London, 1966), 344.

Notes: Figures for 1886 and 1888 are limited to factories of ten or more persons, 1892 figures for companies with 1,000 yen or more in capital. Employment in 1900 differed from 1897 only by the proportion of employment in heavy industry, which grew to 13 percent (59,000 of 435,000) while the other sectors shrank slightly.

[a] Glass-making, paper-making, weaving and cloth manufacture, chemicals, brick-making.

the short time between 1893 and 1896 the scale of silk-reeling firms grew significantly (see table 2). Cotton-spinning mills grew from an average of 2,500 spindles in 1879 to nearly 15,000 spindles in 1897.[26] While heavy industry and mining firms mushroomed, decreasing the average size of these firms slightly between 1886 and 1897, the largest factories and mines continued to dominate both employment and output. In 1886 the top 2 percent of heavy industry factories (two plants, both government-operated military plants) together employed over 5,000 workers, some 40 percent of total employment in heavy industry. In 1900, the top 2 percent of heavy industry factories (nine plants, most government-operated military plants) employed more than 30,000 workers, over half the total employment in heavy industry. Among the top employers remained the Tokyo and Osaka Armaments Works, and the Yokosuka, Kure, and Tsukiji Navy Shipyards.[27]

Through the growth in exports and import substitution, the Japanese government was able to finance its purchases of communication and transportation equipment. The national telegraph network was largely complete by 1885, and railway mileage increased from less than one hundred in 1880 to over two thousand in 1895.[28] This set the stage for high growth in heavy industry after the victory over China in the Sino-Japanese War (1894–1895) yielded a 366-million yen reparation. The war also provided two rationales for continued growth in military spending. First,

Table 2. Scale of Silk-Reeling Factories, 1893 and 1896

	NUMBER OF FACTORIES	
WORKERS EMPLOYED	1893	1896
Over 500	6	36
100–499	138	360
50–99	388	550
10–49	2,671	1,952
Total Factories	3,203	2,900

Sources: 1893 figures from Sumiya Mikio, *Nihon Chin Rōdō Shiron* [Historical treatise on Japanese wage labor] (Tokyo, 1955), 156; 1896 figures from Yokoyama Gennosuke, *Nihon no Kasō Shakai* [Japanese lower-class society] (1898), reprinted in Sumiya Mikio, ed., *Yokoyama Gennosuke Zenshū* [The collected works of Yokoyama Gennosuke] (Tokyo, 1972), 143.

the war had shown the benefits of an expansionist strategy as Japan had gained control of Korea. Second, the Triple Intervention by France, Germany, and Russia, which forced Japan to hand back concessions won on the Chinese mainland, showed Japan was still too weak to resist humiliation at the hands of Western powers. Spurred on by the war's outcome, the Japanese government poured resources into increasing military strength. Heavy industry grew rapidly, particularly after the Shipbuilding Encouragement Acts of 1896 and 1899, and nearly doubled employment between 1897 and 1900.[29]

Japan's increase in industrial output was less significant when measured against the entire economy, however. Industrial workers remained a small proportion of the work force, approximately 1 percent in 1886 and still only 2 percent in 1900. Still, the large scale of factories, the increase in communications and transportation infrastructure, and the introduction of modern equipment, technology, and management had created skilled work forces, open labor markets, and a breakdown of traditional interpersonal relations—which in turn led to the emergence of industrial strife and labor organizations.

The Labor Market

The supply of labor in Japan was dominated by five key factors: rapid population growth, rapid change in the structure of domestic demand for goods, government policies to balance the budget, the growth of the national transportation network, and the continuing strength of feudal customs regarding women. The population of Japan, which grew slowly during the Tokugawa period, began to increase rapidly after the Meiji Restoration in 1868. Japan's population of 35 million in 1872 had grown to 43 million by 1898. Population growth was assisted not only by improved medical treatment and facilities available after 1868, but also by government policies designed to increase the population to provide for a strong military. The government encouraged larger families directly through propaganda and indirectly through conscription. The government extended military service from just the samurai class to all male citizens at age twenty in 1873, which meant that a farmer with only one son would lose his help on the farm during his military service. There was also the possibility of the family dying out if the son were killed in action. In response to conscription, farm families started having more children. Further, the feudal practice of *mabiki* (killing of unwanted babies, primarily girls) gradually died out under disapproval from the government and an increasingly Western-influenced society.[30]

With the lifting of the ban on foreign trade just before the Meiji Restoration, Japan's domestic demand underwent rapid change. Cotton and wool goods from overseas were better-made, cheaper, and more comfortable than the Japanese equivalents. Demand for Western manufactures and machinery increased. The impoverishment of the samurai class led to less demand for traditional luxury wares, such as swords, armor, lacquerware, and Japanese-style paper. Meanwhile, demand for new goods, such as Western-style buildings, paper, suits, and hats, increased rapidly. These changes put severe pressure on traditional craftsmen, whose output and employment were significantly reduced.

Rapid increases in imports quickly led to a chronic trade deficit, while the government's existing obligations to the samurai class resulted in a budget deficit. The government's efforts to reduce the deficits had a dramatic impact on both the agricultural sector, by fostering land tenancy and agricultural poverty, and the samurai class, by wiping out samurai stipends.

During the feudal period in Japan, most farmers owned their land and paid taxes in rice to the government.[31] With the Meiji Restoration, the government put tax revenue on a stable basis by requiring payment of taxes in yen rather than rice, whose value fluctuated from year to year. The government also confiscated common land in the villages and charged farmers for firewood and grazing. In bad years, when a crop was poor or prices low, the burden of taxes and fees remained fixed, and marginal farmers were forced to sell their land to pay their taxes and fees. Unlike much of Western agriculture, where large farms were much more efficient than small ones, Japanese agriculture was essentially a hand gardening activity. Thus, concentration of land holdings did not result in enclosure and the creation of large, efficient farms and reduced agricultural employment as it did in England with the agricultural revolution. Instead, farmers who sold their land stayed on as tenants, paying rent to the landlord.[32]

Under these circumstances it is not surprising that from 1873 to

1900 the number of Japanese farm households stayed constant at about 5.5 million, or that there was little change in the amount of land being farmed by a household. The proportion of households owning land dropped steadily, however, as more and more became tenants. Thus, while only one-third of farm families were tenants at the start of the Meiji period, 40 percent had become tenants by 1893. Tenancy was more widespread in certain farming sectors. For example, fully half of all rice farmers had become tenants by 1893.[33]

Government efforts to reduce the burden of the samurai stipends brought about impoverishment for many of that class. Upon coming to power in 1868, the new government worked to reduce the size of the samurai class. Opponents of the Restoration lost their samurai status, and with the abolition of the feudal territories in 1871 more samurai lost their positions. In all, some 190,000 people had lost their samurai status by 1872.[34]

The government also reduced stipends for the remaining samurai. By 1871 total stipends had been reduced to some 40 percent of the amount paid at the start of the Restoration. Still, the fact that stipends were paid in rice was a severe problem due to price fluctuations, and the stipends represented a continuous drain on the government budget. In 1876 stipends were converted to government bonds. Rapid inflation after 1877 forced samurai to sell their bonds, and many who invested in their own businesses with the proceeds were wiped out by the 1881 depression. Many samurai became beggars, robbers, and rickshaw men, and even prostituted their wives and daughters.[35]

This labor pool of excess farmers, obsolete craftsmen, and impoverished samurai was rendered more and more accessible to industrial employers by the gradual completion of a national transportation and communications system. By 1897 Japan had completed rail, telegraph, and coastal shipping systems linking all major transportation centers quickly and reliably.

Access to the female labor force was determined by the existence of the feudal custom called *jochū minarai* ("learning to be a woman"). This was widely practiced by farm families when there were too many mouths to feed at home. It was simply a custom of sending a daughter to the home of a wealthy merchant, farmer, or landlord for a certain period of time, generally several years. There she would learn etiquette, how to speak correctly, and work at household chores. She might learn a household by-employment such as weaving or silk-reeling. The master of the household would provide her with food, clothing, housing, and a small allowance at festival time. Each summer and winter a small payment was made to the farm family in compensation for the services of the girl. At the end of her service, she was usually given bedding, kitchen utensils, and other items that were to be part of her dowry when she married.

The existence of the custom of *jochū minarai* allowed industrialists easy access to female labor. By adhering to the traditional requirements (small payments to the family, addition to the dowry, some measure of supervision), factory owners could claim that they offered a form of *jochū minarai* where the girl learned a skill —the skills required to manufacture the factory's product. Of course, the work force was thereby restricted to young unskilled girls who could be expected to work for only a few years before marriage. Nevertheless, this custom opened up a potential source of labor that could be recruited over considerable distance, which otherwise would have been kept at home under the watchful eyes of concerned parents. Adherence to this custom meant acceptance on the part of industrialists of the tradition that a married woman's place was in the home, and therefore eliminated access to that source of labor—as well as assuring a high turnover in female factory employment when girls stopped working to get married. Married women had to rely on household by-employment, such as making matches, weaving, teaching, or running a small shop in the front of the home to supplement household income.[36]

The demand for labor in Japan in the Meiji period was strongly influenced by three factors—urbanization, rapid growth of industry, and the nontraditional nature of skills required for industry. Japan in 1868 was overwhelmingly agrarian, with only 10 percent of the population living in urban areas (over 10,000 population). By 1900 nearly 20 percent of Japan's much larger population lived in urban areas.[37] The reason for this was that as agricultural employment became saturated (as evidenced by no increase in agricultural households), the only opportunities to make a living were in the cities and towns. In fact, from 1872 to 1900 agricultural employment was steady at some 15.5 million people, while employment outside the agricultural sector grew from 5.8 million to 8.5 million people. Virtually all this employment was outside the manufacturing industry—in construction, rickshaw pulling, day labor, wholesaling, retailing transportation, government service, and so on.[38]

The Japanese government chose to promote silk-reeling, cotton-spinning, and heavy industry as part of its effort to reduce the trade deficit and become self-sufficient in armaments. Yet these industries were modern rather than traditional, and required new skills that the existing labor force did not have.

The mismatch between the available skills and those required was made worse by the very small industrial base and its rapid growth. Since the base of industry was small, there were few places that could provide training or experience to the work force. The rapid growth of industry served to keep the demand for trained labor much higher than the supply. In cotton-reeling and silk-spinning, the favorable effect of a relatively short training time was countered by the fact that the girls only worked for a few years. In heavy industry, the long training time for skilled workers led to severe shortages. The existence of the national communications and transportation system meant that trained workers could and did quickly change jobs. Many firms found it advantageous to recruit trained workers from other companies rather than to train their own.

Poor working conditions, authoritarian management, and illness exacerbated high turnover. Throughout industry in the late 1890s, those with less than one year of service at their current factory made up between 35 and 50 percent of the work force. Turnover rates in excess of 100 percent were common. In textiles, workers were generally lured away or tricked into leaving, while in heavy industry workers simply left to find a better job.[39]

Labor Relations and Conditions of Labor

Before the Meiji period there were two basic patterns of labor relations. One of these was characteristic of government-operated enterprises, such as the mines and weapons factories, which were administered by samurai. In government-run plants, matters related to the work force were delegated to labor bosses known as *oyakata* or *oyabun* ("parent"). Such *oyakata* controlled and exploited the work force, relying on the power of the samurai to quell any labor unrest. The other pattern of labor relations was characteristic of the family-run firms of merchants, craftsmen, and wealthy farmers (hereinafter called the merchant pattern). In such enterprises the work force was managed like a Japanese family or clan, and in many cases was largely made up of family or clan members. Both of these basic patterns of labor relations relied fundamentally on the concept of *shujū no kankei* ("relations between master and servant"), a philosophy for sustaining the basic unit of Japanese society, the household.

Shujū no kankei maintained that:

1. The basic goal of the household is to continue as a household. The members of the household, while they may be members of a separate or independent family, are not separate from the household. The relationship between a household and its members is for life.
2. Due to the basic goal of continuity, the relations between parent and child take precedence over the relations between husband and wife. Vertical relationships outweigh horizontal relationships.
3. The economic basis of the household is the property of the household. In order to produce the wealth to maintain the household, the household manages this property. To minimize reliance on outsiders, the household produces as much as possible of its own needs.
4. The concept of "the household" has precedence over any individual member. The members exist to preserve the household.[40]

In the Japanese household, it was the obligation of the head of the household to manage the affairs of the household to assure its continuity. In this, his authority was near absolute. It was the responsibility of household members to obey the head of the household. In return, they received sustenance and care. However, the welfare of the individual household members was a secondary concern compared to the continuity of the household. When necessary, individual members were expected to sacrifice their own welfare, even their lives, for the good of the household.

Although these two basic patterns of labor relations both relied on *shujū no kankei,* they had quite different characteristics. At government-run plants the relationship between worker and manager closely resembled the relationship between governing lord and peasant. The manager was responsible for the welfare of the enterprise (realm) and laid out certain proclamations and regulations to which there was no appeal. The manager did as he saw fit and the worker was expected to obey. There was a bureaucracy designed to carry out management's proclamations and regulations, and it also operated to keep order and physically punish those who transgressed. Administrators and workers lived and worked in physically separate locations and did not socialize together. Supervision was left to the labor bosses, or *oyakata,* who handled day-to-day management and training of the work force. A fixed daily wage was common, and workers were expected to provide for their own room and board from this wage, although *oyakata* often provided this to workers they supervised. Working hours were regular, often on a twelve-hour-shift basis.

In the merchant pattern, labor relations were quite different. Rules were informal and enforced by peer pressure or personally by the head of the household, and rarely involved physical punishment. All household members lived, worked, and socialized together. Household elders arranged marriages, attended funerals and festivals, and assisted in times of sickness when household members were involved. Control and supervision of the work force extended to the personal lives of household members outside working hours. There was little distinction between work for the merchant firm and work on the personal affairs of the merchant. Monetary compensation was paid perhaps once a year, with most of the compensation coming in the form of free room and board. Piece rates and forced savings schemes were the norm. Long working hours—up to sixteen and eighteen hours per day in summer or peak seasons and from twelve to fourteen hours per day at other times—were common. The standard method of training was through apprenticeship for boys and the *jochū minarai* system for girls.[41]

With the emergence of large-scale factories in the Meiji period, the two distinct labor relations patterns of the feudal period were gradually integrated and merged, although differences remained from industry to industry. From the samurai pattern came official regulations, physical punishment, daily wages, fixed working hours, responsibility of workers for their own welfare, and physi-

cal separation of workers and managers in their working and private lives. From the merchant pattern came forced savings,
extremely long working hours, supervision of workers' private
lives via dormitory or company housing, use of workers on personal affairs of managers, and training via the apprentice system.
Both patterns reinforced the absolute authority of the manager,
with no recourse or appeal to managerial decisions or rules. The
merging of these two patterns gave the worker the worst of both—
the rigid, uncaring bureaucracy of the samurai pattern along with
the suffocating control and supervision of the merchant pattern.
The worker lost both the relative personal freedom offered by the
samurai pattern and the benevolence inherent in the merchant pattern.[42]

In industries with male work forces and long training requirements—heavy industry and mining—the merging of the two labor
systems left the direct supervision of the work force to the
oyakata. *Oyakata* provided supervision and training, handled pay
and promotion, and did the hiring and firing. In industries with a
female labor force—silk-reeling and cotton-spinning—*oyakata*
had no role. The companies had recruiters, foremen, and dorm
mothers to handle the close supervision called for by the *jochū
minarai* tradition, and training was done on the job.

Cotton-spinning and silk-reeling were two major industries
characterized by the combined samurai-merchant labor relations
pattern. The earliest modern textile enterprises were set up under
the new government after 1868 primarily to provide relief for the
economically distressed samurai class, and to reduce the trade deficit by adding value to Japanese silk exports and reducing imports
of cotton cloth. Virtually all the managers of the first mills were
samurai, and the workers were primarily daughters of samurai.
The early mills were dominated by the samurai style of labor relations, except that since the work was largely mechanized and
training requirements minimal, labor matters were handled directly through rules and a "lead girl" system rather than entrusted to
oyakata. Dorm mothers provided close supervision to girls living
in company dormitories.

Working conditions were fairly good since the government was
trying to support the samurai class rather than make a profit.
Working hours were from dawn to dusk, there was no night shift,
wages were paid regularly, and most workers lived at home and

walked to work. While rules were strict and discipline tight, morale was high since the workers and managers considered themselves to be working patriotically for Japan, as befitted an elite. Pay was good compared to wage rates that later prevailed. The girls worked for several years prior to marriage in order to save a dowry.[43]

As the government sold off the textile mills after 1880 to reduce the budget deficit, private owners with a profit motive came to control the textile industry. The model for the industry was the Osaka Spinning Company, founded by Shibusawa Eiichi in 1883. Founded as a corporation and refusing all forms of government aid, the company set up its first mill on a huge scale—10,500 spindles instead of the 2,000 spindles common in the old government mills. Furthermore, the mill was steam-powered and was directed by a Japanese who had spent time studying management techniques at British cotton-spinning mills. The mill was immediately successful, making profits of nearly 20 percent per year from 1883 to 1889.[44]

Part of the key to this success was Shibusawa's synthesis of the samurai pattern and the merchant pattern in his organization of the mill's work force. From the samurai pattern Shibusawa borrowed the strict authority of management, formal work rules, and the spirit of putting the firm before oneself. From the merchant pattern he borrowed the use of an agricultural work force, low wages, dormitory living, and piece rates. Shibusawa also introduced the night shift, common in Britain, to keep the expensive machinery working twenty-four hours a day. The choice of management personnel similarly reflected the synthesis of samurai and merchant traditions. Shibusawa was born into a wealthy farming family that purchased samurai rank, and Shibusawa himself became a merchant. The other managers included those of samurai, merchant, and landowning background.[45]

The synthesis of these styles of labor management involved some innovation. Since Shibusawa sought numerous low-wage agricultural workers, a system of recruitment in rural areas had to be set up. The farm girls were housed in company dormitories while they worked at the firm. The concept of "household comes first" was appropriated and tied to the goal of making profits, so that although the firm became a household, the well-being of the household was linked solely to investor profit.[46]

As more firms copied the success of the Osaka Spinning Company, competition intensified and firms sought to reduce labor costs. Working hours lengthened to sixteen to eighteen hours per day in silk-reeling, and up to twelve hours in cotton-spinning with alternating day and night shifts each week for each worker. Real wages dropped year by year and moved away from daily wages for the operatives to a piece-rate system. Workers, overwhelmingly young females, earned only twenty sen (a sen is one one-hundredth of a yen) per day, paid monthly. A yen was worth fifty U.S. cents at the time, so wages were equivalent to ten cents a day. Punishments included fines, confiscation of savings, and physical beatings. Sanitation was poor and illness, especially tuberculosis, was rife. Medical care simply did not exist in many factories: sick girls were simply sent home and lost their jobs.[47]

Rapid turnover became an increasing problem as operatives sought better conditions at other plants or simply returned to the farms. Firms tightened security, locking the girls in and chaperoning them on the rare holidays. To replace personnel losses, firms stepped up recruitment efforts and even resorted to kidnapping workers from other factories. The system of incentives and penalties grew more complex and severe. The cost of recruitment, training, and security rose rapidly.[48]

This situation in textiles continued until new concepts of management were tried in the 1920s. The basic dilemma of the textile industrialists was that while they longed for a master-servant relationship with their workers *(shujū no kankei)*, they simultaneously sought the lowest possible wage bill. They failed to realize that the modern factory was not a household and that calling it one was not enough to secure worker loyalty. Until management recognized its human obligations to the workers and created the "social" company that could unite workers and management behind the same goals, workplaces were characterized by high turnover, low productivity, and animosity between labor and management.

Labor relations in heavy industry, while also derived from the samurai and merchant models, were very different from those in textiles because of the important role of the *oyakata*. The dominant factor in labor relations in heavy industry in the period 1868–1900 was the prevalence of "indirect management." Japanese managers in such firms, many of samurai background, exercised no direct supervision over labor and the production process, concerning themselves rather with staff duties, finance, purchasing, and so on. Initially, this was due to extensive training and supervision of the work force by foreign technicians. As the foreign technicians completed their training assignments and were discharged, however, Japanese managers found they did not have the necessary training or experience to manage labor because of the complicated, technical nature of production in heavy industry and the extensive reliance on workers with a range of skills rather than specialized workers.[49]

The reason for this reliance on the multiple-skills worker was the relatively low level of the imported Western technology. Processes had yet to be standardized, techniques simplified, and jobs broken down. Japanese industry, even government-owned industries, did not have the resources to systematically import the latest Western technology. Few workplaces, the limited availability of raw materials and the broad range of demand in Japan meant that production was by small batches. In this environment, an adaptable worker with a low skills level in a variety of jobs was more useful than a specialist.

Supervising crews of such multiple-skills workers was beyond management's capability, and skilled workers trained by the government to be foremen found they could get higher paying technical or management jobs instead. For labor training and supervision, heavy industry relied on the *oyakata*. They got their instructions from managers and directed and supervised the work crews in the completion of tasks. The *oyakata* system originated in the traditional labor relations of the craftsmen (the merchant pattern).[50]

There were three main types of *oyakata* in heavy industry. Initially, the most common was the "apprentice" *oyakata* who instructed his apprentices at work and fed and clothed them in his home, where they lived during their apprenticeship. Although the apprentice signed an employment contract with the firm, wages were given to the *oyakata*, who then doled out a small allowance to each apprentice. This continued for three, five, or seven years until the apprentice became an independent worker.[51]

By the mid-1890s this type of *oyakata* had begun to disappear. The heavy demand for skilled labor caused apprentices to flee their masters before the end of the apprenticeship period since they could get full wages elsewhere. The "subcontracting" *oyakata* then became more common.

The subcontracting system at that time allowed a foreman to subcontract work from the firm, direct laborers in its completion, and divide up the payment for the subcontracting work between himself and the workers. The workers the foreman directed were all employed by the firm, and they customarily received at least their normal daily wage while doing subcontract work. The *oyakata* had discretion over the division of the profits, that is, the difference between the subcontract price and the total wage bill. Usually, he and his righthand men got over half the profits.[52]

The third type of *oyakata*, the "foreman" type, became prevalent by the late 1890s. The foreman *oyakata* had no apprentices and made no wage payments to his men, but still held decision-making power over employment, promotion, pay raises, entering pay levels, and incentives and punishments. The gradual shift from the apprentice type of *oyakata* to the foreman type was as a result of management efforts to curb *oyakata* autonomy and favoritism and exert greater control over the workplace and work force. This was reinforced by the gradual standardization of jobs and expansion of demand, which allowed longer production runs and a more specialized work force.[53]

For example, at the Yokosuka Navy Shipyards before 1893 there had been only a factory manager at each plant and several direct subordinates *(hanchō)*, each of whom supervised several *oyakata* and their workers. In 1893, in each division of ship-building and machine-making there appeared a "numbers man" whose job was to keep track of the comings and goings of the men and regulate all aspects of daily wage payments. In 1898 six new white-collar management posts were created at each division, ranging from a works manager who supervised, budgeted, and inspected all repair and construction work, to a general-affairs manager who handled everything connected with wages and promotion. Thus, the expansion of workplace regulations and the formation of a bureaucracy, key aspects of the samurai management system, were gradually implemented at the expense of *oyakata* control. Labor management came to be an uneasy blend of the merchant and samurai systems. Still, in the late 1890s *oyakata* retained considerable power. Even though managers had been put in place whose responsibilities allowed them to override *oyakata* decisions, managers were not apt to push the *oyakata* when trouble might result.[54]

Working conditions in heavy industry were considerably better than in textiles. Employees worked from ten to twelve hours per day, and in addition to normal holidays the men had two to four Sundays off each month. Overtime premiums of 25 to 50 percent were paid. Wages were some fifty sen per day, paid once or twice a month, with piece-rate or subcontract payments made upon completion of the job. Many firms had forced savings schemes to reduce turnover and provide a security fund in case of damages caused by the worker. Incentives for regular attendance or high productivity were common, as were fines for rule infractions (discharge was rarely used because of the shortage of skilled workers). In case of work-related accident or death, firms adopted the merchant tradition of paying medical or funeral expenses, but there was no tradition regarding lost wages or pensions, so no such benefits were paid.[55]

The mining industry's system of relations between labor and management was based on the customs and practices of the convict labor supervision systems used in the mines by the Japanese government during the Tokugawa period (1603–1868). The mining work force was overwhelmingly male and unskilled, and the working conditions nightmarish. Recruitment of workers was very difficult for the mining industry, and the role of the *oyakata* was much more pervasive than in heavy industry. In mining supervision and recruitment were delegated, not because management was incapable of supervising the multiple-skills worker as in heavy industry, but largely because the supervisory role was difficult, disagreeable, and dangerous.

At most mines miners were housed in long single-story wooden buildings called *naya* ("barns"). There miners would eat, drink, and sleep, always under the supervision of an *oyakata*. Each *oyakata* had several such "barns" under his supervision, for which he set wages, determined promotion and punishment, made work assignments, recruited new men, and determined living conditions. The *oyakata* even arbitrated arguments between his men and lent them money.[56]

The horrible working conditions were a key factor in the mines. Miners worked a twelve-hour shift in 120 degree heat, naked except for a loincloth. They would crawl up to a half-mile through six inches of tepid water to their work spot, wrest coal from the earth with a pickax, then drag or carry 125 pounds of coal in a bamboo basket several hundred yards to the steam conveyor. Although the miners were paid, the *oyakata* would deduct for rent, food, tools, and other expenses. Deductions often exceeded wages, forcing miners into debt. The only escape was for a miner to be ransomed by his family, but even those few who could write were not allowed to send letters home.[57]

The prospect of escape was always on the minds of the miners, but punishment was severe. Workers who disobeyed or tried to escape were often hoisted into the air with their hands tied behind their back and beaten mercilessly. In one case, a fire was started underneath a miner, and when he started to scream, his mouth was sewn shut. The supervisors then thrust small kindling wood up his anus, killing him. Supervisors indeed had the power of life and death. In the summer of 1884 cholera broke out at the Takashima mine, killing nearly half the work force. In an effort to stop the spread of the disease, all who had died or who showed any symptoms of the disease were tied in bundles of five and ten persons. These human bundles were hoisted up on a large iron plate over a huge bonfire. Many miners were burned alive. Word of this got out in 1888, causing a national sensation. The massacre came to be known as the Takashima mine scandal. The responsible company officials were called before a judge, reprimanded, and warned not to murder miners again.[58]

The key job for the *oyakata* working in the mining industry was recruitment. No one willingly went to work at the coal mines. The *oyakata* and his strong-arm men either tricked prospects into thinking they would be working for another firm, such as the railroads, or simply kidnapped them. Once at the mine, exploitation of the miners was simple. Payment for coal produced was determined by a complicated system evaluating quantity and quality, and cheating of the miners was routine. Often payments were in tickets good only at the company store or the *oyakata*'s store, where goods were overpriced.

Conditions were better at precious metals mines, with a work day of from eight to ten hours and better health conditions. Pay was approximately 30 to 40 sen per day before deductions by the *oyakata*. Miners of precious metals could work twenty-five days per month, unlike coal miners who averaged only twenty days because of poor health. Pressure on wages was not as great at precious metals mines due to the higher value of the output and the higher skill level required. Many miners worked willingly and there was some personal freedom, allowing more turnover and mobility for the miners.[59]

Work Stoppages and Labor Organizations

During the period 1868–1900 the nature of work stoppages evolved from spontaneous riots similar to the peasant riots of the Tokugawa period to organized strikes on the Western model. Yet this progress centered solely on male workers and only those within the "new occupations"—those that sprang up after the Meiji Restoration, such as boilermaker, printer, lathe operator, railwayman, and so on. The textile workers and miners were enmeshed in conditions and attitudes that militated against modern labor organization and strike activity. While the dwindling number of traditional craftsmen struggled to maintain their power and prerogatives through their guilds, the work force in the new occupations gradually formed mutual assistance societies and then trade unions. By 1897 the growth in new occupations and the evolution of these labor organizations and work stoppages had reached the point where a labor movement could emerge.

Work stoppages at first mirrored the pattern of peasant riots of the Tokugawa period. After repeated appeals to the bureaucracy to redress grievances (for peasants, generally tax relief), the peasants would finally riot, causing damage to government property but rarely harming government officials. This would serve to bring the peasants' grievances to the attention of much higher level officials, and while the ringleaders of peasant riots were punished and sometimes executed, generally complaints were addressed and the peasants given some relief. In the case of industrial workers or craftsmen, repeated appeals to redress grievances regarding wages, working conditions, or employment were often ignored by employers. The workers would finally riot, cause some damage to company property (again, rarely harming company officials), and demand relief. Usually, this would be sufficient to cause management to take a close look at the situation and would often result in

changes, although riot leaders would sometimes be fired or imprisoned. Throughout, authorities neither negotiated nor bargained
with aggrieved peasants or workers. They simply listened and unilaterally undertook relief action or suppression and punishment of
ringleaders. As in the case of peasant riots, if those in authority
chose to ignore grievances, their only course of action was to use
military or police power to cow the rioters into submission.

Since modern industry sprang up in the space of just a few years
and was by and large unrelated to any traditional crafts, it had no
tradition of labor organization to follow. Thus, it was natural for
the workers in modern industry to look to the West as a model,
where labor unions were common. It was generally progressive
oyakata with significant experience combined with young worker
activists who formed the nucleus of modern labor organizations.
The progressive *oyakata* had the contacts, experience, and often
the education that commanded respect from the other workers.
The worker activists had the energy, the intelligence, and the
untraditional attitude required to organize others and handle day-
to-day union business. Both *oyakata* and activists had an interest
in improving their pay, achieving higher social status, and maintaining their autonomy and ability in the face of rapid technologi-
cal and managerial change.

Traditional craftsmen, on the other hand, sought to maintain
their rights and privileges through their guilds and associations.
This took place even as the traditional crafts were losing business
and importance, so that by the time guilds became anachronistic,
the crafts they represented had almost disappeared and been
replaced by modern industry. This was true of the lumbermen,
ship carpenters, precious metals miners, and masons, whose more
traditional organizations simply disappeared as their crafts were
eliminated or radically modernized.

Thus, in the evolution of the labor movement between 1868
and 1897, there was an increasing sophistication of work stoppages, a gradual education of the modern industrial work force in
the ways of Western unionism, and the creation first of mutual
assistance organizations and then unions. Yet this progress was
largely focused in the new occupations, where free labor markets,
absence of tradition, and the encroachment of management on the
authority of the skilled workers and *oyakata* together created an
environment friendly to labor organization.

Textiles

Although silk-reeling and cotton-spinning were new occupations characterized by new technology and modern industrial work-places, no labor organizations emerged in textiles in the period 1868–1897. The high turnover in the work force made organiza-tion efforts hopeless, as girls worked for a few years, earned a dowry, and returned home under the *jochū minarai* tradition. The men working in the mills, often much longer tenured, were super-visory, maintenance, or management personnel enjoying wages and working conditions far superior to those of the women. In these circumstances the men did not form the basis of a union.

Work stoppages in textiles also had a strong resemblance to peasant protests. One such work stoppage took place on June 14, 1886, when over a hundred girls at the Amamiya Silk-Reeling Company, located at Kōfu in Yamanashi Prefecture, walked off the job. The work stoppage was in response to new rules put into effect by the Yamanashi Silk Spinners Association, an organization of employers formed in February 1886. Under the new rules hours were lengthened from fourteen to fourteen-and-a-half per day, wages for top-grade girls were cut from some thirty-two sen to twenty-two sen per day, and supervision became much more strict.[60]

Under the new supervision rules, the foremen would hurry the girls when they went to relieve themselves or to get a glass of water. Since working hours had been lengthened, the girls had to commute to work while it was still dark. One girl at the mill was attacked by a ruffian while on her way to work, and this sparked a protest by the entire mill. The girls left the mill in a group and pro-ceeded to a nearby Buddhist temple to decide what to do. Manage-ment, surprised by this action, sought to determine the girls' griev-ances and after discussion with their leaders decided to shorten working hours by one hour and to investigate other ways to improve working conditions. Despite lack of planning, organiza-tion, recognition by employers, a strike fund, collective bargain-ing, and all other characteristics of a modern strike, the girls at the Amamiya mill had won concessions from the company. Disputes immediately followed at other mills in Yamanashi Prefecture, and the new rules of the employers' association could not be en-forced.[61]

Another work stoppage typical in its spontaneity but unique in that the strikers were prosecuted took place at the Temma Cotton-Spinning Company in Osaka on January 26, 1894.[62] Up to that time there had been several labor disputes at the company protesting arbitrary treatment by supervisors. After the change of shifts on January 26, fifty to sixty workers remained in the cafeteria making noise and gathering other workers. Those on their way to work were threatened with physical harm if they did not join the rioters, who kicked down and burned the cafeteria doors. The disturbance grew to include some two hundred workers and was led by the male workers although they were a small minority at the mill. The only demand of the rioters was the dismissal of technician Kawai Kiyosaburō and factory managers Ozaki Ryūzō and Ishimaru Masatarō, whom they said they could not work under.[63]

The riot was quelled by the police and six rioters were arrested. They were subsequently prosecuted in the only such case on record during this period under Article 270 of the criminal code: "All workmen engaged in industrial or agricultural labor, who with the object of increasing . . . salaries or changing the conditions . . . of labor, have employed strategem or force against their masters or against other workmen so as to hinder the work, shall be punished with imprisonment with labor for a period of from one to six months and a fine of from three to thirty yen."[64] Of the six rioters, two were acquitted, three received the minimum sentence, and the ringleader received a sentence of two months' imprisonment and a fine of three yen. The fact that such light sentences were handed down in the only legal action against workers in this period shows that the industrial labor force was still too small and disorganized to merit organized opposition and oppression by employers and regulation by government.

Mining

Mining, another major sector of industrial employment, was very different from textiles, and its two major subsectors—coal mining and precious metals mining—were worlds apart. No labor organizations appeared in coal mining during the period 1868–1900. While coal mining experienced more work stoppages than any other sector of the economy during the Meiji period, these stoppages were spontaneous riots rather than strikes. Precious metals mining, on the other hand, had a long history of labor organization through its guild, called the *tomoko* (friends). Work stoppages had a correspondingly more organized character in precious metals mining than in coal mining.

Convict labor was the hallmark of coal mining. Where convict labor was not used, farm lads were tricked or coerced into accompanying labor bosses to the mines. Once there they were forced to work like slaves, falling ever further into debt through the truck system, in which miners were forced to buy their necessities at overpriced *oyakata* or company stores. Miners who failed to escape died through disease, mine accidents, or torture by guards. Under these cruel conditions, labor organizations were impossible to organize, and labor protests accordingly took the form of violent riots.

The Takashima and Miike coal mines were representative of the coal mines of the period. The Takashima mine experienced frequent violent riots—eleven major ones between 1870 and 1889. In the most significant of these, seven miners were killed. Riots at Takashima were sparked by wage cuts, increased use of convict labor, and changes in working conditions, but they also simply erupted spontaneously.

At the Miike coal mine, major riots by convict laborers occurred in 1883 and 1884. In the 1883 riot, miners were enraged by mine officials who refused to help with a problem because it was not their area of responsibility. The convict laborers set fire to the mine office, and the fire spread to the mine, killing forty-six miners. The convicts responsible for the fire made good their escape during the chaos.[65]

Precious metals miners, in stark contrast to coal miners, had a long history of organization dating back to the early 1600s. The precious metals miners' guild, the *tomoko,* actually functioned as the government of the mining community. The *tomoko* owned and produced various essentials, such as eating utensils. It arbitrated household disputes and arguments between miners, judged crimes, and administered punishments to offenders. The *tomoko* also provided assistance in case of death or injury through a levy on the members.

The *tomoko* maintained the apprenticeship system whereby young miners learned the trade. Each apprentice miner was assigned a "father" and "older brother" and served three years, three months, and ten days before he was considered a full-fledged miner who could teach others. A miner who had been a *tomoko* member for many years (twenty-five at some mines, as much as forty at others) became an "elder" *(genrō)* and was exempted from work but continued to lead the community.

The *tomoko* were nationwide in scope, and each mining community could call on the others for assistance. "Gift cards" were issued to those who could not recover from their ailment, and "request cards" to those who might recover but would require long convalescence. A miner could present his gift or request card at any *tomoko* community and receive one night's lodging, a meal, and a small sum of money. Such cards could not be obtained easily, however, since they were a heavy burden on the *tomoko* of the nation. Two or three at most were issued at any mine in a year, and to do so required the approval of both community *tomoko* members and the representatives of other mines.

The heart of the *tomoko* was the fictional parent-child relationship. The "father" not only taught his "child" the trade, but also the ways of the community, its laws and morals, and even a little rudimentary schooling. The "child," in return, was expected to care for his father in everyday life and set up the gravestone after he died. In many cases miners were unable to raise a family, and so their "children" revered their memories and fulfilled the obligations of ancestor veneration as was common in Japanese families. This fictional parent-child relationship was a strong part of the craftsman tradition in Japan and the basis for the *oyakata* ("parent") labor-boss system in mining and heavy industry.[66]

Work stoppages at precious metals mines were rare and never characterized by physical violence. In 1869 and 1871 at the government-owned Ikuno silver mine and in 1872 at the government-owned Sado gold mine the miners rioted over the introduction of Western technology and the discharge of miners. Calm was not restored until the government dealt with the unemployment issue either by expanding operations and hiring back the miners or by giving financial relief to the unemployed. A similar disturbance occurred at the Innai silver mine in 1878. The Tarō mine's practice of reducing wages and hours in winter was successfully opposed in 1889 by means of a strike. The strike was triggered by the rising price of rice, for the miners couldn't feed their families on reduced winter wages. The rising price of rice also triggered a community riot led by miners at the Sado silver mine in 1890.

Throughout these disputes there is no doubt that the *tomoko* played a key role in organizing the protests and preserving their nonviolent character. Yet, with the exception of the well-organized Tarō strike, the *tomoko* used the traditional technique of the riot to bring its problems to the attention of high-level officials. None of the characteristics of a modern union—negotiations, strike funds, and announced economic objectives—were present. Yet the *tomoko* members were able to achieve their objectives. Much later, the *tomoko* became fertile ground for unionization and after 1912 assisted the rise of the Yūaikai (Friendly Society), a nation-wide union movement.[67]

Traditional Crafts

Japan's traditional craftsmen also had long histories of guild organization dating back to the start of the Tokugawa period. These guilds had many similarities to those of the feudal period in Western Europe. They were characterized by apprenticeship systems, ownership of shops by the master craftsmen who were guild members, mutual assistance provisions, and restrictive membership practices. In Japan, a single craft would often have two different organizations—one of master craftsmen, merchants, and *oyakata* (employers), and one of apprentices, journeymen, and *kokata* (employees). Again, the dominance of the fictional parent-child relationship within the craftsman tradition of labor relations is clearly shown by the widespread use of the terms *oyakata* ("parent") and *kokata* ("child") throughout all crafts.

An example of such dual organization was that of the woodcutters' guild. The 1,300 woodcutters of the Tokyo area were organized into two groups—300 *oyakata* in the master craftsmen's group, and 1,000 *kokata* in the journeymen's and apprentices' group. Without a certificate from the guild, a woodcutter could not work in Tokyo. Journeymen elected a total of twenty-one representatives from each ward and *gun* (district) of Tokyo to serve as guild officers. Officers collected dues, kept the members informed, and held monthly meetings at their office in Kyōbashi ward to discuss finances and mediate disputes between members. All the journeymen held a meeting each January and July to decide what proposals to make to the *oyakata,* particularly concerning wages.

The *oyakata* organization of three hundred master woodcutters was run by a president, vice-president, secretary, and treasurer.

Only the secretary was not elected. The officers met once a month to discuss the business of the organization and to consider developments in the journeymen's organization. Each January and July all the master craftsmen would convene to deliberate on proposals from the journeymen, and afterwards negotiate with the wood merchants on pricing. After such negotiations the wages for the journeymen would be set for the next six months. The *oyakata* received 40 percent of the wages of his journeymen and had extensive power over his apprentices, even including the right to recall them after they reached journeyman status if he was short of help. Annual membership dues in the *oyakata* guild was thirty yen per year for grade one, the highest level, twenty yen for grade two, and ten yen for grade three. Grades were determined by number of apprentices and annual income.[68]

Such guilds of woodcutters existed throughout Japan, and on occasion acted to protect their interests. For example, the woodcutters of Wakayama Prefecture disputed the use of convict labor to cut wood. When the practice began in 1882, wages were reduced and woodcutters began to lose their jobs. On November 7, 1882, three hundred woodcutters petitioned the ward chief to discontinue use of convict labor, but he replied he could not break his contract with the wood merchants. The guildsmen then appealed to the wood merchants, who requested that convicts no longer be used to cut wood. The guild did not have to resort to a strike.[69]

Unlike the woodcutters, the masons were forced to strike to maintain their wages. The master masons of Tokyo had enjoyed guild organization since the Tokugawa period and had established branches with officers at the twenty-one wards and districts of Tokyo. The officers met monthly to set wages and administer mutual assistance. In January 1889 a wage dispute sparked the appearance of an organization of twelve hundred journeyman masons who had served seven or eight years with the masters and received a craftsman's certificate. Those who had fled their *oyakata*'s home were excluded from membership in the new organization. The master masons opened wage negotiations with the journeymen in October 1889 and agreed to a minimum wage for journeymen of fifty-five sen per day. When in 1891 this agreement was broken, the journeymen struck for six days. The master masons were forced to give in. Another short strike by granite masons against the Japan Construction Company in December 1891 over low wages was also successful.[70]

Dual organization—one guild for master craftsmen and another for journeymen—also characterized other traditional crafts, such as carpenters and plasterers. As with the masons, the master craftsmen in these groups had a prior history of guild organization, while the journeymen first organized over a wage dispute. For example, the journeyman plasterers of Tokyo won a strike against the master plasterers in August 1892 over the progressive decline in their wages. Five hundred journeyman carpenters of Tokyo struck against the master carpenters in September of the same year over wages. The minimum rate for carpentry had been set at forty-five sen per day, but by 1892 the average pay had fallen to that level and inflation was making heavy inroads into the carpenters' standard of living. A compromise was reached that set the minimum rate at forty-eight sen per day.[71]

Journeymen were increasingly willing to organize and take collective action to protect their livelihood as the nineteenth century drew to a close. Yet this was done largely within the framework of the existing guild system, and the power of the master craftsmen was still very great. In many cases, since the master craftsmen took a share of journeymen's wages or marked up expenses as subcontractors, they had an interest in increasing the wages of the journeymen. These wage disputes and strikes were a reflection of the gradual erosion of the master craftsmen's power to control the market and set wages and prices, rather than a new-found class consciousness or militancy on the part of the journeymen. As long as the master craftsmen honored their traditional commitments to the journeymen, the journeymen were content with the guild system. The wage disputes were, in fact, an effort by the journeymen to restore the guarantees of the guild system in the face of pressure by free-market forces set loose and fostered by the Meiji Restoration. This is in stark contrast to the strikes and organization efforts in the "new occupations"—those occupations that sprang up after the Restoration.

The "New Occupations"

Perhaps the earliest of these new occupations was that of rickshaw man. While the rickshaw is perceived in the West as quintessentially Oriental, it was in fact the first and fastest-growing of the new occupations. Invented in 1869, the rickshaw quickly became the most popular means of transit around Tokyo and Yokohama, servicing the foreign traders, government officials, merchants, and the wealthy. In the absence of trams and railways, the number of rickshaws grew to the point that thousands of men depended on them for their livelihood. Only a few of these men owned their own rickshaw. Most rented one from a boss or *oyakata,* who made his living by renting out several rickshaws and providing room and board to his men. Such *oyakata* relied directly on the income earned by the rickshaw men and had a strong interest in their continued employment.

In 1882 the Tokyo Street-Car Company opened its first line, from Shimbashi to Nihombashi, and announced plans to extend the system to all of Tokyo. The rickshaw men reacted by setting up the "Alliance to Oppose Street-Cars" and holding a mass meeting on October 4, 1882. An *oyakata* named Miura, aided by political activists from the Liberty Party (Jiyūtō) and the popular rights movement, organized the meeting, paid for sake, addressed the six hundred rickshaw men who attended, and formed a new party— the Shakaitō (Rickshaw Party). This was daring, as the government had outlawed another political party, the Oriental Socialist Party, only a few months before. Meetings on October 7 and 9 built membership to several thousand, but police attempts to disperse a morale-boosting meeting on November 24 sparked a riot. Leadership of the party was discredited when one officer of the party got into a fight with the police a few days later, and the organization fell apart.[72]

In 1884 an attempt was made at union organization in the printing trades. Section-chief Ikeda of the Tokyo Printing Company (later the Shūeisha) approached the owner, Sakuma Teiichi, with the idea. Sakuma, originally of samurai birth, had become a minor government official in the shogunate. After the Restoration he decided against working for the new government and went into business for himself, trying several trades before setting up a printing shop in 1876. Sakuma printed the magazines, newspapers, and documents that were the weapons of the popular rights movement. Using his shop for social and industrial experiments, he tried the eight-hour day, old-age benefits, regular week-long summer vacations for employees, and profit-sharing. He was the first public defender of unionism in Japan. Despite Sakuma's support, many printing workers were afraid of the union or thought Ikeda was setting it up for his own personal gain. Ikeda tried for two months, but finally gave up.[73]

In 1887 a friendly society was set up among metal workers (machinists, smiths, lathe operators, forge workers, mold-makers, boilermakers, etc.) to promote education and mutual assistance in case of illness. It was based in Tokyo and its leaders were Ozawa Benzō, his brother Kimitarō, and Aida Kichigorō. At the first meeting gambling began in the audience during the speeches. Order was lost, the meeting disintegrated, and some friendly society members proceeded to the red-light district and did not return home for three or four days. Furious criticism by the members' wives at the next meeting forced Ozawa to disband the group.

Ozawa and Aida, two of the first Japanese to learn Western smithing methods, were prominent *oyakata* of the apprentice type who had taught many *oyakata* and foremen throughout Japanese heavy industry. Ozawa was not to be stopped so easily. In June 1889 he formed the Dōmei Shinkō Gumi (Alliance for the Advancement of Workers), encompassing metal workers at the navy shipyards, the Ishikawajima Shipyards, railways mainte-nance shops, and the Tanaka Works (later the Shibaura Engineer-ing Works). The constitution of the organization provided for dues, assistance in the event of discharge, contracts with employ-ers, and a training factory for unemployed members or those wish-ing to improve their skills.[74]

An important objective of Ozawa and Aida in founding the organization was to help *oyakata* and their men adapt to industri-alization, thus protecting and improving their position. According to Aida:

[My ex-apprentices who are now oyakata] really do not have the knowledge to manage effectively and do not really have the qualifi-cations to be oyakata. Their position is severely threatened by the emergence these days of technicians who have graduated from schools and are increasingly assuming supervisory roles in the fac-tories. Unless these oyakata can obtain the knowledge they need, interpret and apply the new technology, and direct the workers, their position is endangered.[75]

Soon after the founding of the Alliance for the Advancement of Workers, rumors began to circulate that the funds being collected from the members were being used by the officers for their personal expenses. The rumors gradually became widespread, and Ozawa was forced to return all the money that had been collected and disband the organization.[76]

The years 1889 and 1890 marked two more such organizational failures in the printing trades, each time caused by prospective members' suspicions. In one case workers thought the union activist was a tool of the employers and physically obstructed organization attempts. In the other case the newly formed printers' friendly society refused to make public its finances and so failed to keep its members. But about this time public attention began to focus on working conditions and unionism. In 1888 the Takashima mine scandal raised a storm of protest over working conditions in the mines. In 1889 all educated Japanese were horrified by exposure of the appalling working conditions at Western-run tea-making plants in Yokohama. By 1890 publications supporting the popular rights movements had begun to vocally support the union concept in response to the problems of labor exploitation. "By striking, ten weak men together can oppose one strong man," wrote *The People's Friend* (Kokumin no Tomo), a popular newspaper, in 1890.[77]

By 1892 "labor problems" *(rōdō mondai)* had become a topic of daily conversation as traditional craftsmen in the capital—plasterers, masons, and carpenters—went on strike. The Japanese Army, alarmed over the prospect of strikes and pushing to completely replace sandals with shoes for enlisted men, allocated funds in its budget proposal for direct army production of shoes. The need for direct army production and a school to train army shoemakers was explained to the Diet by an army representative: "Up to now we have relied on the manufacturers within the city for shoes, but due to the increasing introduction of Western ideas, there has grown up in army circles a fear that organizations of workmen will appear. In the event of an emergency . . . "[78]

Shoemakers, whose livelihood was at stake, mobilized to oppose the army proposal and were supported by the populist Tōyō Jiyūtō (Oriental Liberty Party) and its suborganization, the Nippon Rōdō Kyōkai (Japan Labor Society), which had been formed only months before. On December 21, 1892, members of the Tokyo Shoemakers Association, carrying banners such as "Down with the Military Shoemakers' School," rioted in front of the Diet building. A representative of the shoemakers was allowed to meet with a proxy for the president of the Diet, who listened and promised an answer the next day. The shoemakers' representative was then arrested, and when the shoemakers returned to the Diet the next day, their demands were refused. Shoe merchants, who had supported the shoemakers, began to fear they might lose not only the shoe business but also the army's trade in hides and other raw materials for shoes. Without the support of the shoe merchants, the shoemakers abandoned their protest and dissolved their association. Thirteen members of the association were arrested by the police and charged with violation of the Public Meeting and Political Party Law of 1890. The Oriental Liberty Party and Japan Labor Society, after failing in attempts to organize plasterers, carpenters, and rickshaw men, also dissolved.[79]

Workplace mutual assistance organizations had begun to emerge in the 1890s in the new occupations. Workers contributed a portion of their daily wage to a common fund to be used as an assistance benefit to workers who were hurt or to the families of those who were killed. While in many workplaces this system was informal, in others an organization was set up, rules laid down, and contributions levied officially. Such was the case at the Ōmiya Factory of the Japan Railway Company, where fitters and lathe operators formed a mutual assistance society in June 1895. The founder of this society was Shin Kichigorō, an *oyakata* of the subcontracting type. This mutual assistance society collected funds from members, elected officers, and paid sick and death benefits.[80]

Another example, again in the metalworking trades, was the Kōgyō Dantai Dōmeikai (Alliance for Industrial Organization), formed in February 1897 and led by Muramatsu Tamitarō, an *oyakata* of the foreman type. The object of this group was to "promote friendship between members, build a factory with capital provided by the members, advance technology, obtain advancement of the rights of the members, educate apprentices, provide mutual assistance and raise the status of the members."[81] Primarily organized at the state-run Tokyo Armaments Works, the AIO also had members at other state-run armaments factories who had been recruited by friends at the Tokyo Armaments Works. The AIO was strong and stable, with hundreds of members. In October 1900 its factory, constructed on land it had purchased, began operations manufacturing machinery.[82]

With the emergence of stable mutual assistance societies, union organization quickly followed. The Yokohama ship carpenters formed a union and executed a well-organized strike of unprecedented duration—from June 17 to July 19, 1897. Ship carpentry, a traditional craft before the Restoration, had become a totally new occupation by 1897. The use of metal in shipbuilding, the emergence of corporations with large-scale docks employing hundreds of men, and rapid change in the tools and technology of ship carpentry had changed master craftsmen into industrial workers. When their wages remained static for two years while inflation raged at 20 percent each year, the ship carpenters united to protect their standard of living.

Four hundred Yokohama ship carpenters with subcontracting *oyakata* at the core formed the Yokohama Ship Carpenters' Union on June 5, 1897. The constitution of the union provided for dues, mutual assistance, and election of officers, and set rules for apprentices and subcontracting.[83] On June 7, the union petitioned the various Yokohama shipyards for a raise from sixty sen to seventy-seven sen per day in view of inflation. Several small yard owners, employing a total of one hundred carpenters, agreed to the petition, but all the rest, led by the Yokohama Dock Company and supported by the Japan Mail Steamship Company (the largest shipping company in Japan), refused. Repeated petitions by the carpenters were ignored and the Yokohama Dock Company threatened to blacklist the petitioners.

In response, three hundred ship carpenters went on strike on June 17. Word was sent to carpenters in other shipyards to stay away from Yokohama, and pickets were set up at the yards of the recalcitrant employers. The ship carpenters refrained from drinking and violence and behaved in such a peaceful way that they even earned the sympathy of the police. Strikers were supported by a levy on the one hundred working members of one-third their income. On June 27 all employers except the Yokohama Dock Company offered a compromise wage of seventy-three sen per day, which was accepted. One hundred fifty strikers returned to work on the 28th.

The strike continued against the Yokohama Dock Company, but the 150 remaining strikers soon found work at the other Yoko-

hama shipyards, which were taking over the work of the Yokohama Dock Company. The company attempted to recruit ship carpenters at distant yards, but most supported the strikers and
refused to go to Yokohama. Only twelve carpenters were recruited, and of these the picketing strikers convinced three to support
the strike. After a month the Yokohama Dock Company gave up
and offered seventy-three sen per day, and work resumed on July
20. This strike was hailed as "stand[ing] . . . in . . . favorable
comparison with those strikes conducted by shrewd strike leaders
in Western countries."[84]

Labor organizations and labor protest in Japan had come a long
way since the feudal period. Confrontation with employers had
evolved from spontaneous workshop walkouts on emotional
issues to fully organized strikes supported by union funds against
multiple employers over economic issues. Labor organizations had
evolved from temporary workplace protest committees to stable
mutual assistance societies and then unions. Yet the progress was
all focused in one sector—the new occupations with a career work
force.

Work stoppages and labor organizations became strong and
modern only where traditional structures had broken down. The
cotton-spinning and silk-reeling girls were constrained by the traditional *jochū minarai* system, which transferred parental household authority from a girl's family to her new household or
employer. The traditional approach to convict labor governed
labor relations in coal mining. The precious metals miners were
well satisfied and served by their guild, the *tomoko,* with its
ancient customs and long history. The traditional craftsmen, both
master craftsmen and journeymen, worked to keep the guild system's rights and obligations viable into the twentieth century. Only
in the new occupations that sprang up after 1868, where no workplace traditions existed and where survival depended upon dis-
carding traditional ideas and technology, did work stoppages and
labor organizations evolve and progress.

In the first instance of labor protest involving the new occupations—the rickshaw men's protest in 1882—the workers allied
with political activists. Yet as late as 1897 not a single example of
this can be seen in the tradition-bound occupations. Even when
the Oriental Liberty Party tried to directly organize traditional
craftsmen such as the Tokyo plasterers and carpenters, they were

spurned. The willingness to utilize political leverage and to see efforts by labor as part of a movement were hallmarks of the men in the new occupations. Perhaps more importantly, the men of the new occupations were willing to directly challenge large corporations, the Japanese Army, and even the Japanese government itself in pursuit of their rights. Tradition-bound workers concerned themselves only with their immediate supervisors or *oyakata*. Finally, the men of the new occupations generally strove to better their situation by means such as mutual assistance, wage increases, or building their own factory, whereas tradition-bound workers reacted only to a worsening of conditions and tried to return to the status quo—maintaining wages, maintaining working hours, or getting rid of convict labor in their craft.

Labor markets also played a key role in limiting progress to the new occupations. In textiles, the workers planned on industrial employment for only a few years before returning to the farms, and turnover was very high. There was no stable work force to organize. In coal mining, the remoteness of the mines combined with the high turnover (through escape and death) of the miners made organization impossible. While precious metals miners were skilled career workers, again the remoteness of the mines inhibited the flow of ideas and the movement of the workers. The traditional craftsmen were tied to their particular district and employer because workplaces were very small and guilds controlled the ability to work in a district through the certificate system. Only in the new occupations was there the combination of free labor markets, career workers, and high demand for labor.

Another key factor was the impingement of management on the autonomy and authority of the skilled workers in the new occupations. If the new occupations and free labor markets provided the opportunity for modern labor organization, management encroachment provided the incentive. Time and again *oyakata* tried to lead organizations of workers in efforts to upgrade skills, maintain control, and keep authority. Yet as these efforts fell short, management pushed the *oyakata* gradually back toward worker status—turning the apprentice-type *oyakata* into subcontractors and then foremen. The waning of *oyakata* authority can be traced by examining the change in the type of *oyakata* leading attempts to organize the workers. In the 1880s, Ozawa Benzō and Aida Kichigorō, *oyakata* of the apprentice type, with the most power in the workplace, were leading organization attempts. By the early 1890s *oyakata* like Shin Kichigorō who had been reduced to sub-contractors were leading the workers. By 1897 *oyakata* power had been further curtailed, and Muramatsu Tamitarō, only a foreman, led the organization effort. The goal of Muramatsu's organization —to build a factory—spoke strongly to the need to maintain the status and authority of the members and resist the encroachment of management.

The introduction of new technology and the emergence of large-scale enterprises were not decisive factors in the evolution of labor organizations and work stoppages in Japan. New technology was the basis for cotton-spinning and mining. Yet labor protests remained primitive in these industries. Large-scale workplaces were common in cotton-spinning, silk-reeling, and precious metals mining, yet these industries did not advance in labor organization.

The combination of new career occupations not bound by tradition, free labor markets, and the growing impingement of management on the autonomy and authority of skilled workers was the basis for the evolution of labor organizations and work stoppages. It is not surprising, then, that it was in precisely these new occupations that the Japanese labor movement would spring forth and flower.

2

TAKANO FUSATARŌ

Takano Fusatarō, the founder of the Japanese labor movement, was born in Nagasaki, Japan, on November 24, 1868.[1] Both the time and the place are worthy of note. The year 1868 marked the birth of modern Japan, when the Emperor Meiji was restored to power and the Meiji era proclaimed. Thereafter, as Japan undertook modern development, the expectations and attitudes of the Japanese people began to change. Old customs and ways of life, seen to be out of step with Western "enlightenment," were ridiculed. The future no longer had the predictable quality it had had in the feudal era. The unknown beckoned from every possible direction. This period would produce men ready to grapple with problems Japan had never previously encountered. Takano Fusatarō was one of these men.

Nagasaki, where Takano was born and spent his childhood years, had been the only link between Japan and the West for centuries during the feudal era. The foreign traders who visited the Dutch trading post at Deshima introduced a trickle of books and Western learning to Japan. Nagasaki was at that time the only city in Japan whose citizens could claim they had actually met and dealt with foreigners ("the barbarians"), and it became a focal point for interest in the West.

Takano's father was a tailor, and from all indications his family was poor. Although large families were the norm in Japan at that time, Takano had only one brother, Iwasaburō, and a sister, Kiwa. By the time Takano was nine, the family was under such financial pressure that his father abandoned tailoring and went to work for Takano's uncle, who ran a ticketing and freight-handling business in Yokohama. Yokohama, because of its proximity to Tokyo, had become Japan's largest port and its chief point of contact with the West after the Restoration. A large community of foreigners lived in the special foreign enclaves that had been set up in Yokohama (where foreigners were subject only to their own and not Japanese laws). Takano's formative years were thus spent in close contact with Western influence.

Poverty and misfortune dogged Takano's family despite the move to Yokohama. His father, who had managed to set up his own business as a shipping agent and hosteler with Takano's uncle's assistance, died when Takano was eleven. Takano's mother worked hard to carry on the family business, but when Takano was thirteen, it was completely destroyed by fire. That year, Takano graduated from elementary school and went to work for his uncle in order to support his mother, brother, and sister.[2]

These childhood experiences of poverty, Western influence, and personal misfortune ignited in both Takano and his brother a burning desire for social and material progress for all Japanese people. Their family had struggled with Japan's low wages and long working hours, and they had suffered from the lack of union benefits and social insurance. Both Takanos chose education as their tool for personal improvement, and they later used education of others as their chief weapon for social change.

Takano chose to continue his education while working for his uncle, entering the Commercial School in Yokohama. Since at that time most Japanese did not pursue education beyond the elementary level, this was equivalent in status to pursuing a college education today. Takano immediately showed his personal drive for progress and interest in economics by forming a lecture club among the students. The club invited lecturers from the Tokyo Specialist School to give talks on politics and economics, and also conducted research and sponsored discussions.[3]

In 1886 Takano's uncle died. Takano not only lost his employer but also a significant source of support for his mother. With five years of schooling at the Yokohama Commercial School completed, Takano decided to go to America. His passport stated that he was traveling to San Francisco to undertake commercial studies. Takano probably felt he could earn extra money in America to help support his mother, younger brother, and sister, and at the same time continue his education by learning English and studying business, labor relations, and the social structure in America.

Takano left Japan for San Francisco in late 1886. He had just turned eighteen.[4]

Takano began his activities in San Francisco by studying the English language. He engaged a tutor, a Mrs. Kingsland, at the rate of three dollars per month for several years. At first, until he learned English, Takano probably supported himself during his stay in San Francisco by doing odd jobs. Later on it appears he made a living running a small tobacco shop. Takano worked hard and regularly sent money to his mother in Japan. He also continued his economics education at a municipal commercial school in San Francisco. During his three-year stay in San Francisco, Takano returned to Japan to see his family once, in 1887.[5]

In the fall of 1889 Takano, by now confident of his English but not doing very well financially, decided to move to the state of Washington to find better employment. First he went to Seattle, but in the spring of 1890 he found a job that paid well in Tacoma. Takano stayed in Tacoma over two years, studying conditions in America, economics, and labor problems. During that time he published several articles in Japanese publications in America and Japan about labor problems.[6] One of the articles he published in Japan, which dealt with American working-class society, introduced the nature of the American labor movement to Japan. It was a careful and scholarly work, and revealed that Takano had rapidly gained a detailed knowledge of the basic character of the American labor movement.[7]

Takano was also studying a number of difficult economic texts during this time. He lost no time in finding out who were the prominent economists of the day, and once his knowledge of English was sufficient, he enthusiastically plowed his way through volume after volume of their works. Takano read the treatises of Marshall and Ricardo, and supplemented this reading with a study of Western industrialization, political economy, and history. Furthermore, Takano apparently obtained the journals of the prominent labor organizations of his day and devoted time to the study of American unionism.[8]

At about this time a group of Japanese in San Francisco organized a group called the Shokukō Giyūkai ("Knights of Labor").[9] The founding members, which included Jō Tsunetarō, Sawada Hannosuke, and Hirano Eitarō, set up the organization as a medium for the study of labor problems in the Americas and to illuminate labor problems in Japan. When Takano returned to San

Francisco in late 1892 he joined this group. There Takano forged bonds of friendship that would later stand him in good stead in his organizing efforts in Japan. Jō Tsunetarō, a shoemaker, set up a shoemaker's association upon his return to Japan in 1893, and later moved to Tokyo where he assisted Takano in his organizing work. Sawada Hannosuke, a tailor, tried to organize tailors in Tokyo after his return to Japan in 1895. He also helped Takano's unionization efforts in Tokyo.[10]

Takano left San Francisco and returned to Tokyo to see his family in 1892. The funds Takano had been regularly sending to his mother had not only supported the family but also provided for his brother Iwasaburō's education. Takano Iwasaburō had at this point entered Tokyo Imperial University, Japan's most prestigious school, and was studying economics and labor problems. During his 1892–1893 stay in Tokyo, Takano Fusatarō wrote an article dealing with labor problems and submitted it to a prominent Japanese economics journal. The article was published in late 1893.[11]

Takano returned to America in 1893 and made his way east, stopping for a short time in Chicago, and then proceeding on to Great Barrington, Massachusetts, where he settled in the spring of 1894.[12] Takano then wrote a letter to Samuel Gompers, president of the American Federation of Labor and the most prominent American unionist of the time. This letter reveals Takano's continuing intense interest in labor problems and his view of the importance of education:

> Dear Sir — Having been attracted by the well doings of American Workingmen since my arrival in this country a few years ago, my thought has been turned upon Japanese laborers whose condition viewed from social and material standpoint is most pitiful and has caused me to determine to try to better their condition upon my return home. In order to do so, I intend to study as much as I can of American labor movement while I live in this country.
>
> Understanding that you had such varied experiences on labor organization and as a head of one of the most powerful unions in this country, your opinion concerning labor matter in its various phase would be most worthy, I venture to seek your advice concerning practical application of labor problem in Japan.
>
> As you are aware, there is no labor organization in Japan at present and the cause of this non-existence, I believe, is the prevailing ignorance among the working people. This being the case, to educate the working people is the most important step to be taken

in amelioration of their condition. I further believe that this educational work must be carried by organized effort, that is to say, we must organize the working people in order to educate them.

Thus far I am firmly convinced of the correctness of my position, but what form of organization to be adopted is the point I am not quite sure. Whether it should on line of trade union such as your order is, or it should be organized by locally irrespective of trade or calling such as the Knights of Labor is. It is clear to me that as a permanent form of organization, the trade unionism is the most desirous form in that it insures stability of the union, but to apply it to Japan under existing condition, the result is doubtful. Under the prevailing condition in Japan ignorance among the working people in the country, it is impossible to form any powerful organization whatever form it may adopt in the course of several years. While such gloomy state is existing, is it wise to proceed to organize by trade, I fear it will result in formation of many small organization too weak to make its educational understanding effective. It may be suggested that those small organizations should be federated. But that means another years effort, meantime the educational work must remain ineffective which ought to be avoided, if there is another way.

I am inclined to consider that it is preferable to adopt the form of the K. of L. as a temporary method in organizing the Japanese workingmen, bringing whatever number of them there is who is willing to join under one organization and start the educational work at once. In course of time when should any trade within organization become strong enough to form separate union, allow it to do so, and affiliate it to the main organization and finally bring the organization on to the basis of the trade unionism. Or, would you advise me to proceed with the plan of the trade unionism regardless of its present consequence?

The reason I am so anxious to select a best plan to begin with is this; — failure of the first attempt to organize means annihilation of another attempt within ten or fifteen years following.[13]

The influence on Takano of the two predominant U.S. labor organizations of the time, the Knights of Labor and the American Federation of Labor, is clear. The Knights of Labor, which organized all workers geographically regardless of craft, industry, or skill level, was the newer organization and growing much more rapidly than the AFL. It reached its peak in the early 1890s. Takano favored its structure, temporarily, as a means to educate the workers. Then Takano proposed organization of individual craft unions, which would remain federated to the parent body, much as the American Federation of Labor was a federation of independent trade unions. Takano, despite the popularity of the Knights of Labor at the time, judged the AFL structure stronger and more advanced, and the ultimate goal of his organization efforts.

Gompers responded immediately to Takano's inquiry with a very kind letter. Gompers strongly urged initial organization by trade and opposed the formation of a general labor organization like the Knights of Labor. He complimented Takano on his high ideals and understanding of labor problems and sent him a number of documents. Gompers went on to invite Takano to his office to discuss labor issues at Takano's convenience. Takano, overwhelmed by such consideration, thanked Gompers repeatedly in his next letter. In his response, Gompers invited Takano to make an appointment to see him and also to write an article on Japanese workingmen and conditions in Japan for the *American Federationist,* which had just begun publication. This article, entitled "Labor Movement in Japan," appeared in the *Federationist* in October 1894.[14]

In early May 1894 Takano moved to New York, where Gompers sent him a number of documents by mail. These documents gave details on the structures and benefit systems of several AFL affiliates, including the Cigar Makers International Union. Takano was particularly interested in the federal labor unions directly affiliated to the AFL and questioned Gompers on the mutual assistance programs of the AFL unions. Gompers assured him that labor organizations with such programs proved to be the most stable.[15]

After corresponding with Gompers for some time, Takano wrote his first letter to the Knights of Labor on August 25, 1894. He asked primarily questions pertaining to organization:

126 Gold St. Brooklyn, N.Y.
August 25. 1894

Mr. J. Hayes,
Gen. Sec.-Treasurer of K. of L.

Dear Sir, — Having endeavored to formulate the best plan to ameliorate the conditions of the Japanese working people, I am convinced that the cause of the existing deplorable state of affairs

among the laboring class of the country is none other than the prevailing ignorance among the same. That being assumed as true, a
step towards their emancipation is to educate them. As educational
work requires concentration, we must bring them under a powerful
organization which can be done only through means such as yours.
To me it seems that to organize the workers of the country where
nothing as yet known, [?]ing such movement upon line of trade-
unionism is a folly. It will only result in the formation of many small
unions too weak to make its work of utility.

With such an understanding, I have watched as best I can, the
working of your order during the last year or two, and am satisfied
of the feasibility and benefits derived thereof, and I propose to
adopt the same plan when I shall begin my active agitation for the
cause upon my return home.

What I am lacking in at present is the knowledge concerning the
detailed plan of the organization. I know there are many forms of
assembly under your order such as State, District, Local and Trade,
but do not know upon what basis they are formed, for instance, as
to how a state assembly is formed. Is it a central body composed of
the District and Local assemblies, or is it formed apart from these?
Is a trade assembly formed by members of Local or District
assemblies according to their trade and calling? Is the rate of the ini-
tiation fee and monthly dues of all your assemblies uniform? How is
the revenue of the central body derived?

It is of the utmost necessity for me to be acquainted with every
detail of the organization which I am seeking to initiate, in order to
ensure my successful undertaking. Beside, under existing conditions
a failure of the first attempt to organize will result in annihilation of
a subsequent one during ten or fifteen years following.

Should you be kind enough to give me the information concerning the detailed form, I shall be greatly obliged to you, and your
kindness will bring a great blessing to the Japanese workers.[16]

The Knights of Labor duly responded to Takano's letter, giving
him the information he requested and a number of documents
containing more detailed information about the structure and
inner workings of the Knights of Labor.[17] Takano received this
response from the Knights just before his first face-to-face meeting
with Gompers. After the meeting with Gompers, Takano stopped
corresponding with the Knights of Labor and decided to rely on
Gompers and the AFL. Clearly Takano had been influenced by
Gompers' thinking and support. Takano continued to write to

Gompers and submit articles to the *American Federationist,* and Gompers continued to support Takano's efforts both through verbal encouragement and financial compensation for his articles. Based on subsequent events, it is clear that Takano was swayed toward the AFL model, with its central federation structure encompassing a number of unions each organized on a trade basis.

Takano's meeting with Gompers took place in early September in New York. Gompers had this to say about Takano: "[Takano] became very much interested in the labor movement and came down to my office to ask me for information on our trade union movement which would be helpful to Japanese workers. After several conferences with him I was convinced of his ability and his sincerity."[18]

Takano and Gompers met several times and discussed labor problems and the labor movement. The two men reached a meeting of minds, and in his next letter to Takano, dated October 22, 1894, Gompers made him a general organizer for the AFL. Takano immediately left for Japan.[19]

Although Takano's philosophy and approach to organization had been strongly influenced by Gompers, he could not apply Gompers' teachings to Japan without modification. The key difference between Japan and the United States in this regard was that workers in the U.S. had individual rights and liberties that they were expected to protect and use to further their own interests. In contrast, Japan's central government and emphasis of tradition worked to undermine efforts by individuals and groups on their own behalf. In Japan, the only valid reason for change was to benefit the entire country rather than a specific individual or group. Two key philosophies were dominant in Japan at that time: laissez-faire and state guidance.

Laissez-faire, favored by many businessmen and some bureaucrats, seemed to be the source of economic prosperity in the West. In the context of Japan's lack of individual rights, however, laissez-faire meant exploitation of labor. The absence of any government regulations protecting the work force combined with the unrestrained drive by employers to maximize profits resulted in low wages, long hours, and unhealthy working conditions.

Japan's rapid population growth and limited arable land meant that the supply of labor remained abundant in spite of low wages and poor working conditions. At the same time, workers and employers had no experience in handling labor relations and management issues arising out of the new industrialization. In this situation, argued opponents of laissez-faire, the only solution was state guidance. Many intellectuals in the Meiji period favored the philosophy of intervention and control by the state of the relations between capital and labor. The Social Policy School, widely respected in government circles, was the chief proponent of this view in Japan.

The Social Policy School (Shakai Seisaku Gakukai), founded in 1896 by a small group of professors and government bureaucrats, centered around Kanai En and Kuwata Kumazō, two prominent professors at Tokyo Imperial University.[20] Takano Iwasaburō, Takano Fusatarō's younger brother, who was then a graduate student at Tokyo University and would later become a professor there, was also one of the founding members of the Social Policy School.[21] The position of the group was set forth in its prospectus as follows:

> Since the spirit of extreme self-interest and of free and unrestricted competition gives rise to widening gulfs between rich and poor, we reject the principles of laissez-faire. We are also opposed to socialism because it plans for the destruction of capitalists and for the overthrow of the existing economic system which would be detrimental to the fortunes of the nation. We believe that, if the present system of private property is maintained and if, within its limits, class friction is prevented by the exercise of state power and by the exertions of individual citizens, we may look forward to the continuation of social harmony.[22]

The founders of the Social Policy School had been taught in Germany under economics professors of the German Historical School, and also received instruction at the famous Verein für Sozialpolitik (Social Policy School), which had been set up in 1872. Kanai En, the first lecturer on social policy at Tokyo University, like the German social policy scholars rejected the concept of labor and capital solving labor problems on their own *(autonome Sozialpolitik)* and from the first insisted on a policy of state-directed social policy *(staatliche Sozialpolitik)*.[23]

The social policy scholars' rejection of an autonomous solution of labor problems by the marketplace brought them into direct conflict with British neoclassical economists. The British economists argued in favor of the "invisible hand" of Adam Smith and equilibrium through supply and demand, and ignored the entire field of social policy. As a result, while neoclassical economic theory is understood in English-speaking countries, social policy ideology is virtually unknown. This lacuna, together with the importance of the impact of social policy on the Japanese labor movement, necessitates a detailed discussion of social policy ideology.

The Social Policy School made the study of labor problems its main object. This represented widespread recognition of the necessity for the state's intervention in labor problems and the immaturity of the labor relations system that had sprung up after the Meiji Restoration. To social policy scholars, this in turn required the entry of the state into social reform through social policy if the state was to avoid revolution, class conflict, and breakdown of the capitalist system. The social policy scholars, in essence, sought to protect capitalism from itself.

Social policy dealt with the basic contradiction and problem within the capitalist system—labor. While the capitalist system required labor as a productive input, the wages paid to labor and the conditions under which labor worked were not necessarily sufficient for the regeneration of labor power, either from day to day, over a single working life, or even from generation to generation. In the short term, workers could be overworked, and through illness or accident, be permanently incapacitated or even killed. In the long term, wages could be held so low that workers would be unable to raise healthy families to provide the next generation of workers. If low wages and poor working conditions continued long enough, it was conceivable that capitalism could destroy its own productive input—labor—while using it to produce.[24]

The concerns of the social policy scholars were particularly appropriate to late-developing economies like Germany and Japan. Unlike Britain and the United States, where emigration or the availability of new land limited the supply of industrial labor so that workers could command a living wage, Japan and Germany both had significant excess labor trapped on the farms as industrialization started. This excessive labor supply and the drive by capitalists to maximize profits led to low wages and poor working conditions. The abysmal working conditions in the mining and

textile industries in Japan were compelling evidence that the fears
of the social policy scholars were in fact being realized.[25]

Social policy was directed primarily toward two goals. The first
goal was to alter the distributive relationships of the existing capitalist system in order to provide for the regeneration of labor
power. This was termed "distributive justice" or *verteilende Ger-
echtigkeit*. An example would be the government legislating working conditions and a minimum wage. The second goal of social
policy was to protect the capitalist system from political or revolutionary threats by fostering harmony between labor and capital.
The government would play a key role in this by promoting conciliation, arbitration, and mediation. The government could also
intervene directly by requiring consultation between workers and
managers, mandating compromises in industrial disputes, or even
outlawing strikes.[26]

From its very first year, the Social Policy School was embroiled
in disputes between scholars over the role of unionism in Japan.
Although social policy scholars agreed that strikes were detrimental because of the damage they caused the economy as well as the
workers and employers involved, they disagreed over the value of
unions themselves. Takano Iwasaburō was the first scholar in the
Social Policy School to discuss unions. Even before the formation
of the first labor unions in Japan, he pointed out the peculiar character of labor as a good, the unequal bargaining stature of workers
and employers, and the need for unions to rectify this bargaining
imbalance. Organizations of workingmen invariably led to organizations of employers, he asserted, and this invariably led to industrial warfare. Constant strikes and lockouts were damaging to the
public, and therefore an alternate method of settling industrial disputes was necessary. Takano Iwasaburō advocated joint committees made up of representatives of labor and capital at the plant or
firm level, which would negotiate contracts based on discussion
rather than conflict. Representatives of the work force would be
selected from the union, which would act as a mechanism for the
workers to reach consensus about their position in discussions
with management.[27]

Other social policy scholars disagreed with Takano Iwasaburō.
They argued that state intervention alone would resolve labor
problems. Takano Iwasaburō's opponents insisted that unions

were superfluous at best and at worst potential hotbeds of radicalism and socialism. Most advocates of state guidance, such as Takano's old teacher Kanai En, fell somewhere between Takano Iwasaburō and his opponents on the question of unionism.[28]

Because of his brother's direct involvement in the Social Policy School, Takano Fusatarō was well aware of the ideological climate in Japan as he considered starting his efforts to organize the workers. Given the prominence of laissez-faire and social policy ideologies in Japan, Takano Fusatarō's challenge was to fashion a philosophy that could command sufficient support to allow him to organize workers into trade unions. Takano correctly judged that those who favored laissez-faire sought to maintain the status quo and would oppose unions. While the Social Policy School seemed equally hostile, Takano saw that by modifying Gompers' philosophy somewhat he could gain the support of the Social Policy School while at the same time remain true to the key objectives of unionism—organization of labor and improved working conditions.

Takano modified the AFL philosophy on two key points. First, he argued, like the Social Policy School, that higher wages and better working conditions for workers were good for the economy as a whole; but he went beyond the Social Policy School by asserting that this was not only essential for the preservation of capitalism, but that it was essential for economic growth as well. The second modification Takano made was to emphasize education of the work force rather than strikes as the key source of wage increases. Takano was forced to relegate the strike to the status of a weapon of last resort if he was to have any chance of winning the support of the Social Policy School. These two changes to the AFL philosophy created a new labor ideology much more in line with that of the Social Policy School. Takano refused to change any part of the AFL philosophy regarding government, however. He opposed state control of labor and insisted on the need for union organization and mutual assistance to improve the status of the workers. Like Gompers, though, he welcomed government legislation to improve working conditions and otherwise help the working man as long as unions maintained their autonomy and power.

Takano skillfully utilized the arguments of George Gunton, a popular American economist of the period 1885–1895, to find a middle ground between the AFL ideology and that of the Social Policy School. Gunton published his most famous and influential work—*Wealth and Progress*—in 1887. This work was so successful that Gunton became president of the Institute of Social Economics and editor of the *Social Economist* in 1890, which became *Gunton's Magazine* in 1896. *Wealth and Progress* provided Takano with an economic framework that demonstrated how the interests of workers, employers, and the state were in basic harmony.[29]

In his book Gunton attacked the neoclassical economists of his day, who asserted that wage rates were fixed at a natural level by the productivity of labor. In their view, any effort to raise wages above this level would be self-defeating since correcting mechanisms such as higher prices, unemployment, or a slower rate of economic growth would offset the change in money wage rates to leave real wages unchanged. According to the neoclassicists, unionists were foolish to try to raise wages.[30]

Gunton based his argument on the need to maintain and expand aggregate demand. He pointed out that production was of little use if there were no buyers of goods and services. Demand could only be tapped if those who wanted goods and services had the money to buy them. Since workers and their demand for goods and services were an important part of the economy, keeping wages low meant restricting demand and therefore also restricting economic growth.[31]

Gunton made other strong arguments in favor of higher wages. He pointed out that higher wages induced capitalists to invest in labor-saving devices, which made workers more productive. Higher wages made possible the large-scale demand that made mass-production techniques economical. In short, Gunton argued that a gradual rise in real wages was essential to provide the demand to fuel industrial expansion.[32]

Takano Fusatarō made Gunton's argument his own:

> If there is an increase in wages, this does not bring about lower profits to the capitalist if it brings about an increase in consumption on the part of the workers. If wages should drop, there is no reason for the employer not to lose profits. Why is this? If the reason for no lost profits in the case of higher wages is higher consumption on the part of workers in the whole body of consumers, then if a fall in wages should take place, due to the drop in consumption the

employer should suffer from lower profits. To put this again in a different way, if wages rise, consumption rises, demand for goods rises and prices rise. If prices should fall, the profits made by the employer by cutting wages will not make up the loss due to the fall in prices.[33]

. . . cheap wages means small consumption, small consumption means small production, small production means small industry and small industry means small wealth, hence no prosperity, no development.[34]

If we look at the condition of Japanese workers in the economic aspect, we would tremble with anxiety for the future welfare of the country. It is not too much to say that the rise or fall of the country depends upon the solution of the problem. Really, I do not argue for the necessity of a labor movement because the condition of the workers is pitiful and their environment is intensely inimical to their interests, nor because of humane sentiment. But I do argue for it because the future prosperity of the nation does demand it and future achievement of civilization does necessitate it. For, a labor movement is a step to better their condition; to better their condition is to raise their mode of living; to raise their mode of living is to increase consumption; to increase consumption is to increase production, and production is the basis of national prosperity. Thus, every effort to better the condition of laborers is of vital importance for the nation.[35]

Takano thus found a middle ground that both Gompers and the Social Policy School could agree on: that higher wages led not only to more prosperous workers (Gompers' objective) and to maintenance of the health of the workers required for a long-term supply of labor for capitalism (the Social Policy School objective), but also to a more prosperous and growing nation by increasing aggregate demand. Takano went on to find a middle ground on the means by which higher wages would be achieved. While accepting the possibility of collective bargaining and strikes to raise wages (Gompers' position) and state intervention on behalf of labor (the Social School position), Takano emphasized worker education, self-improvement, and mutual assistance. Both the AFL and the Social Policy School could support these means to achieving higher wages. Takano outlined his thinking in a letter:

I believe that in course of amelioration of the condition of Japanese workers, or any other class of workers, the rashness will never succeed. . . . What we need is evolution as against revolution. To do injustice to other side in order to right injustice of one side is not a real remedy. We must recognize and respect the rights of employers if we have them regard and respect our rights. With such an understanding, there will result in the labor movement a reduction of much unnecessary controversies. What I think to be essential in the Japanese labor movement is not to incite working people to antagonize the capitalist, but to educate them and their children so as to raise their standard of living. What I propose to do is to enlist the sympathy of employers in educating the employees, which, I believe, is not a thing impossible to do, in view of the existing state of relationship between these classes.[36]

On several other key points, where no middle ground could be found between the AFL philosophy and that of the Social Policy School, Takano agreed sometimes with one, sometimes with the other. Takano stoutly defended the need for unions rather than relying solely on government intervention. Yet he agreed with the Social Policy School on the need for leadership by intellectuals rather than the workers themselves:

What are the conditions required for the organization of the workers? . . . One is the leadership of a famous intellectual. . . . The workers are property-less and ignorant—how are they to set up an orderly and enlightened movement? . . . They lack method and technique. . . . The intellectual plans organization and the workers gladly obey his direction. . . . A strong movement can easily be obtained with the direction of intellectuals.[37]

Takano also agreed with the Social Policy School that strikes were counterproductive, not because they damaged society but rather because the first Japanese unions would be so weak that their strikes would fail and the unions disintegrate. Takano felt that once the workers' unions were strong enough, they could as a last resort use the strike weapon to protect and improve their standard of living. Takano's position on strikes simply could not be as outspoken as that of the AFL because of Japan's authoritarian central government, the Japanese social tradition of harmony, and the Social Policy School influence:

. . . The only methods by which the workers can protect their rights, that is, the strike or boycott, have no effectiveness against the organizations of capitalists now. This presents a major obstacle to the advancement of the organization of workers, as workers are fired as a result of strikes. We have no wish to see this misfortune befall the worker so today we must try for an enlightened and orderly movement. . . .[38]

Takano agreed with both the Social Policy School and Gompers about the inadvisability of political action and the need to move quickly to resolve labor problems and thus forestall revolution or class conflict. Political action was viewed as a challenge to the state and a threat to the capitalist system, and was to be avoided:

But how long will the workers remain in their semi-conscious conditions? Is not the [un]wholesome influence of modern industries enlightening them? Is not the injurious effects of factory life awakening them? Once aroused, realization must follow. Then the strong opposition against the existing order and fallacious economic teachings will show itself. Class conflict, bitter and fierce, will be waged. Anarchism, Communism and Socialism will have their sway. It will be too late then to seek a rational solution of the labor problem.[39]

Thanks to his skillful synthesis of the philosophies of the AFL and the Social Policy School, Takano was able to call on the financial and moral support of both groups. Gompers continued to support Takano in his organizing effort, renewing Takano's commission as an AFL organizer after Takano returned to Japan in early 1896,[40] and continuing to commission Takano to do articles for the *American Federationist*. Takano's brother Iwasaburō was instrumental in fostering good relations between Takano and the social policy scholars. Social Policy School members gave liberal financial support to Takano's early organization efforts. Famous members of the Social Policy School, such as Kuwata Kumazō and Kanai En,[41] spoke at mass meetings and rallies sponsored by Takano. Both Takano and his lieutenant, Katayama Sen—the top labor leaders in the early movement—became members of the Social Policy School.[42] Assured of the backing of these two powerful groups, Takano could now turn his attention to organizing Japan's first unions.[43]

3

BIRTH OF THE LABOR MOVEMENT

AFTER Takano returned to Japan in 1896, he found a job as a translator at the Yokohama *Japan Advertiser.* Throughout the summer, public attention focused more and more on labor problems. Takano sensed the favorable situation and under Gompers' constant urging decided to start organizing the workers in November 1896.[1] Takano notified Gompers of his decision in a December 11, 1896, letter:

> The passing year was most remarkable period in history of the labor movement in this country. It was during the year that a great change has been noted of the public opinion towards the labor problem in this country. There never was such a period as the present year when welfare of the working class was so much talked about. There is very little doubt that the intense demand for labor as a result of industrial advancement on one hand and repeated strikes on the other are the factors which brought the problem to the public prominence. Nor will it be much out of the mark to predict that in the coming year we are going to witness . . . actual efforts being made at every side for the interest of that much abused class. Here let me announce to you that I myself am going to try a hand in it. I have come to the decision a month ago but so circumstanced I was at the time that I have hesitated. As the days passed on it became so apparent that a golden opportunity is at hand, and to allow to pass it off without no effort on my part is a folly. I had no more time to hesitate and leaving the office of the Advertiser a week ago I went up to Tokyo with a view of serving the field in the capital. I have already mapped up a course of my action and will endeavor to attain [my] aim[s]. . . . The plan I have mapped out begins with an

effort to present a memorial to the Lower House of the Diet, which will meet on Dec. 23 and continue in session for three months praying enactment of a law regulating organization of working people by their trade. (I will advocate the law in its simplest form, the law merely . . . an order from the Government upon the working class to form unions and leaving all other matters to union themselves to decide upon.)

Preceding the presentation of the memorial, however, I will hold a series of meetings in Tokyo with object of securing as many signatures of the working people as possible. The presentation of the memorial is so to speak a first gun of our active movement. I shall try in all my power for organizing the workers, whether the enactment is forthcoming or not. At this point I believe an explanation is necessary why I take the step of presenting the memorial. There is no power existing except an order from the Government that is strong enough to arouse the Japanese workers to the burning necessity of combination. The issue of an order from the Government will equal years effort of agitation in respect with formation of trade unions. Once they come under the shield of organization, they will be met with actual benefit of the organization, and necessity of union will become apparent to them. This is somewhat a new departure but such things are often witnessed in a country as this—a law indicating a path for the people. I am now engaged in drawing up the address and hope I shall be able to present it to the [lower] House before the month of Jan. expires.

I am now keenly feeling necessity of providing myself with a fund to carry me through my first active effort and have devised a plan to earn enough to sustain myself by engaging in a work of rendering translation of English to Japanese (and vice versa). This will not deter my active movement as I shall be able to engage in the work in spare time, and hope it will come out as I wish for.

I would like to inquire of you whether I shall not be able by your kind effort to secure one or two labor paper or magazine in your country to which I can send monthly contribution with suitable remuneration, however small it may be. I shall be under great obligation to you if you will make inquiries among your friends to the effect to let me know at any early date. . . .[2]

Takano initially felt the most promising route to organize the Japanese workers was through legislation. He believed that government action would be more effective in promoting unionism quickly than organization attempts by a group of interested individuals. His assessment of the situation was probably correct as far as the effectiveness of government action was concerned, but the chances of such legislation being enacted in Japan at that time were virtually nil. Neither laissez-faire proponents nor social policy scholars could support such a bill. However, Takano's initial recourse to the government was consistent with his ideology, which allowed for government action on behalf of the workers so long as it did not restrict or control unions.

Takano's memorial or petition to the Diet took much longer than he anticipated. While he drafted it and gathered signatures, he was able to make headway in other directions. Through the introduction of his younger brother Iwasaburō, Takano attended a regular meeting of the Social Policy School in February 1897. The meeting not only gave Takano a chance to learn more about social policy, but also provided him with an opportunity to meet and enlist the support of the progressive intellectuals he deemed so important to the success of the labor movement.[3] In preparing to launch his organizing effort, Takano wrote several drafts of a pamphlet calling on Japanese workers to organize labor unions. At the same time, he worked hard to translate the constitutions of U.S. unions, such as the International Cigar Makers and the Locomotive Engineers, into Japanese. He also translated several pamphlets related to union organization.[4]

On the evening of March 22, Sakuma Teiichi, member of the Social Policy School, a progressive employer and pro-union thinker (see chapter 1), visited Takano. He asked that Takano speak at the next meeting of the Kōgyō Kyōkai (Industrial Institute), which was to take place on April 6. The Industrial Institute had been set up in June 1893 with the object of "seeking industrial progress, strengthening close relations between employers and employees, raising the status of the workers, promoting the training of apprentices, and increasing the welfare of employers and employees." The president of the Industrial Institute was Kaneko Kentarō (later minister of state for agriculture and commerce); Sakuma was chairman. Takano immediately agreed to speak at the April 6 general meeting.[5]

Takano lost no time in making good use of his acquaintance with Sakuma. On March 29 he called on Sakuma, who among his other accomplishments also owned and operated a printing company. Takano discussed his preparations for the launching of the labor movement and asked Sakuma to print his organizing pamphlet for the Japanese workers, "Shokukō Shokun ni Yosu" ("A Summons to the Workers").

Takano, as part of his organizing strategy, also called together the men who had helped form the Shokukō Giyūkai (Knights of Labor) years before in San Francisco. Several had returned to Tokyo and joined with Takano to reestablish the organization in the spring of 1897. With their assistance, Takano decided to launch the labor movement through distribution of the organizing pamphlet rather than waiting to gather sufficient signatures for the Diet memorial. Accordingly, in early April 1897, two members of the Shokukō Giyūkai, Sawada Hannosuke and Jō Tsunetarō, began to distribute the pamphlet to factory workers on their way to work.[6]

Excerpts from "A Summons to the Workers" indicate Takano's approach to organizing the workers of Japan:[7]

The year 1899 will see Japan really opened to foreign intercourse. It will be a time when foreign capitalists will enter our country and attempt to amass millions in profits by exploiting our cheap labor and our clever workers. In such a situation, these foreign capitalists, who are not only different in character, manners, and customs, but who are also notorious for their cruel treatment of workers, will try to become your masters within the next three years. In the light of this situation, you workers must soon start to prepare yourselves or you cannot help suffering the same abuses as the workers of Europe and America. . . .

. . . Unless you workers heed the precept of the ancients and prepare for adversity while you are able, and make it your practice to provide for ways to cope with future difficulties while you are strong and sound of body, it will be hard for you to avoid transgressing the fundamental obligations of a human being, a husband, or a parent. . . . With the rise of factories and mills your wives, who should be looking after the home, take themselves off to work in the factories. And since even innocent children work at the machines, the life of the home is thrown into confusion. . . . If you are husbands, you cannot but want to give your wives a comfortable life. If you are parents, you cannot but want to see your children educated. . . .

. . . Some of you will say: "The rich are becoming richer and the poor are becoming poorer. The injustices and ruined circumstances which are the workers' lot are indeed cause for bitterness. Only by a revolution correcting this situation may the differences in wealth be equalized." . . . You workers should think twice before accepting these arguments. The advances of society have always been at a leisurely and orderly pace. . . . As far as equalization of economic differences is concerned, since all men are not equally wise, inequalities in the amount of property individually possessed are inevitable. . . . In view of this, you workers should firmly and resolutely reject ideas of revolution and acts of radicalism. . . .

We would recommend, consequently, that you workers establish trade unions based upon the feelings common to men engaged in the same work and possessed of kindred sentiments. These trade unions, moreover, should be organized on a nationwide cooperative basis. . . . Your internecine strife, the contempt in which the foreigners hold you, and the position in which you find yourselves today, all may to a large extent be attributed to the failure of you workers to act unitedly.

We thus advise you again to form trade unions—but how should such trade unions be organized?

1. A local trade union should be formed whenever seven or more members of a trade gather together in a single city or county.

2. A local trade union federation should be formed by uniting the various local trade unions in a city or county.

3. A national trade federation should be formed by uniting the various local trade unions in a particular trade.

4. The various national trade federations should be united to form a national trade alliance.

Each local union and the national trade federation build up a fund from the monthly dues of the union members, minus union expenses and so on.

Each union establishes rules, deciding the time to make members eligible for assistance (for example, after some number of months of payment of dues) and the lowest limit of yen in the fund beyond which the fund cannot be used to assist union members.

Each union should expand its assistance provisions to include assistance of union members who are unemployed, wish to travel, or are old.

Stand up, you workers! Stand up and organize unions! Endeavor to discharge that important obligation and to preserve your honor as men!

. . . It is the height of folly to degrade oneself in the face of the enemy due to petty emotional matters or internal disputes. . . . If a small group is gathered which realizes the insignificant nature of its position and endeavors to strive for itself and for its wives and children, that is, a band of workers sworn to fight to the death on the glorious field of battle, a glorious movement is the result. . . . It has been our firm belief that the number of workers who are filled with the spirit of heroism, who see themselves as part of this band of workers sworn to fight to the death, certainly cannot be small.[8]

Takano's pamphlet appealed less to the workers as members of a class-conscious proletariat with a revolutionary mission than it did to Japanese attitudes among them. Since the revision of foreign treaties would allow foreigners to live in Japan's interior starting in 1899, "A Summons to the Workers" took advantage of the Japanese people's fear of foreign domination and exploitation. The pamphlet went on to play on the workers' desire for a full and happy family life. It appealed to the honesty and upright character of the workers, their law-abiding nature, their sense of social cohesion and responsibility, and their male pride and courage.

This document, which laid the foundation of the labor movement in Japan, rejected revolutionary tactics and advocated slow and sure organization of the workers. It had a nationalistic flavor as it attempted to arouse fear of domination by foreign employers. This also played on the Japanese feeling of inferiority at not being recognized as a civilized people in foreign eyes, and the feeling of nationalistic pride in Japanese institutions and customs, which foreigners threatened. "A Summons to the Workers" almost seemed to promise that the workers would aid Japan's modernization, gain the respect of foreigners, and save Japan from the threat of takeover by foreign capital simply by organizing unions.

The pamphlet is interesting in several other respects. The foreign employer is portrayed as the main opponent. Opposition to Japanese employers is downplayed, and the break-up of the home is attributed to machines, factories, and foreigners. Workers are urged to make the necessary preparations for bad times: if they subsequently suffer because they ignored such advice, it is their own fault.

More important than the deliberate de-emphasis of opposition to domestic employers is the attitude displayed toward the concept of unions as tools to raise wages, improve working conditions, and control the supply of labor. Nowhere does the pamphlet mention the possibility of affecting wages by concerted action. Takano mentions foreign workers striking, making specific mention of the large sums disbursed by Western unions, even strike payments, but not what issues caused them to strike. Instead of explaining how workers could build up a strike fund and then negotiate for higher wages and better conditions, Takano deliberately avoids this and instead focuses the attention of the workers on mutual assistance.

Although this pamphlet appears to advocate Western-style unionism, the functions of the trade unions explained by the pamphlet are more limited than those of the West. These functions are to help develop the nation, to raise the dignity and independence of the workers through mutual assistance, to help make Japanese equal to foreigners, and to oppose exploitation by foreign employers. The trade unions outlined by the pamphlet do not strike, advocate revolutionary tactics, oppose domestic employers, or attempt to control wages and the supply of labor. This organizing pamphlet represents a compromise between pure and simple American Federation of Labor trade unionism and the ideology of Japan's Social Policy School.

Takano's decision to compromise with the Social Policy School's position on the strike question enabled him to obtain the support of key intellectuals in Japan. Yet his failure to embrace the strike weapon had two major consequences for the labor movement. First, the appeal of unionism to the workers was weakened since direct efforts to raise wages and improve working conditions were ruled out. Second, and perhaps even more important, Takano's abandonment of the strike weapon did not mean that the movement would not wield such a weapon. Instead, it meant that radicals and socialists would capitalize on successful strikes instead of union moderates. Takano's relinquishment of the strike weapon served in the long term to weaken his position and that of moderate progressive unionists and strengthen the standing of the militant radicals Takano was trying to preempt within the labor movement.

Shortly after the distribution of "A Summons to the Workers" began, Takano moved to broaden his contacts and find other means to take his message to the workingmen of Japan. He decided to use the general meeting of the Industrial Institute, to which he had been invited by Sakuma Teiichi in March, as another forum for labor organization. Takano described the April 6 meeting in a letter to Samuel Gompers:

Hongo, Tokyo, Japan, April 15, 1897

Mr. Samuel Gompers,
Pres't American Federation of Labor:

My Dear Sir: I have, at last, the honor to inform you that the first public meeting ever held in this country with the sole object of advocating the cause of labor was held . . . on the 6th inst. at the Kinki-kan, Kanda, this city, when several hundred workmen attended despite a pouring rain and addressed by Messrs. T. Sakuma, a hearty sympathizer with the cause of labor; K. Tajima, a graduate of the Imperial University; T. Takeuchi, a student of social problems, and myself.

Mr. Sakuma broached on the national necessity of bettering the laborer's condition, and gave much valuable advice to the audience, a large majority of which was working people. Messrs. Tajima and Takeuchi advocated: the former, co-operation as the only means to promote the welfare of working people; the latter, the habit of thrift among workers. I myself advanced the organization of workers as the best means to promote the interest of workers, dwelling at considerable length upon the method of formation of trade unions, explaining the plan of American trade unions and the American Federation of Labor. . . .

The "friends of workers" [under whose auspices I spoke] consists of four remnants, members of an association formed years ago in San Francisco by some dozen Japanese living there. The remnant members are a tailor, two shoemakers and myself, all of them, I assure you, are staunch advocates of trade unionism.

At the meeting a pamphlet written by me was distributed, in which the benefit of organized action, the plan of formation, and the beneficiary system in vogue in the United States were fully set forth. I enclose a copy as it is the first of its kind published in this country. . . .

The presentation of the petition to the Lower House of the Diet, of which I wrote you before, was abandoned owing to advice I have received from a member of the House. He, however, promised to present to the House at its next session a bill encouraging the formation of trade unions.[9]

Having made good use of the meeting of the Industrial Institute, Takano and his supporters sought to sponsor a meeting of their own, where they could set the entire agenda. It would be several months, however, before Takano and the "friends of workers" (Knights of Labor) could sponsor their own meeting. The main problem holding up the organization of the workers was financial. Between April and June, Takano worked hard to convince his source of support in Japan—the social policy scholars—to assist his organization efforts financially. By June he had received pledges of financial assistance for his planned series of rallies from certain Social Policy School members. Suzuki Jun'ichirō, an officer of the Social Policy School, was particularly supportive.[10]

In mid-June an office for the Japan Knights of Labor was set up in central Tokyo, and a rally was scheduled for the end of the month. Takano asked Katayama Sen, a social worker, and Matsumura Kaiseki, a noted scholar and lecturer, to give speeches. He then obtained the use of the YMCA Hall in Tokyo for the rally. Takano called on Sakuma Teiichi and asked that he speak at the meeting, and also asked that Shimada Saburō, a liberal journalist and politician, attend. Just prior to the rally, Takano met with Jō Tsunetarō, Sawada Hannosuke, Katayama Sen, and Suzuki Jun'-ichirō to discuss the foundation of the labor movement at the rally. On June 24 Takano personally distributed pamphlets to workers announcing the meeting.[11]

On June 25, 1897, the Japan Knights of Labor held its rally at the YMCA Hall. Despite bad weather, there were over a thousand people in attendance,[12] more than half of whom were workers. Jō Tsunetarō opened the meeting, followed by Takano, Matsumura, Sakuma, and Katayama, who all gave speeches. After the speeches Takano took the opportunity, as representative of the Knights of Labor, to voice the need for the formation of a Rōdō Kumiai Kiseikai (Association for Encouragement and Formation of Trade Unions). Some forty persons from the audience responded to Takano's call, and the addition of Sawada, Jō, Takano, and other sponsors of the meeting brought the total to forty-seven founding members of the Kiseikai.[13]

The Kiseikai was an umbrella organization that allowed workers of all trades and skill levels to join. Once a sufficient number of workers from a particular trade had been recruited, they would be organized into trade unions. Superficially, the Kiseikai resembled the Knights of Labor: both had open membership and a centralized executive body; both sought to promote cooperation and organization, and downplayed strikes.[14]

Yet the Knights of Labor had no provision to break itself up into constituent trade unions. While the Knights had a few subunits that closely resembled national trade unions—for example, the Window-Glass Workers' Association—these subunits were not created by the Knights. Instead, they were accommodations to existing unions of workers who wished to affiliate with the Knights as a group. The leaders of the Knights, in their quest for growth, chose to accept these organizations, even though they were incompatible with the general, mixed structure of the Knights of Labor.[15]

Takano actually modeled the Kiseikai on the federal labor unions of the American Federation of Labor. These, like the Kiseikai, were central, mixed bodies that, when they became large enough, were broken up into trade unions. The AFL described the federal labor unions as "a recruiting ground for the trade union movement and a convenience for the workers in such localities or diverse callings where there is an insufficient number of any particular trade or calling to form a trade union."[16] The federal labor union was basically an organizing convenience. When the AFL started an organizing drive in a given geographical area, it brought both the skilled and unskilled recruits of a number of trades into a federal labor union. When the federal union became large enough, it was broken into locals by trade, and these locals were affiliated with the national trade unions.[17] Takano had found within the AFL structure what he considered to be the ideal approach to labor organizing in Japan.

But Takano added some key elements to the Kiseikai that made it much more than a mere organizing body. Takano had no intention of dissolving the Kiseikai when the constituent unions were formed as the AFL federal labor union had done. He envisioned instead the Kiseikai becoming a federation of trade unions, like the AFL itself. Each union would belong to the Kiseikai, and the Kiseikai would lead the union movement and coordinate the efforts of the unions. To insure that he and his supporters controlled the movement, Takano required interlocking executive boards for the Kiseikai and the unions, and he restricted the activities of the national trade unions to mutual assistance, operating cooperatives, and mediation in labor disputes. The Kiseikai also was much stronger than the AFL since it had its own source of direct financing: a set portion of each union member's dues was earmarked for the Kiseikai and paid monthly by each constituent trade union.

On July 5, 1897, the inaugural ceremony of the Kiseikai was held in a Tokyo working-class district.[18] Over the previous two weeks the forty-seven founding members had been joined by twenty-four new recruits. Takano, Sawada, and Jō were elected temporary directors at this meeting, and work commenced on the constitution of the Kiseikai. Takano and his supporters decided to continue the program of rallies to educate the public and the workers. Members contributed twenty-eight yen for the next rally, which was held on July 18, again at the YMCA Hall in Tokyo. Takano, Katayama, and other Kiseikai members gave speeches, and at the end of the meeting there were over thirty new members for the Kiseikai.[19]

The leaders of the Kiseikai held the first monthly business meeting on August 1. Ten regular officers and five directors, including Takano, Katayama, and Sawada, were elected. Three committees were formed from among these fifteen men: an Activities Committee of eight members, a Rally Committee of eight members, and an Education Committee of five members. Of the five directors, Takano was elected executive director. Suzuki Jun'ichirō, a scholar and officer of the Social Policy School, and Sakuma Teiichi were nominated councilors. The constitution of the Kiseikai was formally adopted, and since the organization showed promise for growth, a continuing program of agitation was agreed upon. The leaders of the Kiseikai were determined to sponsor two or three rallies monthly and expand the area of activity from Tokyo to nearby Yokohama.[20]

The Kiseikai was organized to promote and create labor unions rather than to act as a union itself. It strove to make contact with existing unions and coordinate their activities. The leaders of the Kiseikai thought of it as a "trade union school."[21] Its goal was to recruit future union members, indoctrinate them, and, when a sufficient number of members in one trade or industry had been recruited, to organize a union among them. Kiseikai members, whether workers or intellectuals, were expected to agitate for organization of the workers and to recruit new members for the Kiseikai. When unions were formed, the union members remained members of the Kiseikai and their obligation to recruit new Kiseikai members from any trade continued.

Since the publication and distribution of "A Summons to the Workers," a mere four months had elapsed. Yet in that time the four "remnants" of the Shokukō Giyūkai of San Francisco had launched an organization capable of organizing unions and had obtained support from a wide range of Japanese intellectuals, liberals, and workers. The Kiseikai, with officers, a constitution, and financing, embarked fully into organizing efforts in the fall of 1897. The Japanese labor movement dates from the formation of the Kiseikai, and the promise of the Kiseikai was fulfilled within a few months by the emergence of Japan's first large independent unions.

4

THE METALWORKERS' UNION

THE LEADERS of the Kiseikai were busy through the fall with regular meetings and rallies, and were active in building good relations with existing labor organizations. On August 21, 1897, Takano and Katayama Sen were invited to speak at a meeting of the Tokyo Lithographers' Union. They spoke at a meeting of the Tokyo Ship Carpenters' Union on September 1, and at the inaugural ceremony of the Tokyo Doll-Makers' Union on September 20. Takano and his followers aggressively recruited new members through rallies and personal contacts with Kiseikai members' friends. The Kiseikai grew rapidly, from less than 100 members in July, to over 300 in August, 450 in September, and over 1,000 members in November.[1]

Metalworkers—machinists, boilermakers, casters, forgers, lathe operators, fitters, smiths, and so on—formed the majority of Kiseikai recruits. There were three reasons for this: 1) the prior history of organization by metalworkers; 2) the concentration of metalworkers in large industrial enterprises; and 3) the use of advanced management techniques and the rapid change from indirect to direct management then ongoing at these enterprises.

Metalworkers had been the most active of those involved in labor organization in Japan prior to 1897. Metalworking enjoyed the largest employment among the new occupations and grew rapidly during the Meiji period under government policies designed to enable Japan to be militarily self-sufficient. Lacking any pre-Meiji history of traditional craft organization and forced to rapidly adapt to changing Western manufacturing techniques, metalworkers naturally looked to the West as their model for labor organization.

The popular *oyakata* Ozawa Benzō, his brother Kunitarō, and Aida Kichigorō had attempted to organize metalworkers in the Tokyo shipyards in 1887 and 1889. Muramatsu Tamitarō, an *oyakata* foreman at the Tokyo Armaments Works, had succeeded in forming a mutual assistance organization in February 1897 based at the Rifle Works of the Tokyo Armaments Works. These earlier organization efforts made metalworkers particularly receptive to the Kiseikai's recruitment attempts.[2]

The leaders of these early organization drives joined the Kiseikai and gave their full assistance to helping it grow. Ozawa Benzō, for example, worked with the Kiseikai to establish the Metalworkers' Union. Later, as head of the union's mutual assistance department, he spearheaded efforts to organize the Ishikawajima Shipyards for the union.[3] Muramatsu Tamitarō was elected one of the first five directors of the Kiseikai and later aided Katayama Sen as accounting section chief of the Metalworkers' Union publication *Rōdō Sekai* (Labor World). Muramatsu's mutual assistance organization, the Alliance for Industrial Organization, cooperated fully with the Kiseikai. Most members of the AIO joined the Kiseikai and helped to form the Metalworkers' Union. The core of the AIO's membership was at the Rifle Works of the Tokyo Armaments Works, which became one of the largest and strongest branches of the Metalworkers' Union. Because it was gathering funds to set up its own factory, the AIO continued to maintain its own separate treasury and organize its own activities.[4]

The concentration of metalworkers in large industrial enterprises was a major factor in their rapid organization. Unlike many other new occupations—in the printing and railway industries, for example, where there were rarely more than fifty men at a particular workplace—metalworkers were concentrated at large industrial enterprises employing over a thousand workers. The Tokyo and Osaka Armaments Works, the shipyards at Yokosuka, Akabane, and Ishikawajima, and the Shibaura Engineering Works each employed over a thousand men, with the largest plant employing nearly five thousand. In such large plants labor organization was easier: workers were easier to contact, a critical mass of worker activists more readily assembled, and union business more easily administered.

Finally, metalworkers organized quickly into unions because management pressure on them was intense. The shipyards and government armaments works were among the first to introduce advanced Western management techniques. These techniques served to reduce the authority and independence of the *oyakata* and strengthen labor supervision by management. Indirect management, where *oyakata* were given general objectives and discretion over pay, hours, conditions, hiring and firing, and so on, rapidly gave way to direct management control of personnel functions with close direction of foremen by line managers.

The Tokyo Armaments Works is a characteristic example, where the entire factory, and especially the Rifle Works, adopted mass-production techniques.[5] In 1885 the Japanese army had developed the Murata rifle and set up a mass-production system for it at the Tokyo Armaments Works. That year thirty thousand rifles were produced. Subsequently, with the Murata repeating rifle and the 1897 foot soldier's rifle, the mass-production techniques were improved and their application broadened. In 1897 a number of British machines were purchased and introduced, and the specialization and division of labor was intensified. The metalworkers at the Tokyo Armaments Works and elsewhere reacted to the breakdown of their jobs and tight management control by organizing.[6]

Since the Kiseikai's membership was almost exclusively in the metalworking trades,[7] and the objective of the Kiseikai was to form unions from among their members, the Kiseikai's main effort in the fall of 1897 was to form a union of metalworkers. In late August the Kiseikai sponsored a mass meeting at the Tokyo Armaments Works (Tokyo Hōhei Kōshō), which would later become the stronghold of the Metalworkers' Union. On October 24 Kiseikai leaders met to discuss the rules of the proposed union. With the election of founding members on November 14, worker activists and Kiseikai leaders moved closer to the formation of the union. Among the thirty-six founding members were Iwata Sukejirō, Mimae Kintarō, and Umakai Chōnosuke, three worker activists in the Kiseikai.[8]

These three worker activists were the only workers among the ten regular officers of the Kiseikai elected August 1, 1897. All three were employed in the newest metalworking occupations at government-run plants with advanced supervisory systems. Umakai was a lathe operator in the Ministry of Posts and Communications Factory, which made equipment for lighthouses; Mamie and

Iwata were fitters at the Tokyo Armaments Works. They were young, skilled workers who later founded and joined the Kiseikai Youth Group and played key roles in day-to-day recruitment, dues collection, and the administration of mutual assistance. To a large extent it was the emergence of men like these who, with the support of intellectuals like Takano and *oyakata* like Ozawa or Muramatsu, made Japan's first major union possible.[9]

By December sufficient members had been recruited and preparations made for the founding of the Metalworkers' Union. The inaugural ceremony of the new union was held on December 1, 1897. Takano described the ceremony and the union in a letter to Gompers:

> Hongo, Tokyo, Japan, December 17, 1897. On the evening of December 1st last, with pomp and array, the newly formed union of iron workers held its opening ceremony at the Association Hall of this city with many prominent public officials and capitalists as guests. The whole strength of the union, 1,200 in number, together with an equal number of workers of other trades were in attendance. The ceremony was opened by myself as chairman of the committee on arrangement. Mr. Sakuma Teiichi, sympathizer with labor, delivered the first congratulatory speech followed by Messrs. Shimada Saburo, vice president of the Lower House of Diet; Miyoshi Taizo, ex-chief Justice of the Court of Cassation; Profs. Takano Iwasaburo and Suzuki Junichiro. Mr. Katayama Sen, M.A. of Wisconsin University, was the last speaker and the ceremony was closed amid thundering cheers for the union.
>
> . . . There never was in the industrial annals of this country any workingmen's association formed with so large a membership as the Iron Workers Union, nor has there ever before been any meeting held under the auspices of working people which was attended by public officials and capitalists. . . .
>
> . . . It is height of folly on the part of organized workers to indulge in inflammatory declaration or radical utterances at present stage of our social condition, that is to say, while the workers are not sufficiently organized on one hand and the strong arm of the government is ever ready to crush out organization of workingmen on the other, the founders of the union should be complimented for their wise choice of peaceful and conservative methods as represented in pure and simple trade unionism. . . . What nonsense it would be for a labor organization to declare for any political action while its members are all barred out from political participation by

reason of voting qualification (only those who are paying national taxes to an amount of 15 yen are qualified voters). The best it is able to gain by such action is an enmity of government and hatred of governing classes.

Having steered clear away from all these dangers, the union endeavors to establish a solid basis of its organization by promoting solidarity of its members with a system of benefit which consists of a sick benefit of 20 sen per diem for a period of ninety days within a year; a funeral benefit of 20 yen, and a death benefit of 10 to 30 yen. A moderate sum of 20 sen is uniformly charged as monthly dues. Elementary education of its workers, absence of which is a conspicuous feature among our workers, is entrusted to its mother organization, the Rodo Kumiai Kisei Kwai, thus establishing links of connection with other unions to be formed by the association. This method, it is claimed, will make easier that assiduous task of federating existing unions, enabling them to present a solid front of the army of organized workers as soon as the association succeeds to organize other trades. . . .

. . . While the Rodo Kumiai Kisei Kwai was able to bring only 100 workers of other trades under its banner, 1,200 iron workers flocked to it during the same length of time, which goes to show that their intelligence and higher wage condition made them easier to perceive the necessity of organized effort and susceptible to the influence of agitation carried on by the association. Having these elements of success, nothing but a bright future is predictive at present for the union.[10]

Takano's letter makes several important observations about the Metalworkers' Union (which he calls the Iron Workers' Union). The initial reaction of many public officials and employers to the formation of the union was mixed. The appearance of unionism in Japan represented progress toward the ideal of industrialization—after all, all the advanced Western countries had unions. So the natural opposition to their emergence displayed by employers and the government was tempered by the realization that this was a landmark in Japanese economic development. The Metalworkers' Union thus began its brief history with some degree of support among employers and government bureaucrats, as indicated by their attendance at the founding meeting.

Takano's letter also reveals something of the character of the Metalworkers' Union. The leaders of the Kiseikai and the union espoused gradualism and moderation, not revolution. The basis for union organization was mutual assistance, and elaborate mutual assistance provisions were the heart of the union's constitution. The mutual assistance provisions of the union were relatively generous, especially when compared to the level of dues. At twenty sen, dues amounted to only two or three hours' wages per month. General educational activities were the province of the Kiseikai, which was to become a federation of affiliated unions as new unions were formed. Takano was proud of the higher-paid, skilled membership of the union.

The Metalworkers' Union membership was concentrated in a few workplaces, each of which was highly organized (see table 3). Of the 1,183 members of the Metalworkers' Union at the time of its inauguration, over half (677) were employed at the Tokyo Armaments Works. The vast majority of these worked at the Rifle Works (570 members).[11] The Rifle Works was highly organized, with virtually every metalworker there a union member. At most of the other branches, which were at much smaller workplaces, unionization was also high, with over half of the workers union members.

With the birth of the Metalworkers' Union came the emergence of *Rōdō Sekai* (hereinafter referred to as *Labor World*), its official

Table 3. Membership of the Metalworkers' Union, by Workplace (December 1, 1897)

Location	Membership
Tokyo Armaments Works	677
Kōbu Railway	6
Shimbashi Railway Workshop	86
Ministry of Posts and Communications Factory (lighthouse equipment)	40
Hiraoka Factory (railway equipment)	43
Nakashima Factory (boilers, machinery)	53
Hara Iron Works	11
Tokyo Cotton Spinning Plant	15
Takeuchi Safe Factory	14
Ōmiya Factory (Japan Railways Co.)	53
Yokohama (dockyards)	185
Total	1,183

Sources: The figures and breakdowns are from Katayama Sen and Nishikawa Mitsujirō, *Nihon no Rōdō Undō* [The Japanese labor movement] (Tokyo: Iwanami Shoten, 1952; first published in 1901), 76–77. The description of the products of the various smaller factories is provided by Rōdō Undō Shiryō Iinkai, ed., *Nihon Rōdō Undō Shiryō* [Collected documents on the Japanese labor movement] (Tokyo, 1962) 1:471.

publication. A biweekly averaging ten pages, it regularly ran a half-page labor cartoon, several articles on labor, union news, a full page of news in English, and a page or two of advertisements. Katayama Sen was the editor. The paper's motto admonished, "If any man will not work, neither let him eat."[12] Its slogan claimed: "The Laborer is worthy of his hire."[13] The price of *Labor World* was two sen, or one cent, and its circulation gradually rose to over three thousand by the spring of 1898.[14]

The Kiseikai had a strong influence on the union. The decision-making body of the union was a committee made up of representatives elected from each branch. There was one representative for each fifty members in a branch.[15] The governing body was the Executive Board, composed of the five directors of the Kiseikai and six union officers—the chairmen and vice-chairmen of the mutual assistance, finance, and general affairs departments of the union. One of the eleven board members was selected chairman.[16] This structure magnified the power of the Kiseikai. But in reality, Takano and Katayama became the key decision makers. Headquarters controlled finances and so had relatively strong control over the branches. But this did not prevent the branches from occasionally engaging in autonomous action and bucking headquarters.[17]

The structure of the Metalworkers' Union was based more on industry than individual crafts. All workers in a particular shop would commonly be union members, regardless of their craft. With this inclusive character, the union more closely resembled modern-day Japanese enterprise-unions (where all employees in a particular firm regardless of skill level or trade are union members) than craft unions of the 1890s.

Union members were originally "blacksmiths, forgers, casters, machinists, boilermakers and copper workers," but the constitution was soon revised to allow shipbuilders, electrical workers, and engineers or firemen in metalworking shops to be members. The wording of the constitution allowed even machinists and other workers outside heavy industry to join the union, but in fact virtually all union members worked in heavy industry. There were no membership restrictions on age, years of experience, or condition of service (apprentices could join).[18] This was in sharp contrast to the West, where the restrictions on membership were severe. Nor were Western unions inclusive. There were unions of machinists, forgers, boilermakers, electrical workers, and so on.

In addition to being inclusive, the Metalworkers' Union was overwhelmingly organized on a shop basis. Branches were set up when in one factory, several nearby factories, or a small geographic area there were twenty-five or more union members.[19] Branches were of two different types—geographically based and workplace- or shop-based. A geographically based branch was composed of union members who worked at several workplaces in a single area. The shop-based branch was made up of all union members employed at a particular shop at a workplace. Since there were usually several shops at a major workplace (differentiated by function—one for casting, one for smithing, and so on), there might be several shop-based branches at a single workplace. Only a few branches were organized on a geographical basis, and they never made up more than 5 percent of union membership.[20]

Two examples of geographically based branches are the third (Yokohama) branch and the sixth (Honjo) branch. The Yokohama branch was based on the Yokohama dockworkers and included union members working in small shops in the Yokohama area. The Honjo branch was based on union membership in small factories in the Honjo ward of Tokyo, such as the Hiraoka Works, the Nakashima Works, and the Takeuchi Safe Factory.[21]

Shop-based branches were of two types. One type was a branch covering an entire workplace, with sub-branches for each shop at that workplace. The other type had a branch for each shop. An example of the first type was branch seventeen at the Yokosuka Navy Shipyards. This single branch covered all union members at the entire shipyard. Branch seventeen proved somewhat unwieldy as membership grew. It was formed in April 1898 as a single entity, but by June of that year the branch had created six internal sub-branches for the major shops at the shipyards: Shipbuilders A, Shipbuilders B, Machinists, Boilermakers, Wrought-Iron Workers, and Casters. Each of these subdivisions were made by the branch itself solely for its own administrative convenience. Each sub-branch had its own assistant director, finance officer, mutual assistance officer, and general affairs officer. These officers not only formed the leadership of the sub-branch, but, together with the branch director and branch finance officers, also oversaw the branch.[22] This structure of a branch at the workplace with sub-branches for each shop was common at the large enterprises.[23]

An example of the simple shop-based branch structure is the Tokyo Armaments Works. Here, instead of one workplace branch with shop sub-branches, a branch was set up for each shop. When the union was first organized there were seven branches at the Tokyo Armaments Works, and by the end of 1899 there were eleven.[24] Each shop branch had its own officers. As membership grew, the lack of coordination between branches became an issue, and in February 1898 a federation of the Tokyo Armaments Works branches was set up with headquarters in Kanda, Tokyo.[25]

The federation primarily concerned itself with operating union cooperatives and providing occupational counseling to the membership. As the federation took over and rationalized the various cooperatives set up by the different branches at the Works, it became clear that the federation provided needed coordination.[26] The federation at the Works provided the same support for its shop-based branches as the branch leadership provided at Yokosuka to the shop-based sub-branches. Thus the two types of shop-based branches were virtually identical, the only distinction being the definition of a branch—the shop-based organization or the workplace-based organization.

The shop-based organization structure of the Metalworkers' Union facilitated the educational, cooperative, mutual assistance, and club functions of the union. These functions, by nature inclusive (as compared to exclusive functions such as control of the labor force and restriction of apprentices), caused the structure of the Metalworkers' Union to differ from that of Western unions. The Metalworkers' Union was based on an appeal to workers that was not craft-specific. It's goals—to provide education, mutual assistance, higher status, and representation for the workers—attracted workers regardless of craft, skill level, or industry. This kind of appeal was translated into a structure that did not discriminate against any workers in the industry, but that revolved around the shop unions within which effective recruitment and educational and club activities could be carried out. The evolution of the shop structure indicated that Japanese workers were more "shop-conscious" than job, class, or craft-conscious.[27]

The evolution of the shop-based organizational structure with coordinating units at the workplace level occurred independently of the union constitution and Kiseikai direction. It arose out of the natural affinities and inclinations of the workers at that time. This structure, evident at the inception of the Japanese labor movement, is peculiar to Japan. It forms the basis for organization by company (enterprise unionism) with weak federations of company-based unions within a particular industry. Shop-based structure with groups of shops in the same enterprise coordinating activities is very similar to today's plant-based locals organized into enterprise-wide unions. The labor force in Japan clearly preferred an inclusive, enterprise-based structure in the 1890s, as is the case today.

The Metalworkers' Union itself, spanning several enterprises, is analogous to today's union federation, which groups unions from different enterprises in an industry-wide federation. The Kiseikai, intended as a central coordinator for many unions, has many parallels with the national union centers such as Sōhyō and Dōmei, which are groupings of several industry-wide union federations.

The key functions of the Metalworkers' Union were mutual assistance and the operation of cooperatives. Mutual assistance, heavily stressed in "A Summons to the Workers," was "a solid base of . . . [union] organization" in Takano's eyes.[28] Of the twenty-sen dues required by the Metalworkers' Union, ten sen went to mutual assistance and headquarters expenses.[29] Of the remaining ten sen, half went to the Kiseikai and half to the branch. The mutual assistance provisions in the rules of the Metalworkers' Union were detailed and specific. Benefits were not designed to replace lost wages completely: wages ranged from forty to fifty sen and up per day for workers in heavy industry, while sickness and injury benefits, for example, were only twenty sen per day.

Benefits were offered in case of illness, injury, death, and loss of home due to fire. The death benefits included not only a funeral allowance of twenty yen, but also a one-time family assistance allowance of from ten to thirty yen depending on the number of years of union membership of the deceased. A unionist had to have been a member in good standing for six months in order to receive benefits. In addition, no benefits were paid if the member was at fault. The fire benefits, for example, could only be paid if the fire spread to the victim's home, not if it started there. The mutual assistance provisions required that union officers check and verify every claim.[30]

The dues devoted to supporting these mutual assistance provisions were quite low in comparison with those of Western unions, both in absolute and relative terms. In the West, dues equivalent to one day's pay a month or even one hour's pay a day were standard, between 4 and 10 percent of a worker's wages. In comparison, the Metalworkers' Union dues were only 1 percent of a Japanese worker's wages. The low level of dues made the benefit system quite liberal. For only twenty sen each month a unionist could receive twenty sen per day for up to ninety days each year under the sickness and injury benefit provisions. The Metalworkers' Union, in this sense, copied the scope of mutual assistance benefits in the West but without the accompanying high dues. Maintenance of such benefits over time was particularly precarious since less than half of the monthly dues went to mutual assistance, the rest going to support the Kiseikai, union headquarters, and the branch organization.

In addition to mutual assistance, operating cooperatives was another key function of the Metalworkers' Union. Both Takano and Katayama saw cooperatives as a key means of strengthening the union. According to Takano's plan, the union would have a cooperative for each branch. The cooperatives would be branch-operated and would sell selected items to members. The price for goods would be no higher than 15 percent above the price at which they were obtained or no higher than the market price. Profits from the cooperatives would be used in three ways: capital formation to support the growth of the cooperative, contributions to union activities, and dividends to the workers.[31]

The Metalworkers' Union organized Japan's first union cooperatives. The cooperatives did a significant business and represented a large investment of union funds and energies (see table 4). Several of the stores, such as that in Yokohama, had enough sales to warrant a number of full-time employees. Most union members within range of a cooperative became members and took advantage of the cooperative's attractive prices. But though the cooperatives represented a financial saving for the members, they did not contribute much to the union's finances. Poor cash flow from the high proportion of credit sales to union members combined with low profit margins kept the cooperatives from paying much in dividends or supporting union activities.

Along with cooperatives and mutual assistance, the Metalworkers' Union placed strong emphasis on education of the membership. As one aspect of education, the union set up labor clubs. The purpose of these clubs was for "workers to gather together, exchange ideas, engage in discussion, give speeches, and while

Table 4. Metalworkers' Union Cooperatives (July 1, 1899)

LOCATION	PAID-UP CAPITAL (yen)	MONTHLY BUSINESS (yen)	MEMBERSHIP (persons)
Misaki-chō	250	300	50
Ōmiya	70	50	40
Aomori	600	472	61
Sendai	300	500	90
Kuroiso	300	400	45
Taira	300	150	50
Hara-machi	350	400	40
Matsuda	150	175	100
Iidabashi	3,000	1,500	300
Yokohama	2,000	1,200	350
Ishikawa	200	150	120
Fukushima	1,600	2,000	100
Total	9,120	7,297	1,346

Source: *Labor World*, no. 39 (July 1, 1899): 10.

enjoying themselves absorb the atmosphere of enlightenment."[32] The most representative of the labor clubs was the one at the Ōmiya factory of the Japan Railway Company (branch two). This club engaged in activities ranging from putting on plays to holding a rally to promote the abolition of legalized prostitution.[33]

Mutual assistance, cooperatives, and education—these were the objectives of the Metalworkers' Union. True to Takano's philosophy, the Metalworkers' Union sought to improve the conditions of the workers by providing a framework in which the workers could improve their health and knowledge and increase productivity, thereby earning higher wages and enhanced status. Takano thought that unionism as a tool to redress economic inequality and afford workers the opportunity to bargain with employers on an equal basis was too advanced a concept to introduce to Japanese workers, and one that if introduced and acted upon would lead to confrontation with management and the disintegration of the union.

Japan's first major union showed many of the characteristics for which Japanese unionism is known today. First and foremost, it exhibited the shop-based structure that formed the basis for enterprise unionism. Second, it had an inclusive, industrial character, which allowed all shop employees to join regardless of age, craft, or training. This inclusive, industrial character was also a key support for enterprise unionism. Third, the union had low dues combined with liberal mutual assistance functions, which made it relatively weak financially and unable to undertake a long strike from lack of a strike fund. Finally, the union strongly emphasized social and self-help activities, such as labor clubs and cooperatives. Japanese unions today work with their companies to provide social and self-help activities to employees.

Thus, Japan's first union was a forerunner of Japan's later union structure and ideology. By compromising between pure and simple trade unionism and Social Policy School ideology, Takano traded the union movement's strongest weapon—the strike, supported by a strong central strike fund—for a higher level of outside intellectual and financial support. While tactically a confrontational approach would certainly have been unwise, Takano's failure to prepare for possible labor-management conflict from the first proved a significant handicap for the union. The adoption of liberal mutual assistance benefits without sufficient dues to support them robbed the union of the ability to withstand adversity of any kind. The Metalworkers' Union thus proved a forerunner of today's enterprise unions, which are characterized by low dues, weak finances, aversion to strike action, a preference for labor-management cooperation, and company or shop-based structure.

5

GROWTH OF THE LABOR MOVEMENT

THE LABOR movement grew rapidly in scope and size during 1898. The political situation was unusually conducive to popular movements, since during 1898 Japan witnessed its first cabinet composed solely of popular party politicians, excluding the authoritarian oligarchs who had led the Meiji Restoration. Simultaneously, employment in heavy industry rose rapidly, fueled by an aggressive government armaments program. The boom in activity also led to inflation, particularly in the price of rice. Skilled industrial workers found themselves in high demand, but employers sought to hold wages steady even as prices rose. The result was high labor turnover combined with unprecedented strike activity.

Until 1895 Japanese political life had been dominated by the struggle between the liberal parties and the oligarchs. After 1895, however, the parties sought to gain by cooperation what they had been unable to obtain by direct confrontation. Accordingly, each party began to attach itself to one of the factions within the oligarchy. The advantages to both sides were obvious: the party became a part of the government when its allied oligarchs were in power, and the oligarchic faction received the votes it needed to pass its program in the lower house of the Diet. The Shimpōtō (Progressive Party) allied with the Matsukata faction in the oligarchy, and the Jiyūtō (Liberty Party) allied with the Itō faction. The parties had not abandoned their goal of eroding the power of the oligarchs, however, so a period of political instability followed the emergence of the faction-party alliances.[1]

The Matsukata cabinet formed on September 18, 1896, dem-

onstrated the precarious nature of the new alliances. The Matsukata cabinet was entirely reliant on Ōkuma Shigenobu and his
Progressive Party for Diet support. Ōkuma was given a cabinet
post, but his party demanded more than this. The Progressive
Party had included in its platform three major planks, one of
which demanded a responsible cabinet and the correction of political evils.[2] This plan was hardly subject to identical interpretation
by the party and the bureaucratic groups. Matsukata gave his
pledge to consider the views of the party and then proceeded, in
the eyes of its members, to disregard his pledge. Ōkuma finally
resigned from his cabinet post in disgust in November 1897. The
government tried to weather the storm by reorganizing the cabinet
and seeking the support of the Liberty Party, but its overtures were
rejected and a vote of no confidence would certainly have carried
had not Matsukata first dissolved the Diet. Lacking party support
and thus having no chance for a favorable outcome in the Diet
election, Matsukata resigned as premier, to be replaced by the
leader of his rival oligarchic faction, Itō.[3]

Now it was the turn of the Itō–Liberty Party alliance to founder.
The general election of March 15, 1898, was very quiet, and the
two major parties retained their near equality in Diet seats. Itō had
promised to give Itagaki Taisuke, the leader of the Liberty Party, a
seat on his cabinet, but after the election he was unable to fulfill
this promise because of opposition by his cabinet members. The
Liberty Party swung from support of Itō to opposition. The
twelfth Diet, convened on May 14, chastised Itō bitterly, and the
Liberty Party joined in the attack. The administration's foreign
policy came in for stinging criticism, for Japan seemed impotent
either to control Western encroachment in China or to take part in
dividing China to obtain a Japanese sphere of influence.[4] The
Diet, because of its vociferous opposition to the administration,
was subsequently dissolved.[5]

Both the Liberty Party and the Progressive Party had now had
the bitter experience of seeing their alliances with elder statesmen
dissolved through what seemed to them the callous and indifferent
attitude of the oligarchy toward the programs and welfare of the
parties. Out of this disillusionment came an attempt to unite the
liberal parties and substitute party government for the Meiji oligarchy. The Liberty Party and the Progressive Party resolved their
past differences and joined together to form a new party, the Ken-

seitō (Constitutional Party). When the party was merely a week old, it met with astonishing success. Itō resigned and recommended the party leaders—Ōkuma and Itagaki—as his successors. The first "party cabinet" was formed on June 30, 1898.[6]

During 1898 the liberal parties went from success to success, increasing their influence within the Japanese government. Accordingly, the political atmosphere was more congenial to mass movements and democratic efforts than it had ever been before. The prospects for union organization, and for political efforts by labor, were correspondingly good.

The aggressive government armaments programs also contributed to the growth of the labor movement. This program had been triggered by the Triple Intervention of France, Germany, and Russia after Japan's defeat of China in the Sino-Japanese War of 1894–1895. Through this intervention by the European powers, Japan was forced to give up certain key territories and rights that China had conceded. Japan's humiliation by the Triple Intervention caused the Japanese government to set in motion programs for increasing military strength so that Japan could resist such arbitrary actions in the future.

By 1898 Japan's military boom was in full swing. The Japanese army was expanded and reorganized. Every effort was made to improve equipment and set up facilities for domestic manufacture of military supplies. Similarly, the country was made self-sufficient in naval armaments, and the navy was greatly increased in size. A large naval building program was initiated in 1896–1897. Shipping and shipbuilding were given substantial subsidies, with the object of increasing both the use and construction of modern vessels.[7]

This government policy rapidly brought about a boom in the heavy industry sector, which was strongly anchored in the shipbuilding and armaments industries. Absolute employment in that sector as well as its proportion of total national industrial employment rose substantially. This produced a growing labor force for the Kiseikai and Metalworkers' Union to organize, and also created a shortage in skilled labor in heavy industry, which made it more difficult for employers to confront and oppose unions (see table 5).

The expansionary policy of the Japanese government both before and after the Sino-Japanese War also had an effect on

Table 5. Employment in Heavy Industry, 1893–1898
(thousands of persons)

Year	Total Industrial Labor Force	In Heavy Industry			Percent in Heavy Industry
		Private	Gov't	Total	
1893	297.1	9.8	9.6	19.4	6.5
1894	396.0	16.1	12.2	28.3	7.1
1895	435.8	16.8	15.3	32.1	7.4
1896	456.2	20.7	15.9	36.5	8.0
1897	460.2	15.3	16.8	32.1	7.0
1898	435.1	22.5	18.7	41.2	9.5

Source: Hyōdō Tsutomu, *Nihon ni Okeru Rōshi Kankei no Tenkai* [The development of labor relations in Japan] (Tokyo, 1971), 90.

Note: All figures are for workplaces of ten or more persons only.

prices. From 1891 to 1898 prices rose constantly. The period 1896–1898 witnessed a very rapid rise in the price of rice, the main staple food in Japan. Employers strove to keep money wages down, and stable wages combined with rising prices pushed down the standard of living of industrial workers. The 30 percent increase in the price of rice in 1898 caused many workers to consider untraditional approaches, such as unionism, to protect their livelihoods and families (see figure 1).

The constant rise in prices with no relief through wage increases gradually brought workers to the breaking point. The industrial boom had created a labor shortage, making workers confident that they would not lose their jobs or could find work elsewhere if they did. This paved the way for a wave of strikes, unprecedented in number and scale. For the first time, instead of spontaneously rioting over emotional issues, workers sought higher wages and better working conditions (see table 6). The government, surprised by the frequency and magnitude of the strikes, called for local reports on them from each prefecture.

The most spectacular strike of this period, by the railway engineers and firemen of the Japan Railway Company, took place early in 1898 and catapulted the labor movement forward. Activist engineers and firemen who had been transferred to the far north of Japan by the company as a disciplinary measure had formed the secret Treatment Improvement Association in early 1898. They opposed the preferential treatment given to salaried employees at the expense of the railwaymen. For example:

Figure 1. Consumer Prices, Tokyo, 1891–1898

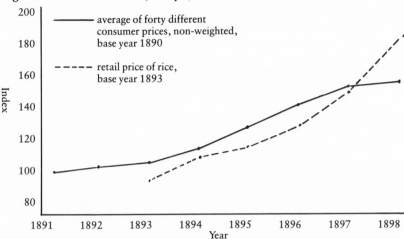

Source: Sumiya Mikio, Kobayashi Ken'ichi, and Hyōdō Tsutomu, *Nihon Shihonshugi to Rōdō Mondai* [Japanese capitalism and labor problems] (Tokyo, 1967), 115.

1. Those considered to be blue-collar workers (such as janitors, firemen, engineers, and so on) received only one-half the semi-annual bonus (relative to their wages).
2. Engineers received nearly twenty sen per night less in travel allowance than conductors.
3. Savings with the company by salaried employees (for retirement) were matched by the company, a benefit not received by blue-collar workers.
4. Engineers were paid less than staff office workers, receiving from fifteen to thirty-five yen per month (apprentice engineers were paid some ten yen per month). In comparison, staff office workers made anywhere between twelve and sixty yen per month, while a stationmaster made from fifteen to forty-five yen per month.[8]

In addition to these economic differentials, the engineers were looked down upon by the salaried employees. Engineers, firemen, and other blue collar workers were subject to poor treatment, criticism, and abuse, such as the requirement that they kneel on the floor while an assistant stationmaster, sitting on a chair, issued instructions.[9] There was indeed ample reason for discontent.

The activist engineers laid out their case in a pamphlet that was

Table 6. Strikes, 1897–1898

REASON	SECOND HALF 1897		CALENDAR 1898	
	STRIKES	WORKERS	STRIKES	WORKERS
Wages Increase	21	2,248	35	5,699
Wages (Other)	6	779	3	381
Shorter Hours	—	—	1	68
Against Foremen	1	155	—	—
About Discharge	2	188	—	—
Other	2	145	4	145
Total	32	3,510	43	6,293

Source: Sumiya Mikio, Kobayashi Ken'ichi, and Hyōdō Tsutomu, *Nihon Shinhonshugi to Rōdō Mondai* [Japanese capitalism and labor problems] (Tokyo, 1967), 116.

Note: "Workers" refers to the number of participants in strikes, not the number of mandays. The only figures available for 1897 are for the latter half of the year.

secretly distributed to Japan Railway Company engineers on February 2, 1898:[10]

Once again we bring you a recommendation of the action stated below, which will be hard on you. We feel you must be of the same opinion. Where there is duty, there are rights; where there are important responsibilities there should be dignity. Yet there are those who unreasonably oppose this. We must become their opposition. As in the proverb, "if there is unfairness, cry for justice," we are unreasonably and unfairly oppressed, so we must cry for justice and cry for it loudly.

It goes without saying that we engineers have great responsibility. . . . The one who is responsible for the entire train is none other than the engineer. The engineer is the only one relied upon to bring the passengers and goods safely to their destination. Our responsibilities are great, and our duties are extensive. . . .

Why does the company treat us so poorly and unreasonably? Even engineers, distinguished modern machine technicians who must undergo training for eight or nine years, are treated poorly. On the other hand, those with schooling but no experience are promoted from telegraph operator to assistant to station master, and receive fair treatment. . . .

If one complains of this situation one invites misfortune, and if one tries to leave one is obstructed and opposed. If one stays in the company one gets low pay. Even though other sections get pay raises due to inflation, we, who work so hard and have such extreme duties and responsibilities, get no pay raises. Our wives weep at the thinness of their clothes, and our children cry from hunger. We, who work hard day and night, get only poor treatment, criticism, abuse, and the laments of our wives and children. . . .

Right now we cannot act openly. This is a good time for united effort. The first step is for everyone who has read this to send an anonymous letter by February 15 to the head of this section asking for a temporary wage increase for engineers. We ask that hundreds of letters from all directions flood into the section head's office.

The next matter is the reform of names. "Drivers" should become "engineers," "driver's assistants" should become "engineer's assistants," "stokers" should become "firemen," and "clean-up men" should become "janitors." It is only natural for a driver, since he is an operative technician, to be called an engineer. . . .

Our alliance has no president and no secretary, and will thus avoid discovery and opposition. We will be somewhat like the secret societies of Russia or the socialist parties of Europe. . . .

If there should be no temporary wage increase forthcoming from the actions taken by February 15, our first action will be the implementation of Article 333. If this article is not strictly put into effect when it is ordered, it will greatly benefit the company. We must finally become angered at the company, which treats us like horses. If, contrary to this article, we should be forced to work, the delay of transportation by two or three hours every day, making schedules useless, will be our insurance.

At the time the Japan Railway Company operated some eight hundred miles of track in northeast Japan. It employed over ten thousand persons, making it the largest railway company in Japan. The company was divided into one department, seven sections, and one factory: the Business Department, General Affairs Section, Roundhouse Section, Accounting Section, Transportation Section, Maintenance Section, Locomotive Section, Construction Section, and the Ōmiya factory. The engineers, firemen, and other blue-collar workers were in the Locomotive Section.[11]

This massive enterprise had to operate as a single organism, which required strong central management. That in turn meant that measures to keep turnover down and foster loyalty to the company had to be effected. The company early on set up a mutual assistance plan, but was unable to come up with an effective labor policy. As a result, labor relations were uneasy at the Japan Railway Company in the late 1890s.[12]

The activist engineers of the Japan Railway Company did not

expect smooth sailing in their dealings with this large company. Expecting an unfavorable reaction on the part of the company, they drafted a petition and sent it to the various station officers on February 13, 1898:

PETITION

On the Matter of Treatment

In comparison with other sections, we are indeed at the lowest level of employees in this company. We are operative technicians, tools of civilization. We are faithful workers who exhibit careful attention to our jobs. We are brave and active engineers. We are patient, industrious strivers. Our actions, as we are the trained heart of the engines, are what determines the company's well-being, trusted as it is by society. In this way, our responsibilities are great. In accordance with these responsibilities, there is no reason why we should not receive the same treatment as staff office workers.

On the Matter of Occupational Names

On the basis of implementation of the previous matter, we desire that the occupational names be changed as follows:

"Driver" should be changed to "engineer";

"Driver's assistant" should be changed to "engineer's assistant";

"Stoker" should be changed to "fireman";

"Clean-up man" should be changed to "janitor."

On the Matter of a Temporary Raise

Due to rising consumer prices at this time, we are finding it extremely difficult to make ends meet. In spite of our previous supplications, brought up after much deliberation, we received no increase in wages. However, we know no relief from rising prices, in spite of the fact that other sections (second and third rank employees also) received a general raise in wages. Not one of us, who work hard and have extreme responsibilities and duties, have received a raise. Our wives weep at the thinness of their clothes, and our children cry from hunger. We ask that, on the basis of your human sympathy, we receive a sufficient increase in wages.

We petition that these three matters, which the branches have all petitioned for under the instructions of headquarters, be implemented by the twenty-fifth of this month.[13]

Meanwhile, communications between the engineers at the various stations of the Japan Railway Company were stepped up, and security measures to prevent the discovery of activists were strictly observed. Preparations for the implementation of "Article 333"— a strike—were accelerated. On February 20 the engineers learned that the company planned to fire the men responsible for the labor unrest and was conducting investigations to discover who they were. On February 21 two conspirators were discovered and suspended, and another was disciplined by transfer to the far northern lines. On the 23rd, the company fired ten activists, five of them at the Ichinoseki station. On the 24th, the five went to the company office to complain that they had been fired without cause. They protested that it was unfair, and "seemed brokenhearted . . . [and] although they had great expectations in their hearts, they did not show this in their faces."[14]

On the morning of February 25, a farewell party was held for those who had been fired, sponsored by about fifty engineers at the Ichinoseki station. While the party was in progress, a coded telegram was received from Sendai reading "dangerous condition: everyone has quit." The men broke up the party and spread the word: Strike! About 350 engineers and firemen all along the line refused to report to work. The morning of February 25 found railroad traffic at a virtual standstill along the main line north of Tokyo. The strike was coordinated from the Fukushima station using coded telegrams to transmit information to other stations. The public was severely inconvenienced, and the attention of all Japan focused on the most organized major strike in its history.[15]

The public had had doubts about the management of the Japan Railway Company for some time, and opinion was firmly on the side of the engineers. Pressure on the company grew as the strike progressed. An influential Japanese publication, *Nihon* (Japan), editorialized: "Those workers who make their living by earning wages and receive their position and wages from their employer must have been unable to bear their condition any longer to declare war on their employer in this way. We hope the Japan Railway Company will reflect seriously on its obligations."[16]

On the morning of February 28, two representatives of the Treatment Improvement Association from Ichinoseki proceeded to the headquarters of the Japan Railway Company in Tokyo. They sought to open negotiations with the company and presented a series of demands: the same ones that had been previously submitted on the issues of treatment, name reform, and wage increases, plus a new one demanding reinstatement of those fired for presenting the demands.[17]

The company appointed Adachi Tarō, head of transportation, as chief mediator to deal with the representatives of the Treatment Improvement Association. In addition, several prominent public figures also acted as mediators. For the next four weeks, twenty-four worker representatives (each station sent at least one representative) were involved in the negotiations with Adachi. Yet the company did not recognize the Treatment Improvement Association as the official representative of the engineers and firemen. Rather, Adachi was appointed go-between and expected to bring about consensus between the opposed parties through separate discussions with each side.

By March 2 negotiations were proceeding so well that it was agreed the striking engineers would go back to work. Although the results of the negotiations had been basically decided by March 6, the formal completion of negotiations and the implementation of the decisions dragged on until March 31. The president of the Japan Railway Company agreed to sign an order reforming the occupational names, but not in exactly the way the engineers wanted. It was agreed that the company would take into consideration a raise in wages for engineers, and engineers were promoted in rank within the company. Further, all those who had been fired, except the two men "responsible for the strike," were reemployed. These two men, Ishida Rokujirō and Ikeda Matahachi, had been the key leaders of the strike and had led the Treatment Improvement Association.[18]

Although the strike ended favorably for the engineers and firemen, their demands were implemented unilaterally by the company. There was no contract, no signed agreement. Rather, the president of the company issued directives altering existing company practices as the engineers wished. The company did not recognize the Treatment Improvement Association, nor did it allow the engineers to escape unharmed from the strike. The public had been inconvenienced and the company hurt financially. The union had to pay, and so two union leaders were dismissed from the company.

Katayama Sen, a leader of the Kiseikai and the editor of *Labor World,* expressed an interesting attitude in his article "Great Strike in Japan," which dealt with the railway strike and the discharge of union leaders:

The strikers proved themselves worthy of praise and admiration. Their leaders heroically upheld the cause of their men and sacrificed their positions to the cause of the engineers and firemen. We can not but admire the spirit and conduct of those men who carried on the strike to this successful end with calm and sound judgement and obtained, moreover, all the points of their demand in spite of that daring and smart arbitrator, the head of the R.R. Transportation Department appointed by the Company to treat with them. . . .

The Labor World congratulates the laborers of Japan on the grand success achieved by the engineers, but at the same time the Labor World warns them not to enter hastily this expensive form of dispute and that they should study the labor problem carefully and realize the true situation. What laborers need is not a victorious strike but a strong union. It was really not by the strike that they were able to get the victory but it was the union, although formed so hastily, that stood so firmly behind them. . . .

We are glad to learn that among the leaders who sacrificed bread and the position which they had held for eleven long years in the Company's service, there was a man who is well acquainted with the religious literature of the day, whose earnestness and skill in the conduct of the negotiations with the Company were effective in winning the victory. His name is Rokujirō Ishida. The Labor World sympathizes with him and his colleagues who lost their position on account of the good work they did in the interest of the engineers in Japan but they will be known in the Labor World as martyrs to the laborer's cause and will gain finally a victory in the estimate of the world![19]

Company demands that union leaders be fired stemmed from the traditional attitude toward those who opposed recognized authority or committed acts that inconvenienced the public. No matter what the circumstances or justification, opposition to authority and harming others was deemed inexcusable. Thus, a union was always seen to be in the wrong no matter how strong its case for a strike, and to atone for its evil had to sacrifice its leaders. Although the public sympathized with the union it did not object to the dismissal of the union leaders.

Katayama, a union organizer and labor movement leader, accepted as natural the discharge of Ishida and Ikeda. Even Katayama felt that the engineers could not expect to inconvenience the public (virtually an antisocial act) with impunity. Further, Katayama's assertion that the union, not the strike, brought victory for the engineers shows how much Takano's compromise with Social

Policy School ideology had moved the labor movement away from pure-and-simple AFL trade unionism. Katayama stressed that a strike, by itself, would not bring favorable results for the workers. A strong union, on the other hand, could obtain victories without striking. Katayama felt at this time that the goal of the workers was not strikes and economic strife but rather union organization that could accomplish gains without such strife, an echo of Takano's labor ideology.

Takano Fusatarō wrote to Gompers about the toll the strike had taken on both the union and management: "It should be noted in this connection that this condemnation of directors by the press bore fruit shortly after. Four days after the strike commenced the chief of the locomotive department of the company resigned his position, and two days after the conference closed the president and vice-president of the company tendered their resignations."[20] Just as the engineers had to sacrifice their leaders, so too did management have to resign because their negligence had allowed a situation to develop where the public was inconvenienced. This too was accepted as natural by the Japanese. In a sense, this reaction to the strike was a continuation of the tradition of the peasant riots of the feudal period, where the farmers brought their plight to the attention of high-level officials by rioting. But when the riot was over and the government had made its unilateral decisions, riot leaders were imprisoned or executed, and government officials resigned to atone for their negligence.

The effect of the Japan Railway Company strike was felt all over Japan. Unrest was reported on the Japan National Railways, which peaked on March 2 when engineers learned they might be transferred to the Japan Railway Company to take over the positions of engineers out on strike. Engineers in western Japan set up an organization to obtain better treatment from their employers. The engineers of the Sanyō Railway in southern Japan, using the Japan Railway Company strike as a model, struck in May 1898, and won. The engineers on the Kyūshū Railways struck on September 21, 1899, and the strike was resolved by the intervention of a mediator. In 1899 the maintenance workers of the Japan Railway Company demanded revision of the method of calculating years of service, the same benefits as salaried employees, and the implementation of semiannual raises. The maintenance crew of the Japan Railway Company, imitating the engineers, set up an organization, presented their demands to the company, struck, and won.[21]

The engineers of the Japan Railway Company disbanded the secret and unofficial Treatment Improvement Association after the strike was over, and on April 5, 1898, formed their own union, called the Reform Society (Kyōseikai), to protect their gains.[22] The Reform Society had a much more militant character than the Metalworkers' Union, although it had a similar structure. Unlike the Metalworkers' Union, which had no out-of-work or strike benefits, the engineers set up provisions for the payment of funds during the strike to those who had been fired. The metalworkers relied on mere expulsion for discipline, while the Reform Society used elaborate punishments, including the silent treatment, for offenders. Reform Society dues were much higher than the Metalworkers' Union dues and were similar to those of Western unions: the Reform Society constitution, Article Twenty-One, called for the "payment of one day's wages a month to the central fund for one year, and a half-day's wages per month thereafter."[23] When members left the company's employ or died, their contribution to the fund was returned to them or their family. There were no mutual assistance provisions in the Reform Society constitution.[24]

Although the second article of the constitution of the Reform Society stated, "Members of this organization will seek only the benefit and prosperity of the company . . . [and] will of course . . . work diligently and behave correctly, and will not engage in violent action,"[25] Katayama Sen described the union as militant. Referring to the fact that the union had built up a membership of a thousand and a strike fund of ten thousand yen by late 1898 and had doubled the fund by the end of 1899,[26] Katayama wrote: "The militant union sees the employer as its foe and readies itself to meet him at any time. . . . This fund is a strike fund and nothing else, which is to say it is set up to protect the rights of members and is for the organization to fight the employer. The strike is their solution. We see this characteristic in the Reform Society of the engineers of the Japan Railway Company."[27]

The Reform Society was characterized by the same shop-based structure as the Metalworkers' Union. The branches of the Reform Society were located at major railway stations where its members reported to work. The Reform Society sought to organize all blue-collar workers in the Locomotive Section of the Japan

Railway Company. These included engineers, their assistants, fire-men, enginehouse workers, and train janitors. These men worked together, relied upon one another, faced the same supervision within the section, and were treated alike. The Reform Society had the same inclusive structure as the Metalworkers' Union. There was no discrimination on the basis of skill, age, or trade, and branches were based on workplace divisions. Again, the struc-ture of the Reform Society is in direct contrast to the structure of Western railway unions, where each particular trade had its own union that spanned many railway companies.

The fifth article of the Reform Society's constitution proclaimed that "engineers, their assistants, and enginehouse workers have an obligation to join." Union pressure on such workers at the Japan Railway Company was so great that nearly all joined the Reform Society, creating what was virtually a union shop. The company was conciliatory toward the Reform Society, and those who did not join were soon fired by the company or otherwise left employ-ment there. Management had been influenced by the fact that sev-eral managers had had to resign after the engineers' strike. Man-agement tried to make it easy for members to attend the Reform Society conventions, and it opened up routes of promotion for engineers, and tried to tie in Reform Society members with the supervisory staff. Because of these factors, labor-management peace continued for several years after the strike, allowing the Reform Society time to grow and become better-financed.[28]

The Kiseikai leaders greeted the strike and the organization of the engineers with enthusiasm. They hoped to bring the Reform Society under the banner of the Kiseikai and thereby increase the strength of the labor movement. Takano and his followers imme-diately laid plans for a series of rallies at the towns where the Japan Railway Company had its workshops. It took the Kiseikai some time to raise the necessary funds, but by July 1898 all was ready and Takano, Katayama, and their supporters left Tokyo for their first tour of northern Japan for the Kiseikai.[29]

Takano and his supporters stopped and spoke at nearly every major station on the northern railway lines. They were given assistance by Reform Society members, who helped in making arrangements for the rallies, played hosts to the traveling Kiseikai leaders, and spoke at the rallies. After a week on the road, Takano and his supporters returned to Tokyo.[30]

Despite these efforts, the Reform Society refused to affiliate with the Kiseikai. The engineers felt they had little to gain by joining the Kiseikai since they had sufficient organization ability to keep the Japan Railway Company nearly a union shop. The Reform Society had no intention of organizing outside the company; engineers elsewhere, in Kyūshū and at the Sanyō railways, were forming their own organizations on a company basis. The Kiseikai at the time had no presence in northern Japan, being focused exclusively in the Tokyo area.

The leaders of the Reform Society realized they might give up much if they joined the Kiseikai. First, a portion of their dues would be funneled to support Kiseikai efforts on behalf of the union movement as a whole. Second, Reform Society leaders saw how they could be drawn into larger issues and their strength dissipated in political and educational activities. Third, and most importantly, the Reform Society leaders did not want to give up leadership of their union to the Kiseikai. Under the system of interlocking directorates, the Kiseikai directors would have a major influence on the Reform Society if the two were affiliated. The engineers were unwilling to give up their independence in return for what minor assistance the Kiseikai could offer.

The Kiseikai rallies in the north did bear fruit, however. The Metalworkers' Union was able to organize metalworkers at a number of railway workshops of the Japan Railway Company. These workers were separate from the engineers, firemen, and enginehouse workers, and were responsible for construction, repair, and maintenance of the rolling stock throughout the system. The major engine factory for the Japan Railway Company was the Ōmiya Factory near Tokyo, one of the original branches of the Metalworkers' Union. In addition to this major plant, there were smaller workshops all along the line to the north, which provided new ground for organization by the Metalworkers' Union and the Kiseikai.

Up until the Kiseikai tour of the north, the Metalworkers' Union had grown through organization efforts in Tokyo. Throughout the spring of 1898, new branches had been formed at plants employing metalworkers in the Tokyo area. In February the metalworkers organized the Shimbashi Railway and Shibaura Engineering Works. In March they started a major organization drive at the Ishikawajima Shipyards with the help of Ozawa Benzō and his friends. By May three branches had been formed there, and the Yokosuka Navy Shipyards and Akabane Navy shipyards had been organized. The metalworkers also extended their reach into the railway plants with a branch at the Kōbu Railway Factory. These were major organization drives—the Metalworkers' Union gained hundreds of new members at both the Yokosuka Navy Shipyards and the Ishikawajima Shipyards—and membership grew rapidly.[31]

With the successful strike by the engineers and the organizing rallies by the Kiseikai in the north, the Metalworkers' Union was able to add new branches at the Japan Railway Company. In May a branch was formed grouping the metalworkers at the Fukushima, Kuroiso, and Sendai workshops. In August branches were set up at the Aomori and Morioka workshops of the Japan Railway Company. The tour of the north also contributed to the later founding of three branches of the Metalworkers' Union in Hokkaidō, Japan's main northern island. With these new branches, the Metalworkers' Union during 1898 was able to more than double its membership, from some 1,300 to 3,000 (see table 7).[32]

Given that total employment in heavy industry in 1898 was around forty-two thousand, the membership of the Metalworkers' Union represented a significant organization level for the industry —some 7 percent. Since the Kiseikai had not organized at all in western Japan, where several major heavy industry plants were

Table 7. Growth of the Metalworkers' Union, 1897–1898

DATE	BRANCHES	MEMBERSHIP
December 1, 1897	13	1,183
February 1, 1898	13	2,000
March 15, 1898	18	2,400
May 1, 1898	19	2,500
August 1, 1898	24	2,700
September 1, 1898	27	2,700
October 15, 1898	30	2,700
December 1, 1898	32	3,000

Sources: Labor World, no. 5 (February 1, 1898): 4; ibid., no. 8 (March 15, 1898): 5; ibid., no. 11 (May 1, 1898): 10; ibid., no. 17 (August 1, 1898): 10; ibid., no. 19 (September 1, 1898): 10; ibid., no. 22 (October 15, 1898): 10; ibid., no. 25 (December 1, 1898): 12; Katayama Sen and Nishikawa Mitsujirō, *Nihon no Rōdō Undō* [The Japanese labor movement] (Tokyo: Iwanami Shoten, 1952; first published in 1901), 76–77, 80.

located—the Osaka Armaments Works and the Kure Navy Shipyards, for example—the Metalworkers' Union had an even higher
organization rate among metalworkers in Tokyo. Of course, at the
particular plants the metalworkers had organized, the organization rate was even higher, approaching nearly 100 percent at the
Tokyo Armaments Works' Rifle Works, for example. The Kiseikai
counted its organization efforts during 1898, despite the failure of
the Reform Society to affiliate, spectacularly successful.

The Kiseikai leaders felt that printers could be another organizational success for them, since in numbers printers ranked second
to metalworkers among Kiseikai members. During the spring of
1898 the Kiseikai began efforts to organize a union among printers, compositors, lithographers, and others in the printing trades.
Since there were fewer than fifty printers in the Kiseikai, however,
the Kiseikai could not organize a union from among the members.
Instead, the Kiseikai sought to work through its members to set up
a union. The first attempt was to organize printers at the Tokyo
Printing Company, who had struck on their own in February 1897
to obtain better treatment.[33]

The efforts of the Kiseikai soon bore fruit. A Printers' Union
was formed on March 20, 1898, and held a general meeting on
April 3. Although the Kiseikai supported the union, only a minority of the new union members belonged to the Kiseikai. The
Kiseikai did not have sufficient influence within the union to control it, and so it was from the start independent. Shortly after the
union was founded seven of its organizers were discharged by the
Tokyo Printing Company. Management refused to give good reason for the discharges, so over one hundred printers went out on
strike at the Tokyo Printing Company. The union did not have a
broad base of support among printers as it was organized mainly
in the Honjo and Fukugawa wards of Tokyo. The company's attitude was unyielding, and by bringing in outside workers to fill the
vacancies created by the strike, it managed to hold out. The strike
collapsed and the seven leaders were blacklisted.[34]

Stung by this failure and reinforced in their view of strikes, the
Kiseikai leaders continued to work to promote unionism in the
printing trades. Yet Kiseikai influence remained minor. Only a few
printers were affiliated with it, making recruiting difficult. About
three months after the demise of the Printers' Union, Ezawa
Saburō managed to persuade eleven members of the old union to

reorganize.[35] On August 4, 1898, these twelve men founded the Printers' Friendly Association (Kappankō Dōshi Konwakai)[36] and agreed to publish a newspaper with their own funds. The first issue of this newspaper appeared September 27, 1898.[37] Significantly, these men sought no financial or other aid from the Kiseikai, preferring to remain in secrecy.

The Printers' Friendly Association gradually grew in size. Its membership list, however, was kept secret "since the capitalists do not yet understand the real intentions of this organization."[38] By October 2, 1898, the association had some 350 members, and in the following months efforts to recruit influential managers in the Tokyo printing houses met with some success. In December 1898 an influential capitalist, Takeuchi Shinji, became president of the association. In this way, the printers hoped to achieve their goals through cooperation with management rather than confrontation.[39]

These activities by the printers, railwaymen, and metalworkers —all new occupations established since the Meiji Restoration— had brought Japan's labor movement into prominence during 1898 and focused public attention on the factory legislation debate raging in the autumn of 1898. Industrial strife was sweeping the country, and the public was acutely aware of the importance of labor problems. The outbreak of strikes after the Sino-Japanese War and rapid industrialization were factors bringing the Japanese government to a serious consideration of the possibility of enacting factory legislation.[40] The first Japanese factory legislation was drawn up within the Ministry of Agriculture and Commerce under the government of Count Ōkuma in the fall of 1897. This legislation was to be submitted to the Diet in November of 1898, thus allowing ample time for review of its provisions by interested businessmen and bureaucrats. Arrangements were made to place the proposed legislation before chambers of commerce throughout the country for consideration. Further, the legislation was scheduled to be reviewed by the Higher Agricultural, Commercial, and Industrial Board in the fall of 1898. This would allow opportunity for recommendations to modify the bill. It was clear from these efforts at consultation that proponents of the bill did not wish to antagonize propertied interests. They saw no reason to diminish the bill's small chance for enactment, since many laissez-faire bureaucrats and businessmen would oppose such a law.[41]

The four major sections of the proposed legislation were as follows:

Under the first head, it is stipulated that the proposed law will be applied to factories employing over fifty workmen and apprentices. . . .

The second contains provision subjecting owners of factories to go through a rigid examination by authorities, and requiring safety provisions for dangerous machinery and for preservation of health and morality.

Under the third, several important features for protection of workmen and children are to be noted. They are:

(a) Prohibition of employment of children under ten years of age. For industries with special circumstances, application of this clause will be suspended or limited by public ordinance.

(b) Limitation of working hours to ten for children under fourteen years of age. However, this limitation will be modified with the approval of authorities when there exist special circumstances.

(c) Suspension of work on at least two days in each month and on three national holidays, and an hour of meal time during a working day. These requirements are also to be modified by consent of authorities where there exist special circumstances.

(d) Provision of educational facilities by the employer at his own expense, for children under his employment whose ages are below fourteen years, and who have not completed common school education.

(e) Liability of employer in case of accident, fatal or otherwise, or employee in discharging his duty. Exceptions noted for cases resulting from intentional purpose of workman himself or his fellow-servant, and from calamity of nature.[42]

(f) Issue of certificate of authorities or by masters' association who previously applied to and granted the power to issue the certificate by the Minister of State for Agriculture and Commerce, when issue of such certificate is deemed necessary for regulation of workmen, requiring of workmen to deposit his certificate with his employer while he remains under the employment, and of employer, to employ none but certificate holders.

Under the fourth head it is provided that the employer who maintains an apprentice system in his factory must get permission of authorities for rules and regulations governing the system in the factory. Necessary provisions to be made in such regulations are also indicated.[43]

Close examination of the proposed factory act by the leaders of the Kiseikai convinced them that, although the law singled out some of the more glaring abuses of the factory system for correction, it was not only totally inadequate but in some cases inimical to the best interests of the workers. Takano, leader of the Kiseikai, outlined his objections as follows:

> Considered from the view-point of working people there are many defects in the proposed law. In the first place, the scope of the law is not wide enough to include factories where there exist grievous evils which endanger health of working people. In the second place, those exempt clauses for prohibition and limitation of child labor and long working hours [cripple these protective provisions]. In the third place, while the proposed law requires of employer to provide for educational facilities, no punishment is provided for its violation, thus making the provision non-obligatory upon employer. Fourthly, the issue of certificate tends to hinder free movement of workmen while it gives to employer the power to compel his employee to remain under his service through unjust withholding of the certificate.[44]

The Kiseikai immediately launched a campaign for revision of the proposed factory law. The first step was taken at the regular monthly meeting of the Kiseikai on September 23, 1898, when Kiseikai leaders agreed on their own proposals for factory legislation:

> 1. That the sphere of operation of the factory regulations shall involve premises where steam power of various kinds is in operation and where more than five workmen or apprentices are employed.
> 2. That youths below the age of ten shall not be employed in such establishments under any circumstances.
> 3. That a child under fourteen years of age shall not be employed for more than eight hours per day under any circumstances.
> 4. That operatives over fourteen years of age shall not be employed for more than ten hours a day except under special circumstances.
> 5. That the laborers shall have a rest on every Sunday or one day in seven, but under extraordinary circumstances it may be pro-

longed if the employer gets the necessary permission from the government.

6. That apprentices under fourteen not having passed the whole course of an elementary school shall have some necessary instruction imparted to them by their employers who failing to do so shall be subjected to a fine of 200 yen.

7. That for the case of accident resulting from intentional purpose of fellow-servant, the employer shall be held responsible.

8. That a workingman's certificate shall only be issued to apprentices.

9. That inspectors of factories shall be appointed. [45]

The provisions of the proposed factory law stopped far short of the legislative protection of labor then in force in Great Britain, Germany, France, and the United States. British workers were protected by workmen's compensation, fair-wage provisions in government contracts, a 56.5-hour maximum work week, factory inspection, and limitations on the hours of labor of women and children. German labor legislation was even more advanced, including national health insurance and old age and disability insurance. France's first factory act was passed in 1841, but successive legislation was slow in coming. Factory inspection and limitations on the hours of work of women and children were only supplemented by an employers' liability law in 1898. Japan's new factory law would not even bring it up to the level of protection of labor in France, the most backward of the industrialized countries in this respect. [46]

Comparison between Japan, where there was no protective legislation, and the United States, where it was fairly advanced, indicates the gap between Japan and the industrialized countries. Employers' liability was fairly extensive in the U.S., where the first such act was passed in 1856. By 1896 the federal government and eight states had enacted eight-hour-day laws and thirteen states had women's labor laws. By 1899 most states had limited the hours of work of children and provided a minimum age before which children could not work. Old age pension laws had still to be enacted in the United States. [47]

Once the Kiseikai had established its goals for revision of the proposed law, it began its campaign to change it. First, the Kiseikai appointed a petition committee of five (including Takano, Sawada, Katayama, and Ozawa) at its regular meeting on Septem-

ber 23, 1898. This committee was to present the amendments outlined above to the government, Diet, and the Higher Agricultural,
Commercial, and Industrial Board. It was also to petition the government and the Diet, as well as call on each member of the
Higher Board, which was to meet and begin evaluation of the proposed factory law on October 20, 1898. The Kiseikai leaders also
decided to hold a large procession through the capital on November 3, as well as rallies in support of the amendments to the proposed factory law.[48]

The Kiseikai swung into action. On October 23, the Kiseikai
held a rally at Yokohama under the auspices of the third branch of
the Metalworkers' Union, whose members gave most of the
speeches. Over 1,300 workmen attended the meeting, and the
speeches were tinged with an attitude of indignation at what was
deemed political oppression. The speakers expressed the opinion
that the government needed to realize that the law did not protect
the workers. On October 26, the Social Policy School held a rally
on the proposed factory law at which Takano, his younger brother
Iwasaburō, Katayama, and Kanai En spoke. Another rally in
opposition to the factory law was held November 6, and although
the crowd was small since it was a religious festival day, the speakers fervently pressed home their points.[49] Unfortunately, the large
procession through Tokyo scheduled for November 3 was prohibited by the police.[50]

The main effort of the Kiseikai was directed at persuading the
Higher Agricultural, Commercial, and Industrial Board itself. The
petition committee called on the members of the board in a series
of visits or interviews. The first set of interviews began on October
3. The petition committee first called on Mr. Ariga, head of the
board, and had a very satisfactory interview with him. The committee next called on Shimada Saburō, member and ex-vice-president of the lower house of the Diet, who agreed with the Kiseikai's
amendments on the questions of child labor and workmen's certificates. Next, Sakuma Teiichi, in spite of the fact that he was seriously ill, met and agreed with the petition committee, encouraging
them to continue their campaign to revise the proposed factory
law. The first series of interviews also included unsuccessful
attempts to call on other members of the Higher Board, and visits
to the Congress of Chambers of Commerce and the Home Ministry.[51]

A week later a second series of interviews with board members began. First the petition committee called on Mr. Tejima, who approved of the protection of child workers. But Mr. Taguchi opposed the bill on the grounds of laissez-faire. Kanai En, a professor at Tokyo University and Social Policy School member, was about to leave for the university so there was insufficient time to discuss the amendments proposed by the Kiseikai. A third set of interviews was attempted, but the committee was unable to arrange any more meetings with members of the Higher Board.[52]

These were not the only activities conducted by the Kiseikai. Takano wrote:

> During the last two months our association directed its entire attention to amending the proposed factory bill, and active steps were taken to achieve the end. A petition signed by all the [Kiseikai] members[53] was presented to the Minister of State for Agriculture and Commerce. A committee was sent to interview the members of the Higher Agricultural, Commercial and Industrial Board. Mass meetings to herald our demands were held in this city and adjoining towns. Pamphlets explaining our demands were printed and mailed to each member of the Higher Board.[54]

Takano went on to relate the deliberations of the Higher Board when the bill came before it on October 26:

> While we were making all these efforts, the bill came up, on October 26, before the Higher Board, for its consideration. After two days of general discussion, the bill was sent to a special committee of nine. For the five days following, the committee was busily engaged in amending the bill, and on November 1 it reported the bill to the Board in an amended form, which was finally passed by a vote of 15 against 13.[55]

Takano was pleased with the revised bill. He wrote:

> A glance at this amended bill convinces that all our efforts were not made in vain. For the amended bill extended the application of the bill to factories using motive powers of every description while those most objectionable clauses concerning the workingmen's certificate were entirely left out. Furthermore, the bill stipulated the amount of compensation to be paid by employers in cases of accidents to employees while in the discharge of duty. This was a signifi-

cant victory for our association as well as workingmen in general, and we are satisfied with the amended bill, though there is much to be desired with regard to protection of child laborers.

Not only are we pleased with the bill itself, but we are particularly pleased with the fact that a body composed of such well-known capitalists as the Higher Board is, has passed a bill protecting working people, and this fact will go to weaken the opposition for the bill on the floor of the Diet.[56]

The Kiseikai, through incessant lobbying, had managed to make key changes in the proposed factory legislation. Not only had the Kiseikai proved skillful in the political processes of its day, it had also been accepted by government officials as a valid spokesman for workers as a group. The success with the factory legislation seemed to vindicate the gradualist philosophy of Takano, with its avoidance of strikes and confrontation. It also showed that the Social Policy School and labor movement could work closely together as allies to achieve mutual objectives.

The Kiseikai did not get caught up in political controversies, but stuck to the issue at hand—the factory law. Kiseikasi leaders chose this course of action wisely, for the basis of the Japanese political system was the emperor, who stood above all vested interests and represented the interests of the nation itself. Under such a system the government was obligated to give all interested parties a fair hearing so that what constituted the national interest could be correctly perceived by the emperor and his advisors. If the emperor appeared to act arbitrarily or in the interests of a few at the expense of the nation, the governing power of the emperor's advisors, the cabinet, would be seriously undermined. The government could not have ignored the Kiseikai completely, although it could have decided that, on the basis of all the facts, the national interest would not be served by implementing the Kiseikai's proposals.

The Kiseikai's political power was, in a sense, the result of its own weakness. The politicians were all well aware of the Kiseikai's impotence in the political arena. It could not deliver votes, provide funds, or influence key bureaucrats. The Kiseikai represented no threat to the political system. These facts relieved the Kiseikai from any suspicion that its efforts were merely a political ploy. Had the Kiseikai been stronger, its motives would have been suspect, and its actions viewed as the selfish attempts of specific individuals to enhance their own power and political influence. Since the Kiseikai had no power, its leaders' efforts were seen for what they were—an attempt to represent the interests of all workers in Japan. As an emissary from a number of the people of Japan, the Kiseikai deserved a fair hearing by government and advisory bodies.

Success with the proposed factory legislation was the highwater mark for the early Japanese labor movement. No sooner had the Kiseikai succeeded in making changes in the bill than the liberal-party government fell. On October 31, 1898, the Ōkuma-Itagaki cabinet was forced to resign. It had failed to firmly take control of the government.

Government officials, technically subordinate to the cabinet, acted as they wished without fear of loss of office, as they controlled the real heart of the administration. The military men were still powerful and independent, and would not bend to popular rule. Personal rivalries over the question of whose supporters would get what posts in the new government created cabinet disunity. The collapse of the party government in late 1898 signaled the return to a harshly antidemocratic conservative government, which dramatically altered the prospects for unionism.[57]

Unionism also lost one of its key supporters, Sakuma Teiichi, owner of the Shūeisha, the largest printing establishment in Tokyo. Sakuma died on November 6, 1898.[58] With the change of government and loss of Sakuma, the initiative passed to the employers and conservatives who opposed any kind of government regulation of industry. As a result, the amended factory bill passed by the Higher Agricultural, Commercial, and Industrial Board was not placed before the Diet. Instead, the government decided to form a special committee of factory owners and other specialists to investigate conditions and present a new draft law.[59] The subject of factory legislation was effectively tabled for another decade.

The campaign for the amendment of the factory bill had been too successful. By altering the provisions of the law in favor of the workers, the campaign eliminated the small chance the bill had for actual adoption. This was a bitter defeat for the labor leaders who had worked so hard for amendment of the bill. The labor movement began to sink into dissension, disarray, and decline.

6

THE TURNING POINT

THE DEFEAT of the factory act was a bitter blow to the main leader of the labor movement. Takano Fusatarō had just turned thirty, and it must have seemed to him that all his study and efforts had been overwhelmed by a minor change in the political climate. His ability to achieve his goals seemed to depend on the whim of government officials. Directly after the factory act defeat, Takano left his leadership position in the Kiseikai to go to Yokohama to run the largest cooperative for the Metalworkers' Union. The Social Policy School's interest in and support of the labor movement was also diminished by the defeat of the factory act. Shortly after Takano's move to Yokohama, his brother Takano Iwasaburō decided that it was a good time to leave for Germany to undertake several years of postgraduate studies. This left the Kiseikai bereft of its main contact with the Social Policy School.[1]

Katayama Sen now became the most prominent leader in the movement. He had played an important role as editor of *Labor World* and a director of the Kiseikai. Now, with Takano spending all his time in Yokohama, day-to-day direction of the Kiseikai fell to Katayama, who became head director of the Kiseikai.

Originally Katayama's views had been similar to Takano's. Katayama initially favored gradualism, self-help, and harmony between labor and capital. As the labor movement grew, however, government opposition and police interference became more pronounced. The defeat of the factory act was only the culmination of a series of events that pushed Katayama toward a more radical and militant philosophy.

From the first, the Japanese government and police obstructed

112

and harassed the labor movement. Those in power feared the development of any organized group that could oppose government policies or support the popular rights movement and liberal political parties in their efforts to wrest political control of Japan from the Meiji oligarchs. At the first Kiseikai meeting to organize workers, held on June 6, 1897, police interference was pronounced:

> . . . [the police] instituted a close watch on those who were instrumental in bringing the meeting into consummation. Private residences of the leaders were made objects of frequent calls of detectives. Their past records were secretly investigated. Their daily movements were closely followed as if they were suspected criminals. The peaceful home life of the leaders was ruthlessly disturbed and their woeful tales thus commenced. However, the authorities have again failed to find in this direction any pretext to crush the movement. Their next move was toward obstructive tactics for the successful consummation of meetings and covert threats against those who joined the movement.
>
> At one time, uniformed police were stationed in our meeting, under the cover of preserving order in the meeting room, but in reality, to overawe attending workingmen, and at the same time to watch the utterances of speakers. At another time they covertly forbade the renting of a hall for our meetings. On another occasion they demanded all the names of those who joined the movement, which was meant to scare the enrolled members away from the movement.[2]

Another example of police interference occurred in the spring of 1898. The Kiseikai planned an athletic meet to be held in Ueno Park in Tokyo. Though the purpose of the meet was to promote solidarity and raise morale among Kiseikai members, Takano and Katayama, who was chairman of the athletic meet committee, also planned to make a public show of the growing labor movement. In an attempt to prevent possible police intervention, elaborate rules were laid down governing all behavior from the assembly of workers until the end of the sports meet. The date of the gala event was scheduled for April 3, a national holiday.[3]

In late March the Tokyo Metropolitan Police Board refused to grant permission for the sports festival to be held. Kiseikai leaders protested and offered to make whatever changes were necessary to gain police approval. The police superintendent agreed to discuss the matter with the chief of police and to inform Takano and Kata-yama of the result. When nothing more was heard, the Kiseikai leaders mistakenly assumed that tacit permission had been given. On the eve of the festival, when all preparations had been com-pleted, the police refused permission to hold the meeting.[4]

Katayama, writing in *Labor World,* attacked the obstructive actions of the police:

> The disappointment and loss produced by the abrupt prohibition is very great. [The union] made many preparations for the occasion, such as ordering luncheons for fifteen hundred, employing three music bands and making the uniform caps and many other articles which involved much money. The financial loss to them is very great but their disappointment is far greater. The inimical attitude assumed by the Prefect of Police in the case before us will inflict the severest blow upon the healthy grow[th of] the labor organization. It is very much feared by the leaders of the laborers that it may cause an unnecessary discontent among them and lead them to assume a hostile position which may ultimately generate an undesirable ele-ment of anarchism and nihilism in Japan.[5]

While the police did allow the sports meet to be held on April 10, many workers could not attend because it was not a holiday.[6] The actual event became a mere shadow of what had been origi-nally planned and was a direct slap in the face to Katayama, who had worked so hard as chairman of the athletic meet. Up to that time Katayama had been a peaceable and law-abiding citizen, and would have resented imputations against his patriotism and loy-alty to the state, but the high-handed and arbitrary actions of gov-ernment officials on the occasion of the sports festival gave him a severe jolt. After April 1898 his passive annoyance with arrogant officials and bureaucrats gave way to resentment and antagonism. His writings in *Labor World* began to be colored by scornful and derisive comments on the thought and behavior of imperial offi-cials.[7]

The decision by the government to table the factory act was the last straw for Katayama, who felt that little could be achieved as long as the government and police chose to frustrate the legitimate objectives of the workers. Katayama turned his attention to means by which the government itself could be successfully opposed or changed. For Katayama, socialism became the long-term solution to the problems of the workers.

Katayama helped found the Shakaishugi Kenkyūkai (Society for the Study of Socialism) in Tokyo in October 1898,[8] the first organization in Japan for the study of socialism. Its members were a dissatisfied minority of the Shakai Mondai Kenkyūkai (Society for the Study of Social Problems), which had a much too diversified membership to accomplish anything constructive. The founding meeting of the Society for the Study of Socialism was held at the Unitarian Church in Shiba ward, under the auspices of Reverend Murai Tomoyoshi.[9]

The Society for the Study of Socialism, modeled on the British Fabian Society, was made up almost entirely of Christians.[10] Some members, such as Abe Isō, were academics, while others, such as Kōtoku Denjirō, were journalists.[11] Many had been overseas, and some had studied there. Katayama Sen, however, was the only member who had any practical experience in social work and social problems: he was active in both the Kingsley Hall settlement housing project in Tokyo as its director, and the labor movement as head director of the Kiseikai. Only twenty or thirty persons attended the first meeting of the Society for the Study of Socialism, which was devoted to lectures and preparations for the next meeting.[12]

The second meeting, held November 20, 1898, saw Murai elected president, rules set up, and a magazine, the *Rikugō Zasshi*, made the official organ of the society. Lest the purposes of the society be misunderstood by the government, the aims of the society were stated as "the study of the principles of socialism and whether or not they may be applied to Japan."[13] Membership was declared to be open to those who were "in accord with the objectives of the Society, whether or not they agree with the teachings of socialism."[14] It was thus made unmistakably clear that the Society for the Study of Socialism was devoted to study and not to the propagation of socialism, although all of the members were in fact proponents of socialism. It was agreed to hold a regular meeting once a month. In addition, the members planned to have several small discussion meetings and a tea every month, and a large public rally every few months. Meanwhile, Katayama began to educate Kiseikai and Metalworkers' Union members about socialism through a regular column in *Labor World*.[15]

Takano's absence and Katayama's turn toward radicalism and militant action caused the Kiseikai and Metalworkers' Union to adopt a much more aggressive stance toward employers. The first demonstration of this new trend came immediately after Takano left his leadership post. In November 1898 the branch of the Metalworkers' Union at the Ōmiya Factory of the Japan Railway Company became embroiled in a dispute that enabled Katayama to begin to assert the rights of the workers.

From the inception of the union at Ōmiya, union members had run up against severe obstruction from reactionary *oyakata* who feared the union as a threat to their authority. A mutual assistance association for lathe operators and fitters had been set up at the Ōmiya Factory in June 1895. This organization was led by an *oyakata* named Shin Kichigorō, who directed work for the Japan Railway Company on a subcontracting basis.[16] Every month each member contributed 20 percent of one day's wages to a mutual assistance fund.

The Metalworkers' Union had successfully organized the Ōmiya Factory, forming its second branch there in December 1897. Since the Metalworkers' Union also provided mutual assistance benefits, the functions of the union and the Ōmiya Factory Fitters' and Lathe Operators' Mutual Assistance Society overlapped considerably. There was also considerable overlap in the membership of the Metalworkers' Union and Shin's mutual assistance society. In fact, the core of the second branch of the union was made up of members of Shin's mutual assistance society. In the March 1898 election of branch officers for the Ōmiya branch of the Metalworkers' Union, no less than eight of the ten officers elected were lathe operators or fitters. Of the fourteen directors of Shin's mutual assistance association (excluding the president and secretaries), seven were branch officers of the Metalworkers' Union. In addition, a secretary of Shin's mutual assistance association was a founding member of the union.[17]

The worker activists who formed the Ōmiya branch of the Metalworkers' Union were fighting against the despotism of *oyakata* Shin in his workshop and his mutual assistance association. These activists opposed Shin's use of the mutual assistance association as a support for his control of the workplace, and attempted to reorganize it into a more inclusive organization that would strengthen organization among metalworkers, not simply

lathe operators and fitters. Shin reacted to this by discrimi-
nating against the union activists, as the formation of the union
branch meant a fundamental realignment of power in the workplace.[18]

Shin saw a major opportunity to discriminate against union
members and weaken the union when a fitter who was a union
member was killed at the Ōmiya Factory in November 1898. The
union sent 20 yen to the family of the union member. In addition,
the company sent 150 yen under its mutual assistance plan and 16
yen as a special reward for service. However, by February 1899,
the 15 yen entitled to the family of the deceased from Shin's
mutual assistance association had not been sent.[19]

Katayama was quick to take a militant stance. In the February
15 issue of *Labor World,* he attacked the unfairness of Shin's
mutual assistance association at Ōmiya. The failure to pay a death
benefit was underscored by a listing of the rules of the organization and its officers. Katayama dealt harshly with the excuse of the
association—that the funds were unavailable due to nonitemized
"miscellaneous expenses."[20]

Katayama chose to pressure Shin by bringing the issue to the
attention of management. Katayama saw this as a good opportunity to resolve a number of standing grievances, such as the issue
of holidays observed at the Ōmiya plant. Accordingly, he led an
effort to redress the grievances of the workers, using Shin's obvious unfairness as a rallying point for the union members. Katayama correctly guessed that the management of the Japan Railway
Company, having just been stung by public criticism over the engineers' strike, would not be able to oppose union demands in the
face of Shin's blatant oppression.

On the 25th ult. the [Kiseikai] went down to Ōmiya where the
workshops of the Japan Railway Co. are. The managers of the factory have always been a stumbling block to the progress of the
union and have on many occasions interfered with the conduct of
the union men. Patience and firm determination on the part of the
members have broken down the stubbornness of the managers and
foremen. The latter recently confessed their former conducts to be a
great mistake and have promised to support the union hereafter.
Ōmiya workshop now rests on Sunday and all the national holidays, which is a great gain to the working men. The meeting has
resulted in the increase of membership more than twice.[21]

Katayama's use of Shin's unfairness as a weapon against the Japan Railway Company, combined with excellent timing and a shrewd sense of the public mood, brought him success in his negotiations with the company. But Katayama did not rest on his laurels and instead kept applying pressure. *Labor World* continued to be the medium for attacks upon the faulty accounting of Shin's mutual assistance association. Under such pressure and with the company management in a weak position, Shin's mutual assistance association dissolved in March 1899. The membership of the Ōmiya branch of the Metalworkers' Union grew rapidly.[22]

Not all of Katayama's efforts had such favorable results for the labor movement. Katayama's militancy created divisions within the movement as he began to oppose the labor-capital harmony philosophy of the Printers' Friendly Association. The printers' organization had been growing rapidly in 1899, primarily because employers had begun to support it instead of obstructing it. The employers favored the cooperative nature of the friendly association, which contrasted with the previous belligerent printers' groups. Membership in the Printers' Friendly Association increased month after month, and the activities of the association became more open. By the spring of 1899, the association felt confident enough to begin activities on a broader scale.[23]

At the joint committee meeting of committeemen and councilors of the friendly association on March 3, 1899, it was agreed to make public the membership list of the association. On April 3, the spring convention of the association was held in Tokyo. Employers were allowed to attend. The printers, desiring friendly relations with the Kiseikai, invited Katayama Sen to be one of their speakers at the convention. Katayama took a militant stance at the convention, speaking out against cooperation between capital and labor. The printers, enjoying rapid growth, ignored Katayama's advice and continued their policy of cooperating with employers. By May 1, a head office and nine branches—seven in Tokyo, one in Saitama Prefecture, and one in Yokohama—had been set up.[24] Katayama, increasingly concerned by the position of the printers, became even more assertive. In the May 15, 1899, issue of *Labor World,* Katayama attacked the printers for their cooperative attitude toward management. Pointing to their disavowal of strike tactics after the unsuccessful strike of April 1898, Katayama likened the association to "one who, having been bitten by a black dog, is afraid of straw!"[25]

This attack deeply offended the printers, and a motion to defend the association was brought up at the association's directors' meeting. It was decided that Katayama's virulence was not worthy of a reply. Katayama's remarks only served to further strengthen the opinion among printers that they should not join the now militant Kiseikai. The association newspaper replied to articles in *Labor World* urging affiliation with the Kiseikai with "Why should we rely on the Kiseikai?"[26]

Undismayed by Katayama's continued opposition to their policies, the printers continued to welcome employers to their meetings and ask their advice. Shimada Saburō, a prominent politician and labor sympathizer, was persuaded to become the president of the Printers' Friendly Association on May 17.[27] Meanwhile plans were laid for the association to become a union, as its rules required when membership reached fifteen hundred. On July 9, the Printers' Friendly Association held a rally at the Kanda Youth Center, and prominent members of the Kiseikai and the Social Policy School gave speeches. The printers, anxious for support within the labor movement for their position on labor-capital harmony, invited Takano and his supporters, including Social Policy School conservatives, to speak at their rally. The printers also asked Katayama to speak, primarily to show how isolated he was and thereby undermine any influence he may have begun to wield among their own more radical members.

The two opposing ideologies were both represented at the printers' rally: Katayama as the militant agitator, and Takano, supported by Kanai En and Kuwata Kumazō of the Social Policy School, as the pacifists. Katayama outlined his views in his speech at the rally:

> . . . I feel that those who direct capital and affect capital cannot be allowed to carry on as they are carrying on today. No matter who owns capital, it must not be allowed to have preference over the workers employed to operate it. To go one step further, I feel that if the workers cannot obtain capital, then it should be given to them. . . .
>
> I hold a view directly opposed to that of those seated here on the stage. I believe that socialism is good. I believe the railroads should be nationalized. As in the case of municipal ownership of the waterworks, I feel that it is better for society as a whole to own something than for an individual to do so. . . .
>
> Who is gradually destroying the capitalists? Capitalists are de-

stroying the capitalists. Even in Japan those who are capitalists are gradually reduced by competition, and as a result the numbers of workers are increasing. Harmony between labor and capital is not, as our goal, harmony between workers and capitalists. If there were sincere harmony between the things [capital] in the workplace and the people who work in the workplace, I believe that not only all Japanese but everyone everywhere would happily make a living. . . .[28]

In response, Kanai En rose to speak:

What is the reason for the success of unionism? It lies in the pursuit of economic objectives, not political action. . . . What we should make clear . . . is that we oppose Mr. Katayama's socialism. Socialism seeks to destroy the present structure of the state. People today speak of socialism, individualism, liberalism and emancipation, but if you ask what these things mean the answer is very vague. Even if there are socialist theories in books by European scholars and arguments between them, in the final analysis they recognize that the entire economic and social structure is one of private property. Today, everyone operates on the private property system, the capitalist getting his interest from capital, the laborer his wages from work. Socialism seeks the destruction of this system, and the implementation of a system of common ownership. Since socialism attempts to fundamentally destroy the organization of the state, it must not be put into practice.[29]

The Social Policy School conservatives had already reacted to Katayama's socialist philosophy by expelling him from the school in May.[30] Then the Takano and Katayama factions reached an open break at the July 9 meeting of the Printers' Friendly Association. Katayama's strident militancy in *Labor World* had already provoked counterattacks by the Takano faction, such as this article entitled "A Warning to *Labor World*":

Labor World is socialist in viewpoint. It advocates political action, seeks to stir up the workers, and makes political comments. It hurts the weak and inexperienced movement by aiming the point of its arguments at capitalists. Even if we believe such articles spring from *Labor World*'s fervor for the workers, there is fear that the Kiseikai will be seen as militant and socialist, and as advocating the use of the strike as the one weapon of the workers, like *Labor World*.[31]

In response to these attacks on his socialist views, Katayama strengthened his criticism of the "harmony" or gradualist faction. He began to insist upon serious consideration of the importance of the strike weapon and collective bargaining, and to clearly advocate the need for and the efficacy of such tactics. Katayama wrote:

> In order for a union to get results, to be and function as a union, it must make demands of the employer, and when he does not listen, it must strike. This is the true union . . . to carry out mutual assistance, to promote friendship between members, and to avoid opposition of capitalists . . . to have as a goal harmony between capital and labor—these are but empty words to cheat society and avoid the violence accompanying union development.[32]

Continuing poor relations between the printers and Katayama, along with the first signs of financial difficulties at the Kiseikai, prompted Takano to return to Tokyo. With the support of the Kiseikai gradualists, Takano replaced Katayama as head director of the Kiseikai in August 1899. Katayama's position as editor of *Labor World,* as well as his continuing role as a director of the Kiseikai ensured that he remained a strong force in the movement. After his success with the Japan Railway Company and the growth of the union branch at Ōmiya, Katayama enjoyed support from a number of metalworkers within the Kiseikai, and Takano simply did not have enough support within the Kiseikai to remove or expel him. Katayama continued to use *Labor World* as a platform for advocating militant tactics.

Despite the developing split within the labor movement, the Printers' Friendly Association continued to grow after the July 9 rally. Committees were chosen to handle the establishment of the Printers' Union and to draw up a tentative constitution in August. The printers from the very start had wanted good relations with the Printers' Employers' Association. They presented their proposed constitution and unionization plans to the employers' association for approval. The employers expressed their agreement with the unionization plan on September 11, but asked that some changes be made in the constitution.[33] The committee revised the constitution as instructed. Then the employers wanted other changes made in the constitution. The printers invited volunteers from the employers' association to participate in the revision of the constitution, which was approved by the constitution committee of the Printers' Friendly Association on October 14. All was ready for the launching of the union.[34]

The printers gained real advantages by their policy of cooperation with management. In their revised constitution, the following articles are notable:

(a) When a union member is laid off at the convenience of the employer, he shall pay the wages of the union member during his period of lay-off. (Article Fifty-Five).

(b) When an employer employs a worker he shall inform the union. (Article Fifty-Eight).

(c) The work day shall be limited to ten hours in shops employing union members. (Article Fifty-Nine).

(d) There shall be a twenty percent night shift allowance. (Article Sixty).[35]

The printers had thus obtained a victory in their negotiations with the employers' association. Membership grew rapidly as news about the constitution spread. In this atmosphere the inaugural ceremony of the Printers' Union was held on November 3, 1899, and with the formation of the union the Printers' Friendly Association was dissolved.[36]

At the inaugural ceremony speeches were given by members and President Shimada, and after the ceremony ended officers were elected. Shimada Saburō was reelected president, and Takano was named an honorary member. The union, with two thousand members, was second only to the Metalworkers' Union in all of Japan. Branches would be established in Tokyo, Yokohama, Kyoto, Nagoya, Osaka, and Nara.[37]

The Printers' Union adopted the same inclusive structure as the Metalworkers' Union and the Reform Society. Lithographers, compositors, and printers, organized in different craft unions in the United States and Britain, in Japan all belonged to the Printers' Union. There were no restrictions on membership based on age or skill level. The printers chose, like the metalworkers and railwaymen, to organize in such a way as to allow all of those men working in the same shop to be union members.

The structure of the Printers' Union was less shop-based than that of the Metalworkers' Union or the Reform Society. There were several reasons for this. First, printing establishments were, on average, smaller in scale than workplaces in heavy industry and the railways. The largest printing firms in Tokyo employed only a hundred men or so, and most publishing companies were much smaller. This made union organization on a workplace basis difficult, and some union branches were formed geographically to allow for sufficient membership to support the branch infrastructure. While there were also geographic branches in the Metalworkers' Union, they were few in number since usually enough members could be found in one workplace to support a branch.

The second reason for a less shop-based structure was related to the printers' desire to cooperate with the employers. A geographic structure diffused employer fears of workplace-based confrontation such as they had experienced in the Tokyo Printing Company strike. This was particularly important since many union activists came from the Tokyo Printing Company and a workplace-based branch there would have been perceived as a threat by management.

Finally, the Printers' Union had achieved rapid growth after the announcement of the favorable terms of its constitution, and many of the new members had joined for opportunistic reasons. There was little solidarity predating the formation of the union among these new members as there had been at the Rifle Works of the Tokyo Armaments Works in the case of the Metalworkers' Union or in the Ichinoseki station of the Japan Railway Company prior to the formation of the Reform Society. For these reasons there was less pressure on union leaders for shop-based branches from the membership.

Despite these factors, a shop-based effort had started the organization effort in the first place, as the twelve founders of the Printers' Friendly Association were all from the Tokyo Printing Company. Had the union lasted longer, shop-based branches would no doubt have appeared, as occurred in branches of the Metalworkers' Union that started with a geographic or workplace-based structure.

Katayama, while congratulating the printers, continued to antagonize them by stressing the importance of strikes:

The Printer['s] Union has grown enormously in its membership. The Union will celebrate its organization on the third inst. It has over 2,000 men and has entered into an agreement with masters. This is a great gain to the cause of the labor movement. From henceforth the printers will get better wages and exercise the power of the union for excluding non-members from their own fields. The true harmony between labor and capital will be realized so long as the latter keeps the agreement. We *hope* they do otherwise the result will be a *strike*. At any rate we heartily congratulate the printers for their brightest prospect.[38]

Takano, meanwhile, worked hard to improve relations between the Kiseikai and the printers. His gradualist philosophy was attractive to the printers, and with Takano in charge the printers proved willing to accept advice from the Kiseikai and its supporters. Takano wrote about his role in advising the printers:

It is proposed that within the coming month [the Printers' Association formed by some printer members of our association] will change its constitution so as to conform to the strict trade union requirements with benefits similar to the iron workers. Ways and means of affiliation with our association are carefully considered by the prime movers of the union, and I am advising them on all the matters relating to trade unionism and its federation.[39]

Takano had returned to lead the labor movement and assist in the formation of Japan's third large union, the Printers' Union. The printers, by joining the metalworkers and railwaymen in forming unions, seemed to light the way for the labor movement and unionization in Japan. Momentum seemed to be building, as one after another of the new occupations developed large, modern labor organizations. Each union had achieved concessions from employers—the railwaymen and metalworkers from the Japan Railway Company, and the printers from their employers' association. Success seemed assured regardless of whether confrontational or gradual tactics were used.

Yet already the movement was split along ideological and tactical grounds. The railwaymen were firmly wedded to confrontation and were building up their strike fund. In stark contrast, the printers had asked employers to help them draft their union constitution. Takano continued to push for evolution, opposing strikes and favoring harmony between labor and capital. Katayama championed militant strikes. The metalworkers and the

Kiseikai were hopelessly split between the Takano and Katayama factions. Meanwhile, the Kiseikai and Metalworkers' Union were isolated from the other unions. The printers were put off by Katayama's militancy, and the railwaymen avoided Kiseikai affiliation in an effort to maintain their independence and non-political philosophy. As serious challenges to the movement arose, Takano and Katayama found themselves unable to work together to overcome them, and the unions could not assist each other. The movement, isolated into camps and rent by ideological controversy, would prove too weak to withstand growing government and employer opposition.

7

CRISIS AND COLLAPSE

THE METALWORKERS' UNION and the Kiseikai were already under siege prior to the formation of the Printers' Union. The problem was finances. By August 1899 the Metalworkers' Union had been running a deficit for six months, totaling 570 yen. Headquarters and branch expenses, such as rallies, salaries, and the publication of *Labor World,* were absorbing 75 percent of all dues. Mutual assistance payments were rising at the rate of 10 percent per month. In short, expenses were outrunning income (see table 8).

Katayama's militancy together with these financial pressures prompted Takano to return to lead the Kiseikai and the Metalworkers' Union. Under Takano's leadership the union moved on August 20 to deal with the deteriorating financial situation. Out of each member's dues of twenty sen, the allowance for branch expenses was reduced from five to three sen, the Kiseikai allowance was cut from five to two-and-a-half sen, and union headquarters was advised to conduct activities within a limit of three sen per member. The union also made three decisions concerning members who were lax in paying their dues, to take effect September 1, 1899:

a) Those who missed paying dues were thereafter to be denied mutual assistance benefits.

b) Even if a member paid up his back dues, he would still not be eligible for mutual assistance benefits until two months had passed and he had faithfully paid his dues those months.

c) Those members who currently were behind on dues were to

126

Table 8. Financial Condition of the Metalworkers' Union, December 1897–February 1900 (yen)

| | | ORDINARY EXPENDITURE | | | |
PERIOD	ORDINARY INCOME	HQ AND BRANCHES	MUTUAL ASSISTANCE	TOTAL	SURPLUS OR DEFICIT
Dec.–Feb. 1897/1898	772.80	461.60	—	461.60	+311.20
Mar.–May 1898	985.40	560.57	134.20	694.77	+290.63
June–Aug. 1898	—	—	—	—	—
Sept.–Nov. 1898	898.40	531.38	299.00	830.38	+ 68.02
Dec.–Feb. 1898/1899	—	—	—	—	—
Mar.–May 1899	1019.00	878.82	400.20	1279.02	−260.02
June–Aug. 1899	1255.00	884.50	684.40	1568.90	−313.90
Sept.–Nov. 1899	1098.60	487.69	832.25	1319.94	−221.34
Dec.–Feb. 1899/1900	554.80	425.88	123.45	539.33	+ 5.47

Sources: Labor World, no. 9 (April 1, 1898): 9; no. 15 (July 1, 1898): 8–9; no. 27 (January 1, 1899): 11–12; no. 40 (July 15, 1899): 4–5; no. 46 (October 15, 1899): 8; no. 55, supplement (February 15, 1900): 5–6; no. 62 (June 1, 1900), 5–6.

pay prior dues along with current dues at the rate of one month's back dues per month. Those who failed to do so were considered lax in paying dues and underwent the provisions (a) and (b) above.[1]

The union also tightened procedures for the payment of mutual assistance benefits, although no change was made in the amounts. These economies provided more funds for mutual assistance benefit payments, but mutual assistance expenses continued to grow, outstripping the growth in funds available. September was a deficit month for the union. The rapid rise in sick benefits was highly concentrated in several branches whose membership was dropping fast. These branches made up only a third of the dues-paying members, but accounted for 60 percent of the sick benefits paid out from September to November and half of the union's membership loss in the period September to December 1899 (see tables 9 and 10). Members in these branches had simply decided to recover their dues by claiming illness before the union collapsed finan-

Table 9. Membership in Metalworkers' Union Branches Paying High
Sick Benefits, September–November 1899 (persons)

| | MEMBERSHIP | | | | SICK BENEFITS |
BRANCH NO.	SEPT.	OCT.	NOV.	DEC.	PAID *(yen)*
2	210	151	114	51	27.40
9	172	102	76	—	57.85
10	161	60	43	22	52.70
11	64	57	57	57	53.85
17	404	143	138	99	77.00
21	77	17	17	14	26.70
Total	988	530	445	243	305.50

Sources: Labor World, no. 46 (October 15, 1899): 8; ibid., no. 55, supplement (February 15, 1900): 5–6; ibid., no. 62 (June 1, 1900): 5–6.

Notes: Branch membership is dues-paying members. "Sick Benefits Paid" shows the amount of sick benefits paid between September and November 1899 for a particular branch. Total sick benefits paid for all Metalworkers' Union members in the period were 495.25 yen. See *Labor World,* no. 55, supplement (February 15, 1900): 5–6.

cially. These members then left the union to avoid paying further dues, convinced that it had no future.

The leaders of the Metalworkers' Union, under continual financial pressure from mutual assistance benefits, felt they could not raise dues or institute a levy since such actions would prompt more members to leave. There was as yet no strong union tradition, and loyalty to the union was weak because of the transient nature of the membership of the union and the short tenure of the officers. The union was made up of and supported primarily by "travelers" —workers who moved from shop to shop to polish their skills and improve their pay. The turnover in branch officers shows the high proportion of travelers in the union.

Branch one, at the Tokyo Armaments Works, started out with eight officers in January 1898. At the next election, in July 1898, only two of the eight were reelected, and the number of officers was expanded to nine. In January 1899 only one of the original officers was reelected. Five of the seven incumbents who had served since July were reelected, and the number of officers was expanded to ten. In July 1899, of the fourteen officers elected (the number had again been expanded), only three had ever served as officers of that branch before.[2]

Other branches show even higher turnover rates. Branch two at the Ōmiya Factory, for example, started out with eight officers in

Table 10. Membership in Metalworkers' Union Receiving High and Low Sick Benefits, September–December 1899

	MEMBERS *(percent)*			
SICK BENEFITS	SEPT.	OCT.	NOV.	DEC.
High	988 (41%)	530 (34%)	445 (28%)	243 (25%)
Low	1,430 (59%)	1,006 (66%)	1,094 (72%)	717 (75%)

Sources: Labor World, no. 46 (October 15, 1899): 8; ibid., no. 55, supplement (February 15, 1900): 5–6; ibid., no. 62 (June 1, 1900): 5–6.

Note: Branches receiving high sick benefits are those shown in table J-2. Branches receiving low sick benefits are all other branches. Figures are for dues-paying members only.

January 1898. In July the number of officers was expanded to fourteen, and five of the original eight were reelected. By July 1899 there were thirty-eight officers at this branch, twenty-seven of which were totally inexperienced. Only two of the thirty-eight had been officers of the branch from the beginning. A similar situation existed at branch seventeen at the Yokosuka Navy Shipyards. In July 1898 only twelve of its forty-six officers had served as union officers before.[3]

Turnover in union membership was also high. Metalworkers changed jobs in search of higher wages, better conditions, or to improve their skill level. Under heavy industry's booming demand, turnover at many workplaces exceeded 100 percent per year. The Metalworkers' Union experienced similar turnover rates, as members went to nonunionized plants or left Tokyo completely for work in western Japan. From March to September 1899, a period in which the number of dues-paying members averaged some 2,000, the Metalworkers' Union recruited 2,150 new members and lost 1,486 who stopped paying dues. The Metalworkers' Union was experiencing a turnover rate well in excess of 100 percent per year, and significant recruitment success was required simply to offset membership losses (see table 11).

The union leadership felt that a levy or dues increase would only accelerate turnover and make it more difficult to recruit new members. Having already trimmed headquarters and branch expenses, the leaders of the Metalworkers' Union had no choice but to cut benefits to balance the books. The union sickness allowance was cut from twenty to fifteen sen per day and paid thirty days after the union member claimed the benefit. The funeral benefit was cut

Table 11. Metalworkers' Union Membership
and New Recruits, 1898–1900

DATE	MEMBERSHIP	RECRUITS
September 1898	1,360	509
October 1898	1,283	263
November 1898	1,849	456
March 1899	1,754	287
April 1899	1,191	302
May 1899	2,150	447
June 1899	1,735	265
July 1899	2,164	318
August 1899	2,376	267
September 1899	2,418	264
October 1899	1,536	127
November 1899	1,539	132
December 1899	960	108
January 1900	849	89
February 1900	965	77

Sources: Labor World, no. 27 (January 1, 1899): 10–11;
no. 40 (July 15, 1899): 5; no. 46 (October 15, 1899): 8;
no. 55, supplement (February 15, 1900): 5; no. 62 (June 1,
1900): 5–6.

Note: Information for December 1898 through February
1899 is unavailable.

from twenty to fifteen yen and paid for union members with at
least one year of membership instead of only six months. The
death allowance was cut from ten to five yen and granted only to
families of members with at least two years of membership instead
of one.[4]

The reaction of the membership to the cuts was immediate.
Dues-paying union members dropped from 2,400 to 1,500 during
October. The number of new members, which had been at least
250 per month, dropped to 127 in October and never again
climbed above 150. Claims for mutual assistance continued
unabated as members tried to cash in before the union went under.
The union struggled with another deficit for September–November
1899.

In early November another labor dispute broke out at the
Ōmiya Factory of the Japan Railway Company—and this dispute
broke the rapidly weakening Metalworkers' Union. Sawano Ki-
chijirō, an apprentice-type *oyakata* at the factory, had been dis-
criminating in favor of his followers, giving them easy work and
promoting them quickly. On November 1, 1899, Sawano took

direct action against eight blacksmiths who, through a mediator, were attempting to rectify the situation. Sawano openly discriminated against the blacksmiths and verbally abused and threatened them.[5]

Sawano was so intimidating that the eight union members immediately left work and did not report to work the next day. Meanwhile, the Japan Railway Company had learned of the workmen's mediation attempt and immediately demanded that they apologize, in writing, to Sawano. The eight union members refused, declaring the company's action to be unfair, and on November 7 all eight tendered their resignations. That evening the company rejected their resignations and fired them on the basis of their one-day absence from work without permission. Without giving the usual one week's notice, the company ordered that the men be moved out of company housing by November 9. Further, the company refused to pay the special service allowance required in cases of discharge at the company's convenience. The company also confiscated the mutual assistance funds the eight workers had accumulated through the company program. The incident became known as the "Ōmiya affair."[6]

The Metalworkers' Union immediately sought to rectify the situation. On the evening of November 10 an emergency conference of the union directors was called. It was agreed that the next day six of the directors, including Takano, Katayama, and Sawada, would proceed to Ōmiya to investigate. A meeting was held at Ōmiya with the Ōmiya branch officers and representatives of the discharged men, and the directors returned to Tokyo the same day.[7]

Takano's control of the Kiseikai meant there would be no strike action or confrontation with the company. Instead, the Metalworkers' Union tried to rally public opinion against the company's unfairness. The militant Katayama faction had little choice but to go along with Takano's tactics because the Metalworkers' Union had been caught off guard by the developments at the Ōmiya Factory. Although the eight discharged men were union members, they had neither consulted with nor acted as representatives of the union.[8] The union decided upon a tame "moderator" role and verbal assault tactics; it could not have organized a strike on such short notice with no funds in its treasury.

On the fourteenth Takano and Katayama called on Superintendent Awaya of the Ōmiya Factory, but he refused to listen to their appeals. The next day a third meeting of union members was held and the resolve of the union strengthened. On the eighteenth the union held an emergency meeting of branch representatives, and they had no choice but to raise funds for a campaign or give in to the company's unfairness. The branch representatives decided to run the risk of alienating the membership and made a levy of five sen per member. The use of these funds and the direction of the campaign in opposition to the unfairness of the Japan Railway Company was left to the union's executive board.[9]

That evening branch representatives assembled again and decided, given the risks associated with a levy, to give the company another chance before opening the campaign. On November 20 Takano, Katayama, and Sawada met with Baron Sōga, the president of the company. The baron agreed to reply to their appeal after an investigation of the facts. On the twenty-fourth he replied that he had found, on the basis of investigation, that the discharge of the eight blacksmiths had been entirely proper. Stung by strikes by the engineers in 1898 and the track maintenance crews in 1899, managers felt that at last they were on strong ground in opposing the unions since the blacksmiths had left work without permission.[10]

The union then launched its campaign with a petition distributed to the newspapers. *Labor World* published a special issue attacking the company for the unjust and corrupt activities condoned at the Ōmiya Factory. The union held a rally at Ōmiya and filed a suit against the president of the company to recover the workmens' mutual assistance funds. The company put up fierce resistance, asking the owners of public halls not to rent their halls for the Kiseikai rally, and posting bills proclaiming Takano and Katayama to be "dogs" who "should be killed."[11]

Public opinion again supported the workers, and the union campaign took its toll. The company again was forced to make concessions. First the company agreed to allow workers who did not show up for work ten days of such behavior before they were discharged. Later, the company returned the mutual assistance funds of the workmen, and the union then dropped the suit against the company president. The discharge of the eight blacksmiths was rescinded and they were allowed to resign instead, and the company laid off Sawano, the offending *oyakata*. Although the union achieved some of its objectives and claimed a major victory, the blacksmiths were not returned to their jobs. Essentially, the company could get rid of union members at will.[12]

Meanwhile, the Katayama faction took advantage of the crisis situation at Ōmiya to alter the nature of the mutual assistance function of the union. When the union held a directors' meeting at Ōmiya in December 1899, the Katayama faction pushed through a resolution to give assistance to the eight discharged men under an 1898 union resolution stating that members who could not work due to a union-related event or act would receive an assistance payment of fifty sen per day." The eight men, over a period of weeks, received a total of fifty-two yen under this decision. This represented a major change in the concept of mutual assistance and reflected a shift away from the idea of a simple mutual assistance society toward that of a labor union.

The Takano faction mounted a counterattack at the next branch representatives' meeting in January 1900. Its proponents pointed out the extreme financial burden that had been imposed on the union, and many representatives expressed fear that the union would be unable to meet its obligations if a number of union members were thrown out of work.[13] The Takano faction managed to have the previous decision overturned. This was a warning against financial and militant involvement in disputes between labor and capital, and reflected a feeling among the majority of union members that the eight discharged men had been careless, impudent, and hence disloyal to the union. Given the financial difficulties of the union, the timing of the dispute could not have been worse.

It was clear by late November that union pressure would not reinstate the blacksmiths in their jobs, and that the company could fire union members at will. Not only had the union failed to achieve its major objectives in the campaign, but the membership had had to pay a levy to finance the campaign. As the union leadership had feared, the reaction of the membership to a levy was disappointing: only 36 yen 50 sen was collected. At the rate of five sen per person, only 730 union members, or less than half the dues-paying membership, had paid the levy.[14]

The failure of the union to preserve jobs for union members at Ōmiya together with the levy to finance this failure caused another dramatic drop in members paying union dues—from over 1,500 in

November to 960 in December. The knowledge that managers could fire union members at will hurt recruitment. The number of new inductees dropped to one hundred per month and continued to decrease. Membership at the Ōmiya branch was particularly hard hit, dropping from 151 in October to 51 in December (see tables 9 and 11).

The dismal failure of Takano's tactics spurred Katayama to undertake a new approach designed to prevent the union from ever again being caught off guard and forced to accept a company discharge of union members. In mid-December he toured northern Japan for several days in an effort to reach an understanding with the other unions at the Japan Railway Company.[15] Three different unions represented Japan Railway Company employees at this time. One was the Metalworkers' Union, which represented metalworkers in the workshops of the company. The Reform Society represented employees in the company's Locomotive Section—engineers, their assistants, firemen, and train janitors. A union of the manual workers in the track maintenance crews had been set up in September 1899, shortly before the Ōmiya affair.

Katayama was working for united action on the part of the various unions at the Japan Railway Company. He was able to bring back to the metalworkers satisfactory assurances of support from other union members in the event of another confrontation between the Metalworkers' Union and the Japan Railway Company. Katayama's trip not only solidified relations between the existing unions, but also made them much more self-confident and bold.

The first result of this diplomacy was a threatened strike for better wages by the engineers and firemen of the Japan Railway Company during the period January 7–16, 1900. The strike was averted by the promise of the head of the Transportation Section that action would be taken to improve the situation. In February 1900 the engineers at the Fukushima station planned a strike, but Katayama insisted that priority be placed on strengthening organization and solidarity, so the plan was dropped.[16]

The initiative then shifted to the metalworkers at the Japan Railway Company. In March 1900 they united to form a "Workers' Alliance," which was led by Katayama. These metal workers chose to work outside the Metalworkers' Union because they wanted to pursue militant tactics, which Takano, still in control of the union, would not allow. The new organization listed its demands in a petition given to the stationmaster or superintendent in charge of each of the sixteen workshops of the Japan Railway Company:[17]

PETITION

All of the Company's workers, including we humble workers, do sincerely feel that deep gratitude for the many life-sustaining benefits the Company has bestowed upon its workers must be expressed. However, pressed by circumstances, we open our hearts on the following points, and wonder if we might not wish for them:

That all workers be treated fairly and impartially.
That a training school for young workers be set up.
That the occupational names be reformed.
That better treatment be given to the workers.
That hourly pay be reformed to daily pay.
That public holidays be observed at the workshops.
That Company housing be given to the workers, except that this
be limited to those who live in the country [rather than the cities].

We humbly point out that it would be most fortunate if the Company would, on the basis of its consideration of the situation, judge the above points, and if it accepts them, implement them with haste.

With thanks and
a hundred bows[18]

Several of the demands embodied within the petition are of interest. The demand for fair treatment for all workers was a direct attack on *oyakata* favoritism. The demand for a training school for young workers was designed to shift training out of the hands of the *oyakata* and make it the responsibility of the company. The issue of hourly pay and its reform to daily pay was basically one of status: hourly workers were the lowliest of workers in Japan. The demand for company housing was meant to eliminate long-distance commuting for workers who lived in the country because of the absence of suitable housing for their families near the workshops. Thus the major demands of this petition were directed against *oyakata,* not management.

The Japan Railway Company took a strong stand against the petition. At some shops the petition was ripped up by management, and at Ōmiya the company went so far as to fire ten members of the petition committee. In response, the Workers' Alliance backed up its petition with a strike. At Ōmiya over 500 of the 1,300 workers struck. At Morioka over 400 and at the smaller workshops some 100 workers struck. Altogether, of approximately 2,300 metalworkers at the Japan Railway Company, 1,087 participated in the strike.[19]

In April negotiations were opened with management. The company maintained that while the demands of the strikers were correct, the method of demand was inappropriate, and that the strikers should return to work and wait for treatment reform. Management also threatened to invoke the recently enacted Peace Police Act, which provided for imprisonment of strikers. The worker representatives, unable to make any progress, returned to the workshops in disgust. The company thereupon fired forty-five representatives of the Workers' Alliance—twenty-eight at Ōmiya, fifteen at Morioka, and two at Fukushima. Support for the metalworkers by the railwaymen and maintenance workers was impossible under the Peace Police Act. The Workers' Alliance was unable to withstand the combined oppression of both management and government, and the strike collapsed.[20]

The Peace Police Act of 1900 had its origins in the fall of the first liberal party cabinet in late 1898. The conservative Yamagata faction of the oligarchy dominated the new cabinet. Yamagata strove to reverse the liberalization of the laws that had taken place during the period the liberal parties controlled the cabinet. For example, the Peace Preservation Regulations of 1897, which gave the government sweeping powers to suppress all political activity in a given area, had been repealed by the liberals in June 1898. This liberalization of the law threatened to erode the power of the oligarchs.[21] Yamagata moved quickly to restore oligarchic control. The Yamagata cabinet began to draft a law to restrict the political parties. In addition, the government decided to add regulations to the law making strike activity illegal. The result was the Peace Police Act of 1900.[22]

The specific articles giving the government and employers legal weapons to destroy unions and break strikes were as follows:

ARTICLE 17: No one shall commit violence or threaten others or publicly slander others for the purposes of the following paragraphs, or tempt and incite others for the purpose of paragraph two below:

(1) In order to let others join, or prevent others from joining an organization which aims at collective action concerning conditions of work or remuneration;

(2) In order to let the employer discharge workers, or to let him reject an application for work or to let a worker stop his work, or to let a worker refuse an offer of employment with a view to organizing a lockout or strike;

(3) In order to compel the other party to agree to conditions of remuneration.

ARTICLE THIRTY: Those who violate Article 17 shall be liable to a heavy imprisonment of 1 to 6 months and in addition a fine of from 3 to 30 yen. The same shall apply to those who commit violence on, threaten, or publicly slander persons who have not joined the employer in a lockout or the union in a strike.[23]

The need for these provisions relating to labor unions was outlined by an official who had written and supported the passage of the Peace Police Act:

Because the railway workers organized and struck, causing cessation of transport for several days, the public suffered losses and was inconvenienced. In the country today this has reached a level which cannot be tolerated . . . when workers strike, they not only cause the company to suffer losses, they cause society, in many cases, great harm. Should workers in war industries strike, they would have no small effect on the progress of a war. If, for example, the workers at the Tokyo Armaments Works should strike, our army would undergo a great handicap. Not only is there loss to the country, there can be problems in foreign trade [as export orders cannot be met]. In spite of the opinions of scholars who advocate the right to strike, it is high time . . . by means of this Act, for such actions to be restricted.[24]

The fact that the Tokyo Armaments Works—the heart of the membership of the Metalworkers' Union—is specifically mentioned here is of major significance. The Japanese government, readying itself for the decisive conflict with Russia, could ill afford the coddling of unionism when it meant that a handful of workers might determine the fate of the nation. Although Western scholars have stated that "it is improbable that the Meiji government was frightened by the 'power' of a working class which constituted not more than one per cent of the total population,"[25] they fail to note where the strength of Japanese unionism lay at the time. It lay in the railroads, the shipyards, and the arsenals, with its very core at the government's largest weapons complex—the Tokyo Armaments Works. Thus as the government prepared for war, it was also compelled to attack the labor movement.

Clearly, the Japanese government did not view the labor movement as a harmless phenomenon. The conservative oligarchs and bureaucrats saw the labor movement as a possible obstacle to government economic and military policy. The ruling elite realized that the unions, just like the political parties, were independent democratic entities representing an alternative way of organizing society and the nation. Such alternatives could not be allowed to flourish.

Takano's ideology and Social Policy School support had failed to win over the Japanese government. Takano's compromises between "pure and simple" trade unionism and the Social Policy School position, designed to show how unionism could benefit society and increase economic growth, did not address the basic reality of Japanese politics. The government, which was oppressive and centralized in character, would brook no possibility of organized resistance to government policy. Thus, the potential for union opposition to government policy was sufficient to cause the government to restrict unionism, regardless of the avowed position or ideology of union leaders. Takano's compromise was not enough to save the Metalworkers' Union and the Kiseikai, and the government's power proved sufficient to overwhelm Katayama's militant approach as well.

While Katayama was being crushed in his challenge to the Japan Railway Company, the Printers' Union was in crisis. In the face of the growing size and power of the Printers' Union, the employers' association had quickly revised its conciliatory attitude. The key to the counterattack of the employers was the fact that the employers' association had not formally given its approval to the constitution of the Printers' Union. True, the association had made some recommendations for changes, and the printers had invited volunteers from among the employers to help them revise the constitution. But the employers had not given formal approval of the revised constitution, and the volunteers who had assisted in the revision were not recognized as representatives of the employers' association by either the employers or the printers.

The Printers' Union was acutely conscious of the fact that the employers had not approved the constitution of the union. Until approval was given, no provisions of the constitution, such as the ten-hour day, would be put into effect by the employers. Accordingly, the Printers' Union wrote to the employers' association in January 1900, shortly after the union had been formed. The printers requested that the employers' association approve the constitution of the union at the association meeting on January 27, 1900.[26]

The employers, however, decided to reorganize their Printers' Employers' Association into the Tokyo Printers' Employers' Association at the January 27 meeting. This was carried out with two objects in mind. First, it facilitated a change to a more confrontational policy toward the Printers' Union, and second, it allowed the employers to avoid approval of the Printers' Union constitution. The employers decided that, because of their reorganization, they would have to discuss the matter of the Printers' Union constitution with their entire membership.[27]

The employers chose to confront the Printers' Union after the January 27 meeting. A Tokyo daily reported:

> The Tokyo Printers' Employers' Association, comprised of employers in the printing trades in Tokyo and Yokohama, along with forming this new organization simultaneously began to produce workmen's certificates to restrict the mobility of workers in the printing trades. In response to this, various types of arguments in opposition to this have gushed forth from the printers, and at the headquarters of the Printers' Union an emergency officers' meeting has been held to deliberate the policy of the union with respect to these workmen's certificates.[28]

The employers' association, by implementing a system of workmen's certificates, went on the offensive and wrested the initiative from the Printers' Union. Members of the employers' association agreed to employ only workers who held a workmen's certificate. Workmen's certificates were then issued to workers, who were required to deposit them with their employers. Employers could then prevent the workers from leaving their employ by refusing to return the certificates.

In the face of employer opposition, the leaders of the Printers' Union were forced to change their policy of cooperation with the employers. The union published an emergency issue of its newspaper, announcing the decision of the union to adopt a tough stance against the employers. The union focused on the newly issued certificates, demanding that the employers reconsider their policy and attacking their methods as unfair.[29]

This shift in employer policy and the militant union response quickly frightened away many union members who were interested in the ten-hour day and the 20 percent night-shift allowance only if they could get them with no effort. Resignations and dues delinquency began in January and increased rapidly. The Peace Police Act in March came as another severe blow, preventing union militants from undertaking a strike for fear of imprisonment. By May, the union could no longer hold on and the union constitution was suspended. The union quietly disappeared.[30]

The promulgation of the Peace Police Act was a severe setback to the labor movement, which was already in decline. The only way for the movement to overcome this obstacle to progress was to have the law repealed, and that required political action. The leaders of the Kiseikai, especially Katayama Sen, were convinced of the need for a political response to this oppressive law. They decided to form the Futsū Senkyo Kisei Dōmeikai (Universal Suffrage Association[31]) on March 10, 1900.

The goals of this new organization were to bring the problem of universal suffrage to the attention of the people and obtain amendment of the election laws to allow universal adult male suffrage. The leaders of the movement felt that if the workers were enfranchised, their political clout would be sufficient to repeal the Peace Police Act and revive the labor movement. Anyone could join the Universal Suffrage Association, and those wishing to help foot the expenses of the association were made special members who were charged fifty sen a month. The main activity of the association was to prepare and present to the fifteenth Diet a massive petition requesting universal male suffrage.[32]

At the first meeting of the association officers were elected. Three directors were elected—Takano Fusatarō representing the Kiseikai, Kōtoku Denjirō from the socialists, and Onose Fujito representing liberal and progressive elements. Between March 11 and March 17 three meetings were held to build up support for the suffrage movement, and the Tokyo Barbers' Association rallied to the cause. Regular rallies were held each month, but after March the movement gained few members and no momentum.[33]

As the leaders of the labor movement linked up with socialist and progressive groups, the workers continued to abandon the unions. The Printers' Union disappeared in May. The Metalworkers' Union, at its June 9 branch representatives meeting, was forced to admit defeat. Membership was shrinking and financial deficits continued. At the June 9 meeting the death allowance was cut from fifteen to ten yen, and all assistance payments for sickness, disability, and fire damage were discontinued.[34] With the cessation of these mutual assistance payments, the Metalworkers' Union faded away.

Mutual assistance had failed to bond the workers to the union. According to *Labor World,* of the 251 union members who had received mutual assistance payments by April 1900, 26 had died, 65 had left the union, 57 had been expelled from the union, and 82 no longer paid their dues. Only 21 members, less than 10 percent, still paid their dues faithfully.[35] As mutual assistance failed, so did the union cooperatives and labor clubs.

The cooperative stores set up by the union, so promising in earlier years, all failed within a few years of their establishment. The cooperatives collapsed for a number of reasons. First, competition from other merchants offering sales, better quality goods, and easy credit presented a difficult challenge to the cooperatives. Second, union policy on pricing (a low 15 percent markup), together with inexperienced management and poor accounting techniques, led to low profits or losses. Finally, cash flow was very poor since union members invariably demanded they be allowed to charge their purchases, and it was difficult to restrict such credit sales.[36]

The labor clubs set up by the union also disbanded as the union declined. The Ōmiya club, for example, suffered from opposition by the Japan Railway Company's management. In May 1900 the company set up its own club for workers in order to destroy the union club. Membership in the company club was required of all workers and 5 percent of their pay went to its upkeep. Under this pressure the union club was dissolved in August 1900.[37]

The demise of the Metalworkers' Union had a decisive impact on the Kiseikai. Kiseikai funding was nearly eliminated by the loss of the steady flow of dues from the Metalworkers' Union. *Labor World,* the union newspaper, had also doubled as the organ of the Kiseikai, and its expenses could not be supported from what remained of the Kiseikai resources. In June 1900, *Labor World,* for years a biweekly, became a monthly, and in September its staff was reorganized. Katayama Sen became the sole publisher and editor, and the support staff was disbanded.[38]

As the unions and the Kiseikai weakened, and the Universal Suffrage Association failed to attract support, Takano and the other moderates gradually gave up and left the movement. Takano, convinced by government repression that the movement had no future, left for China in August 1900. Shimada Saburō, once president of the Printers' Union, became involved in Christianity and social reformism after the collapse of the Printers' Union. Ozawa Benzō, who had led the organization of the Ishikawajima Shipyards by the Metalworkers' Union, left Tokyo in July 1900.[39]

With the departure of the moderates, what remained of the movement came under the control of the radicals. Led by Katayama Sen, they set to work in the fall of 1900 with new energy. The first move was to revitalize the Universal Suffrage Association. The radicals took control of the group at its November 18 general meeting, when Kawano Hironaka and Fukumoto Makoto were elected directors and Katayama was made one of the five secretaries. Preparations continued on the project to present a petition to the Diet.[40] After months of hard work, the Universal Suffrage Association presented its petition to the Diet in March, calling for the right to vote for all Japanese men over the age of twenty. The petition caused no major comment in the Diet and was quietly ignored.[41]

Katayama had been hard at work persuading the last remaining major union in Japan, the Reform Society of the Japan Railway Company, to change its independent policies and join in his efforts for political and social reform. That spring, shortly after the Universal Suffrage Association presented its petition to the Diet, Katayama met with success. On March 23, 1901, the officers of the Reform Society, which numbered around a thousand members at that time, prepared new policies for presentation to the Reform Society's convention. Among these new policies were central financial control rather than control by the branches; publication of a newspaper; efforts at organization of all engineers and firemen in Japan; and opposition to the Peace Police Act. More importantly, however, the Reform Society decided to join the Universal Suffrage Association and espouse socialism. These proposals were presented to the annual convention of the Reform Society on April 17–19, 1901, and were accepted by the membership.[42]

The Reform Society opted for socialism and political action because as a solely economic entity it had little future—particularly in the face of the Peace Police Act and the repressive policies of the increasingly confident Japan Railway Company. Katayama's influence on the Reform Society was also relatively great at this time. The Reform Society thus turned to political action under a combination of unceasing persuasion by Katayama and continued oppression by the Japan Railway Company and the Japanese government.

Katayama had also turned his attention to organizing a socialist political group to replace the Society for the Study of Socialism. Not only had the Society for the Study of Socialism been relatively inactive since early 1900, but there also seemed to be no possibility of converting the group into one that would espouse political action. Accordingly, Katayama organized a "socialist coalition" around a small band of social reformers: himself, three Christian socialists (including Abe Isō), Kōtoku Denjirō, and Sakai Toshihiko.[43] They realized that their protests would remain unheeded unless they were made in a more direct and positive way. Accordingly, they held meetings at the headquarters of the nearly defunct Metalworkers' Union and laid plans for the organization of a new political party.[44]

Despite the outward appearance of teamwork, the socialist coalition formed in the spring of 1901 rested on precarious ideological foundations. Four of the members, including Katayama, were Christians holding socialist convictions that were fundamentally humanistic. However, the social thought of Kōtoku and Sakai, inchoate as it was at the time, was largely derived from radical French liberalism and materialistic French and German socialism. The differences between the two groups went beyond mere ideological tension, since Kōtoku went out of his way to make derisive comments about the spiritual idealism of the Christian majority. It was clear that only an immediate and common goal held this disparate socialist group together.[45]

By May 1901 a platform for the newly formed Shakai Minshutō (Social Democratic Party), proclaiming immediate and long-range objectives, had been hammered out. The final text of this platform was written by Abe Isō, who used as a model the *Communist Manifesto* of Marx and Engels.[46] The opening paragraphs singled out for stinging criticism many chronic abuses in the Japanese social and economic system. After the preliminary remarks the eight ultimate aims of the new political party were listed: universal brotherhood; disarmament and international peace; abolition of political and economic distinctions; public ownership of land and capital; public ownership of communication and transportation facilities; equitable distribution of wealth; equality of political rights; and free state-supported education for the people. Since the organizers of the Social Democratic Party understood that these goals could not be quickly attained, they concluded their manifesto by presenting twenty-eight demands for immediate social and political reform.[47]

The manifesto presented an indictment of the existing system rather than a program for a new social order. Nine of the specific demands called for the enactment of legislation to protect the basic interests of workers, particularly of women and children, and to outlaw inhuman conditions of labor. An additional six insisted upon political reforms such as universal suffrage for men, secret ballot, proportional representation, and the introduction of the referendum. Most of the remaining items in the party's platform were socialist but of varying degrees of extremism. The proposals for the abolition of the House of Peers (the upper house of the Diet) and for reduction of the size of the armed forces were clearly the most controversial.[48]

Counting on the support of trade union members, unorganized workers, and progressive citizens, Katayama and his five allies announced the launching of the Social Democratic Party on May 21, 1901. The declaration of aims was published in *Labor World* and other metropolitan Tokyo newspapers. But scarcely had these papers appeared on the newsstands than the organizers of the party learned that their efforts had been for naught. By order of the government, the Social Democratic Party was suppressed, circulation of the newspaper editions carrying the offensive manifesto was prohibited, and charges of violation of the national press laws were lodged against the responsible editors. Katayama's socialist party had existed for only a few hours.[49]

Why had the government suppressed the Social Democratic Party when many other expressions of social and political dissent had been tolerated during the Meiji period? The government could afford to ignore the socialist rantings in the manifesto, assured that the population of Japan would not support such proposals.

But the socialists had struck a raw nerve when they called for reduced government expenditures, political reform, and a smaller military. Potent democratic forces could rally behind such concepts. The government could take no chances as it struggled to limit Russian expansion in Manchuria and Korea. There is no question that the democratic and antimilitarist position of the Social Democratic Party caused its demise.[50]

Another reason for the suppression lay in the fact that Germany was a model for Japan at this time. Clearly Katayama and his colleagues were well aware of the German experience and consciously sought to imitate it, not only in the name of their party but also in their platform and the nature of their first manifesto. Many Japanese government bureaucrats had studied in Germany during the 1870s and 1880s, so the government was also well aware of the success of the German Social Democratic Party during the period 1870–1900, and it recognized the potential for a repetition of the German experience in Japan. Exercising every precaution, the Japanese government promptly suppressed Katayama's effort to recreate the success of the German socialists.

With the suppression of the Social Democratic Party, all that remained of the movement was the Reform Society of the Japan Railway Company. The Japan Railway Company had begun to take an oppressive stance against the Reform Society in 1900, partly because of the company's success against the metalworkers' strike in the spring of that year, and partly because of the Peace Police Act. The oppression split the Reform Society into two factions: one faction favored dissolution of the union, the other supported the union and insisted on opposing the company oppression. By the end of 1900 the pro-union faction controlled the Reform Society.[51]

The company was unable to destroy the Reform Society because of its union shop character, which made discrimination in favor of nonunion engineers impossible. Unless the company was willing to risk the entire staff of engineers quitting, it could not attack the Reform Society directly. Accordingly, the company took advantage of an opportunity to let the power of the state crush the engineers. On November 10, 1901, the emperor set out by imperial train for Sendai to observe the large-scale fall military maneuvers to be held in northern Japan. The emperor was preceded by a military train.[52] Unfortunately, the military train's engine broke down between Kogota and Semine—two stations on the route to Sendai—and the train remained stationary on the tracks. The engineer who had driven that engine the previous day had warned that it should not be used until it was repaired. Unfortunately, he had been ignored.[53]

The imperial train was thus held up at Kogota station awaiting the "track clear" signal, which would be given when the military train reached Semine station. As time passed and the signal did not come, the head of the Locomotive Section, growing impatient and realizing the inconvenience being caused the emperor, asked the stationmaster to allow the train to continue. The stationmaster refused, citing the iron rule of "no 'track clear' signal, no departure." The head of the Locomotive Section then ordered the stationmaster to send the imperial train on to Semine.

Under these circumstances it was hardly surprising that the imperial train very nearly collided with the military train. The accident was avoided only by the skill of the imperial train's engineer, who managed to stop in time. Although the blame for the danger to the emperor properly lay with management, the Japan Railway Company made it clear to the police that the entire affair was the result of a plot by the Reform Society.

The police ordered the Reform Society to dissolve itself by November 25, or have it done for them. The fact that the company had to resort to government power to destroy the union demonstrated the weakness of management power at this early stage in Japan's industrialization. The Reform Society quietly dissolved itself, returning funds collected to the members. The last major union in the labor movement was gone.

All three unions of the period had suffered from worker apathy, employer opposition, and government oppression, but the heart of the problem was apathy. The members of the Metalworkers' and Printers' unions failed to rally behind their unions and use them to protect their livelihoods. When financial problems or stiff employer opposition threatened, the mass of union members quit the union. All three unions suffered from the passage of the Peace Police Act, which strengthened the employers in their dealings with the unions, yet no unionist was willing to risk imprisonment and so demonstrate the unfairness of the law. Apathetic members, hoping to win better wages and working conditions without a struggle, caused the downfall of the Metalworkers' and Printers' unions. Even the tough, disciplined engineers of the Reform Society would not challenge the unfair Peace Police Act, and hoped to avoid dissolution of their union by abiding by the law. But such an unjust law was bound to lead to unfair actions by employers and the eventual elimination of the union, regardless of the union's strength or law-abiding character.

The decline of the Kiseikai and the Metalworkers' Union, however, preceded government and employer opposition. Low dues and liberal benefits were required to attract members, creating an unsound financial base. Had the Printers' Union survived it would have doubtless suffered from similar financial problems, given the similarity of its dues and benefit structure to that of the Metalworkers' Union. Union members simply refused to pay their way and would not invest in their own organization. The Peace Police Act only served to deliver the coup de grace to a movement that was already faltering from an apathetic membership unwilling to make financial or personal sacrifices to assure themselves and their families a brighter, more secure future.

It was not the high sickness rate, employer opposition, or government oppression that sealed the fate of the labor movement. Rather it was a union membership unequal to the challenges of its day. Given the short history of the unions and the lack of any tradition of organization in the new occupations, it is not surprising the workers failed to show strong loyalty to their unions and the labor movement. But the failure of the members to take a strong united stand for their own interests contributed to the failure of the unions to work together and the growth of rivalry between the Takano and Katayama factions. However, the seeds of future labor unions had been sown, and a tradition of labor organization begun. The courageous early efforts of Takano and Katayama should be measured by the ferocity of the opposition they aroused rather than the paucity of immediate results. The tragedy of the union movement was the acceptance by the mass of Japanese of a governmental system that allowed a Peace Police Act to be passed. The acceptance of the oppression of free democratic unions doomed Japan to absolutist government for nearly a half-century thereafter, and it took crushing defeat in a world war to overcome this complaisance of the Japanese people.

8

LEGACY OF THE MOVEMENT

TAKANO FUSATARŌ left the labor movement in the summer of 1900 and proceeded to Tientsin, China, where he opened a store with his friend Jō Tsunetarō. The store did not flourish, and Takano moved on to Peking where he stayed for some time. He worked as a reporter for the *Yokohama Advertiser* for several years, but then developed an abscess of the liver. He entered the German hospital in Chintao, China, where he died on March 12, 1904. He was thirty-six years old.[1]

Takano's death met with little publicity. Other than a short obituary in *Shakaishugi* (Socialism),[2] only a brief article by Yokoyama Gennosuke, the social reformer, mourned his passing.[3] The father of the Japanese labor movement, who had spent thirteen years of his short life studying or directing labor movements, was promptly forgotten. Today, whenever his name appears in works on the labor movement, it is buried among the names of other leaders: Sawada Hannosuke, Jō Tsunetarō, and Katayama Sen. Often he is not mentioned at all, and others, particularly Katayama Sen, are given credit for achievements that were Takano's. It seems a cruel fate indeed for the man who started Japanese unionism.

Katayama Sen, the key figure in the gradual leftward shift of *Labor World* and the labor movement, is far better remembered. After the collapse of the movement in 1900 and the destruction of left-wing political groups in 1901, he led a long and productive life. In August 1904 he attended the Sixth Convention of the Second International at Amsterdam as the representative of Japanese socialism. In 1916 he began to lean toward bolshevism under the influence of S. J. Rutgers, a Dutch revolutionary in New York.

148

There he became known to Trotsky and Bukharin, and was given a position of leadership in the regrouped left wing in the United States.[4]

Katayama then assembled a band of followers among the lonely and forlorn Japanese immigrant workers in New York. This group gradually returned to Japan after 1919 and laid the foundation for the Japanese Communist Party. By 1921 Katayama was on assignment in Mexico under the direction of the Third International. In 1922 he became a functionary of the Communist International and was elected to the executive committee of that body. He died on November 5, 1933, at the age of seventy-three.[5]

On November 8, 1933, a crowd of some 150,000 poured into the famed Red Square in Moscow to pay their last respects to Katayama. His pallbearers included Stalin and other dignitaries of the Russian Communist Party and the Communist International. After orations had been delivered by the leaders of world communism, Katayama's coffin was closed and he was borne to the crematorium. He became the first Asian ever accorded the honor of having his ashes interred in a crypt in the Kremlin Wall.[6]

The major leaders of the labor movement thus left Japan after the collapse of the movement. But although the labor movement was extinguished, labor organization itself did not completely disappear. The early thought of Takano Fusatarō and the experiences of 1897–1900 had been carefully recorded in the hearts and minds of thousands of workers. Both would have a major impact on the rebirth of the labor movement in 1912.

The emergence of the Yūaikai (Friendly Society) in 1912 was entirely the work of a man named Suzuki Bunji, who renewed the labor movement and led it for many years after 1912.[7] An investigation of Suzuki's early life and the foundation of the Yūaikai reveals the influence of the earlier movement. While Suzuki was studying at Tokyo University (from September 1905 to July 1909), he took many courses under Professors Kanai and Kuwata. These men, members of the Social Policy School, had often spoken at Kiseikai rallies. They supported a labor philosophy similar to that of Takano.[8]

Suzuki also received instruction from Takano Iwasaburō, Takano Fusatarō's younger brother. Although Professor Takano did not lecture on the labor movement in his statistics course, the students were well aware of his relationship with the founder of the Japanese labor movement. Suzuki sought an opportunity to meet and talk with Professor Takano. Suzuki wrote, "I had a chance after graduating to meet with him and become his friend. He told me of his older brother's hardships, how he sacrificed himself and was suppressed. I could feel the deep emotion with which he spoke."[9] Suzuki was deeply moved by Takano's impassioned account of his brother's life.

After he graduated from Tokyo University, Suzuki worked for eight months at the Shūeisha, the printing firm founded by Sakuma Teiichi, one of the first to promote and defend the concept of unionism and a supporter of the Kiseikai. Suzuki obtained his job through the introduction of Shimada Saburō, who had served as president of the Printers' Union and had actively supported the Kiseikai.[10]

Suzuki often discussed his plans for a new labor organization with Abe Isō and sought his advice. Abe had been a close associate of Katayama Sen, and had worked with him to set up the Society for the Study of Socialism in 1898.[11] When the Yūaikai was finally established, Takano Iwasaburō and Kuwata Kumazō were among its official advisors and councilors.[12] Its headquarters was located in the same building that had earlier housed the meetings of the Society for the Study of Socialism.[13] The organizational strategy Suzuki followed closely resembled that which Takano had pursued: first set up a general organization all workers could join, then, when membership was large enough, reorganize it into trade unions.

The similarities between the Yūaikai and the Kiseikai are many. Both were led by intellectuals, not the workers themselves. Both were general labor organizations and made no distinctions between workers based on skill level, age, or trade. Neither organization was politically oriented or revolutionary. Both worked to educate and enlighten the workers rather than to direct strikes and regulate conditions of labor. Both were involved in the same activities: conducting rallies, operating cooperatives, publishing a newspaper, and attempting mediation and conciliation.

The labor philosophies of Suzuki and Takano also shared many similarities. Suzuki objected to strikes while the organization of the workers was weak. He sought the cooperation of management, and indeed, did not set up a branch of the Yūaikai at a plant unless the managers of the plant approved the action. Clearly, although Suzuki, like Takano, espoused a "harmonic" vision of society in which the interests of labor and capital were basically the same, conflict was to be avoided, and cooperation between labor and management was the goal of unionism and modern society.[14]

How much of Suzuki's organizational strategy and labor philosophy can be traced to the earlier movement is a question that must remain unanswered. Conditions in Japan had changed by 1912, but they were still such that peaceful organization of workers was the safest and surest road to success. Perhaps Suzuki, like Takano, merely adapted his strategy to the times. Nevertheless, the presence in Suzuki's early years of so many players from the drama of Japan's nineteenth-century labor movement indicates that Suzuki organized the Yūaikai in full recognition of the history, strategy, and philosophy of Takano and the Kiseikai.

The Kiseikai and Takano Fusatarō early on established several trends and viewpoints that came to fruition later in the history of the Japanese labor movement. Of course, it cannot be asserted that the first attempt at unionism determined the future of the labor movement. Rather, certain characteristics of the early movement came to dominate the Japanese labor movement as it developed. Many factors—social, cultural, economic, and political—worked to sustain these characteristics.

The first and most remarkable of these trends is that toward enterprise unionism: unionism organized on a company basis rather than a geographic or trade basis. The early movement laid the basis for the later development of enterprise unionism in the following ways. First, craft unionism and any kind of unionism limited to a certain group of workers within a workplace was rejected. Unions were designed to include all the workers at a particular workplace or shop, regardless of trade or skill level. Thus there were no structural obstacles to unionism based on the workers at one workplace or firm.

Second, the basic organizational unit was the shop or workplace. Although some branches of the early unions were regional, most were organized on the shop basis. The Tokyo Armaments Works, a single complex of factories, nevertheless had a branch at each factory. This meant that all the members of a particular branch worked for the same company.

In fact, it seemed that Japanese workers wanted unions that

allowed them to participate as a group with all those at the same workplace. Once an inclusive workshop-based unit was formed, Japanese workers sought to organize workers at other shops within the same company, as happened at the Japan Railway Company and the Tokyo Armaments Works. Once an organization spanned the entire company, Japanese unionists looked beyond to their industry or trade, as was the case with the printers and metalworkers from the first, and the railwaymen after the spring of 1901. This organizational philosophy parallels the present structure of Japanese enterprise unionism: factory-based branches formed into company-wide unions, which join together in a loose industry-wide federation. This industry-wide federation belongs to a group of such federations, called a national union center (similar to the AFL-CIO). Thus, from the first, the Japanese labor movement exhibited a unique organizational structure totally different from that of craft unions: enterprise unionism.

Takano's labor philosophy and organization efforts were not mere copies of American Federation of Labor "pure and simple" trade unionism on a craft basis. Takano was not simply influenced by American unionism; he utilized it for his own purposes. Even before he became intimately knowledgeable about the American labor movement, Takano knew he wanted stable unions that could grow rapidly. He simply needed to understand the inner mechanics and structure of American labor bodies that brought about stability and rapid growth. When queried, Gompers told him that mutual assistance and organization by trade contributed to AFL stability. And Takano came to realize that a general mixed-type labor organization was behind the rapid growth of the Knights of Labor and had the greatest potential for growth. When he found the AFL used a similar approach with its federal labor union structure for organizing drives, he decided to use that method in Japan.

Takano definitely based what he did in Japan on his knowledge of the American labor movement. He was not, however, working from an "AFL model" or a "Knights of Labor model." Rather, Takano chose structural aspects of each labor organization that contributed to his goals and fostered and supported his labor philosophy. Thus he was able to institute an organization technique that allowed the formation and growth of shop-based and then enterprise-based units. Takano's philosophy was successful in part because it allowed the formation of unions of the inclusive, shop-based type that Japanese workers wanted.

Why did Japanese workers so strongly prefer this shop-based structure? All three of the first unions in Japan were designed to allow the wage earners who worked together in one workshop to be members of the same organization. Anyone in a printing workshop could be a member of the Printers' Union. Every kind of worker in heavy industry was eligible for membership in the Metalworkers' Union. The wage earners of the Locomotive Section of the Japan Railway Company were all members of the Reform Society. In all three unions, apprentices could be union members. The Reform Society organized every worker in the workplace—engineers, firemen, and even train janitors. This indicates that Japanese workers were strongly "shop-conscious" rather than "job or craft conscious"; in other words, they sought to organize all those in their workshop regardless of skill level or craft rather than organize all those with a given skill level or craft regardless of workplace.

Five factors contributed to the "shop-conscious" nature of Japanese workers. First, Japanese social organization is basically hierarchical. Human relationships tend to be built within a superior-subordinate framework rather than among equals. In a shop unit the informal workplace hierarchy (based on age, experience, etc.) was transferred to the union branch. Hierarchical relations were more difficult to maintain between workers in different shops where there was no common frame of reference.

Second, most of the unionists of the day were "first generation workers." Their parents had not been factory workers, and they had had little preparation for life in the factories. They thus tended to build social relationships without regard to skill level or occupation, because they all faced the same problems in adjusting to factory life, learning a trade, and dealing with supervisors. The labor organizations of these men therefore reflected the social reality that there were no significant divisions between them on the basis of skill level and occupation.

Third, most of the unionists were employed in the new occupations created by the importation of Western technology. This technology disrupted existing craft distinctions and required workers to be able to perform tasks spanning a broad range of occupations. The nature of production by small batches meant that tomorrow's job might be different from today's. Thus the workers in these new occupations had no real concept of "craft" distinctions within their industries.

Fourth, the unionists in Japan were employed in larger-scale enterprises employing fifty to ten thousand employees. There was less need for these men to go outside their workplace to build social relationships. In contrast, Western journeymen in the skilled trades often met with journeymen in the same occupation who worked at other shops. This was due, in part, to the small size of many Western workplaces when unionism began to emerge, as well as the affinity brought by similar occupations. In Japan, one hundred workers might be working together at similar jobs. Under such circumstances social relationships tended to revolve around the workplace.

Finally, the rapid growth in the industrial sector had kept trained skilled labor at a premium for years. Despite the national labor market, skilled workers felt no need for protection from rate-cutting by nonunion labor. There was little need for a national union to regulate wages so that a unionist in Tokyo would not be put out of work by a lower-paid nonunionist in Kyoto. All skilled workers could find work. There was little incentive to go beyond shop, enterprise, or local structures under these circumstances.

These five factors contributed to "shop-conscious" unionism and operated to discourage job or craft consciousness. They also set Japan apart from the West. Early Western unionism arose in a more egalitarian social structure and in traditional occupations, among journeymen who worked in small shops (many of whose fathers had been similarly employed), and in the face of fluctuating demand for skilled labor. Thus Western unions developed an exclusive craft-based character, while Japanese unions developed an inclusive workplace-based character.

Of course, the unionism of 1897 cannot be called enterprise unionism. Yet the structure adopted by the unions not only revealed the strong shop consciousness of the workers, but also made it easier to move toward enterprise unionism rather than another type of unionism. It is significant to note this phenomenon at this early point, for the labor-market structure and management practices at that time were not conducive to the promotion of enterprise unionism. In fact, they were more conducive to the formation of industrial unions or perhaps even craft unions. Thus enterprise unionism was clearly a product of factors other than the common explanations of a segmented labor market and management "paternalism," since these phenomena emerged decades after the formation of Japan's first shop-based unions. From the very beginning, the "shop" and "enterprise" organizational structure appealed to Japanese workers.

Several other important if less fundamental trends also date from Japan's nineteenth-century attempt at unionism. One of these was the prevalence of the idea that unions were social rather than economic tools. The Social Policy School, Takano Fusatarō, and Katayama Sen all saw eye to eye on this point. The only justification for unions was that they helped to bring about a better society—by allowing for the recuperation of labor power (the Social Policy School view), by making possible higher production and a wealthy nation (Takano's view), or by helping to bring about social reform (Katayama's view). No union leader ever attempted to justify unions on any grounds other than that they were good because of their ultimate effects on society.

This idea had important consequences later. The union movement constantly had to prove its social worth and could be opposed on broad social grounds. Unions were held ultimately responsible, not to their members, but to society in general. The actions of unions were greatly circumscribed. No union leader could advocate a simple philosophy of "more, more, more, now." Leaders were required to show that a particular activity was for the good of the nation, would raise production, or assist the public, and so on.

The most important result of this ideological standpoint was the peculiar view society held with respect to the strike. A strike obviously causes great loss to management, labor, and the public. Thus it is difficult to defend as a socially desirable phenomenon. To the Social Policy School and Takano, strikes were things to be avoided for both ideological and opportunistic reasons. Their ultimate aims were higher production and a guaranteed supply of labor to the capitalist system, both of which would be impeded by strikes. They extolled a position of "harmony" and kept the strike weapon at arm's length.

Katayama, on the other hand, saw strikes as the true key to

bringing about social justice, recognition of the rights of the workers, and their proper treatment. Unfortunately, even as he became convinced of the importance of strike action, he also began to drift toward socialism. This made him a radical and an outlaw in Japan. There is no reason to presume that his attitude toward the strike caused him to become a socialist or vice versa. The two trends, toward socialism and militant advocacy of strikes, occurred together largely by circumstance.

Katayama's shift produced a major ideological split within the labor movement that continues to this day. On the one hand, there were the harmonists or moderates, who supported the capitalist system and deprecated strikes. On the other hand there were the radicals, who sought the abolition of the capitalist system and advocated strikes. Strike action thus became associated with antisocial, antistate, and anticapitalist views—and ultimately, through the connection with socialism and political and economic reform, it also gained an antigovernment image.

This fundamental social attitude toward the strike remains strong today in Japan. The major economic rationalizations (such as balancing power between worker and employer) and the major moral rationalizations for the strike (such as a worker's right not to work) have never been strongly asserted. Instead, the social benefits of unionism have been extolled by the moderates and radicals alike. Thus, today we see the legacy of the moderate philosophy in the actions of the Dōmei national center, and the legacy of the radical (and socialist) ideology in the actions of the Sōhyō national center. Dōmei unions downplay strike action and usually undertake only short token strikes on economic issues, seeking compromise with management and joint efforts to raise productivity to allow wages to increase. Sōhyō unions embrace strike action and often undertake long strikes on political issues (such as the right to strike for public sector employees), seeking confrontation with the government and political advantage.

The early union movement thus produced several important trends that affect unionism to this day. In spite of government repression, employer opposition, and worker apathy, Takano Fusatarō and his supporters helped create an organizational structure, philosophy, and tactical approach for unionism that became powerful tools in the hand of later unionists. Furthermore, the workers themselves gained a tradition of organization and the experience of successfully opposing employers and influencing government through independent democratic unions. When the political situation in Japan finally favored unionism after World War II, the hard work and sacrifices of the early activists provided a foundation for the sudden flowering of the unions—and the rapid growth of the Japanese labor movement into the second-largest in the free world. Judged by this result, the efforts of Takano and his supporters cannot be found wanting.

APPENDIXES

APPENDIX A

CONSTITUTION OF THE ALLIANCE FOR INDUSTRIAL ORGANIZATION

ARTICLE ONE   The organization shall work at establishment beginning February 1897.

ARTICLE TWO   This organization makes its headquarters in Tokyo at Koishigawa-ku, Omote-machi no. 8 (as of July 1899). However, for convenience divisions may be made (revision of August 1898).

ARTICLE THREE   This organization seeks to promote friendship between members, to build a factory with capital provided by the members, to advance technology, to obtain advancement of the rights of the members, to educate apprentices, to provide mutual assistance, and to raise the status of the members.

ARTICLE FOUR   This organization seeks to recruit pattern-makers, woodworkers, smiths, casters, forgers, lathe operators, boilermakers, engine workers, electrical workers, and those who handle metal. However, if those outside the trade wish to enter, they must obtain the permission of the officers' council, and apply in writing in accordance with procedures described below (revision of May 1899).

ARTICLE FIVE   Those who wish to become members shall apply in writing at headquarters and the branches, and shall receive a certificate of membership. However, those who move elsewhere after joining should inform the organization in a timely manner that they will do so.

ARTICLE SIX   Members shall promise not to leave without cause or to incite others to leave.

ARTICLE SEVEN   Members shall respect and protect the rules and decisions of this organization and bear financial responsibility for it.

ARTICLE EIGHT   Members shall pay twenty sen per month in a lump sum to the fund and may voluntarily pay more than this into the fund. Those who pay more than their share shall decide how many person's shares they shall pay when they first pay. Also, in such cases there is no obstacle to collecting the fund payment in halves, one-half on the fifteenth of the month and the other on the thirtieth.

ARTICLE NINE   When members, due to illness or injury they did not inflict on themselves, are unable to pay their month's fund payment, they should inform a branch head or headquarters officer of such fact. They may resume fund payments the next month without obstacle. However, those who, without informing officers, fail to pay the fund payment for five months are considered expelled from the organization. Those who are expelled shall receive 40 percent or less of their outstanding fund, the remainder becoming the property of this organization.

ARTICLE TEN   Those expelled from the organization under the provisions of Article Nine must apply for the return of their portion of their outstanding fund within thirty days. If they do not comply with this procedure their entire fund will be confiscated.

ARTICLE ELEVEN   Fund payments shall be exchanged for a clear receipt. In places where it is so done, a separately established receipt certificate may be used, which is later exchanged for appropriate stock, after consultation, when the factory is established (revision of May 1899).

ARTICLE TWELVE   This organization shall hold four conventions each year, in February, May, August, and November, at which deliberations and talks will be held. However, in time of dire need emergency meetings may be held.

ARTICLE THIRTEEN No Articles shall be established in this constitution concerning the implementation of Article Twelve. These shall be left to the regular meetings to decide.

ARTICLE FOURTEEN Should members meet with accident and be unable to attend deliberations, they shall send an appropriate substitute and give that substitute power to speak and vote in their stead. However, those who fail to comply with this procedure shall not be able to protest decisions made in their absence at a later date.

ARTICLE FIFTEEN For the organization the following officers shall be elected from among the members: one president, one vice-president, several finance officers, several branch heads, several auditors, and several secretaries.

ARTICLE SIXTEEN At each branch there shall be one branch head, several officers, one auditor and one mutual assistance officer. However, officers in rural departments are not limited by this.

ARTICLE SEVENTEEN All officers, excepting secretaries, shall serve for a term of one year.

ARTICLE EIGHTEEN The president, vice-president, and finance officers shall be elected at conventions by signed ballot. In case of a tie, the older candidate shall be considered the winner.

ARTICLE NINETEEN Branch heads, officers, auditors, and mutual assistance officers shall be selected by branch members from among themselves.

ARTICLE TWENTY When an officer in the middle of his term is forced to resign due to unavoidable circumstances or is ordered to resign due to inappropriate conduct by the decision of this organization, a substitute shall be selected in accordance with the previous two Articles. However, the substitute may not serve longer than the remaining term of the officer who left office.

ARTICLE TWENTY-ONE The president of this organization shall represent it and execute all duties in accordance with its decisions.

ARTICLE TWENTY-TWO   The vice-president shall assist the president in his duties and shall represent him should he be unable to execute his duties.

ARTICLE TWENTY-THREE   Finance officers shall assist the president and vice-president as they see fit, and shall handle finances and report to the convention on finances.

ARTICLE TWENTY-FOUR   Branch heads shall assist the president and vice-president as they see fit, and shall assist in and supervise financial matters.

ARTICLE TWENTY-FIVE   Branch officers shall assist the branch heads as they see fit, and shall represent their branch head when he is unable to execute his duties. In cases where there is more than one branch officer, the branch officers shall select from among themselves a regular branch officer who shall represent the branch head.

ARTICLE TWENTY-SIX   All officers should always attend the officers' meeting with the object of discussion of business and execution of business.

ARTICLE TWENTY-SEVEN   The chairman of all meetings shall be either the president or vice-president of the organization.

ARTICLE TWENTY-EIGHT   All deliberations shall be decided by majority vote of those present. In case of a tie, the chairman shall cast the deciding vote.

ARTICLE TWENTY-NINE   All who wish to present proposals shall present them to the branch head or headquarters prior to the opening of the meeting. However, emergency deliberations are not bound by this provision (revision of November 1898).

ARTICLE THIRTY   The fund payments of the members, once collected, shall be deposited in the Mitsui Bank. However, the actual deposit procedure shall be done by the president and one finance officer selected from among the finance officers, who will deposit the money in a joint account.

ARTICLE THIRTY-ONE   The funds of members, no matter what the circumstances, may not be withdrawn without approval by a regular or emergency meeting.

ARTICLE THIRTY-TWO   Should a member meet with an accident and leave the organization, he should designate a representative who, with a letter from the stricken member, shall inform a finance officer and comply with the procedures for return of the fund. Should there be no representative, the fund of the stricken member will be confiscated under Article Nine. This may be altered by the decision of three-quarters of the attendants at the regular meeting.

ARTICLE THIRTY-THREE   Should a member die, the representative should comply with the provisions of the previous article. If there is no representative the fund of the member, with appropriate interest, shall be returned to his family.

ARTICLE THIRTY-FOUR   All funds to be returned shall be returned within fifteen days of the application for their return.

ARTICLE THIRTY-FIVE   The deposit book of this organization and accounts may be seen by the members at any time.

ARTICLE THIRTY-SIX   The establishment of the factory being foreseen in three years, the purchase of land, construction of the factory, and purchase of machinery should be prepared for in one and a half years. This provision shall be enforced by the decisions of the regular meetings or emergency meetings, however.

ARTICLE THIRTY-SEVEN   When the factory is to be opened it shall be called the Alliance for Industrial Organization Company, and provisions governing it shall be set up.

ARTICLE THIRTY-EIGHT   This organization, in order to set up a mutual assistance fund, shall collect three sen per month from each member. However, when a lack of funds arises from the implementation of Article Thirty-Nine an emergency levy shall be made (revision of May 1899).

ARTICLE THIRTY-NINE   When members meet with the misfortunes listed below, they shall receive the money sums listed below from the mutual assistance fund. However, those who have not been a member for three months may not receive assistance under these provisions (revision of November 1898).

1. Those whose houses burned down in a fire which spread to their homes shall receive five yen. However, assistance shall not be given unless the burnt residence was the address given by the member as his residence.

2. Those who due to illness must cease working for over fifty days shall receive five yen.

3. Those who, in continuity, must cease working for one hundred days, shall receive five yen in addition to the fifty yen under the above provision.

4. Those who due to work or disaster became permanently disabled and are determined as being no longer capable of their original work shall receive twenty yen. However, in this case determination of capability is decided at an officers' meeting.

5. Those who due to illness or disaster die shall receive twenty yen.

ARTICLE FORTY   All those who wish to receive assistance shall make two officers their guarantors and shall present a doctor's examination certificate. However, members under the jurisdiction of headquarters require two highly trusted members and a doctor's examination certificate. Further, those who receive aid under provision four of the above Article may not receive assistance under provisions two or three (revision of May 1899).

ARTICLE FORTY-ONE   In order to supplement or revise these rules the approval of three-quarters of the membership is required.

Source: Katayama Sen and Nishikawa Mitsujirō, *Nihon no Rōdō Undō* [The Japanese labor movement] (Tokyo: Iwanami Shoten, 1952; first published in 1901), 205–211. My translation.

CONSTITUTION OF THE TOKYO SHIP CARPENTERS' UNION

Goals and Methods

ARTICLE SIX   The members of this union seek to promote mutual friendship, to learn and make use of the techniques of the various countries, to reform old abuses, to promote the development of this craft, and of course to promote public and private trust and welfare.

ARTICLE SEVEN   In order to set a standard for the work that shall be done by the members, the following three grades will be set up among the members: grade one workers, grade two workers, and grade three workers.

ARTICLE THIRTEEN   Members, whenever they make use of their own wood when subcontracted to do ship construction, shall select appropriate, sound, and durable material and will now and then undergo inspection by the customer.

ARTICLE FOURTEEN   Members shall not, in order to satisfy their own demand for profits, bid for or do work for another person's customers, nor shall they submit lower bids for work if they have learned of the bids of other persons, and thus cause them harm.

Only the articles that appear here have been preserved in the original source. The rest have been lost.

ARTICLE FIFTEEN   Members shall, in conformance with written procedures indicated by the president, submit a detailed report of their work every six months, in January and July, and shall submit it to the union office by the fifteenth of the month.

ARTICLE SIXTEEN   Members, when training apprentices, shall give them appropriate training and shall compensate them in accordance with their production.

ARTICLE SEVENTEEN   Should the apprentice of a member run away or leave without permission, the member shall inform the president who shall inform the members. Members who have been so informed may not employ the runaway apprentice without the permission of his original master.

ARTICLE EIGHTEEN   When an apprentice of a member has finished his apprenticeship, the member shall so inform the union office. The president shall then inform the union members.

ARTICLE NINETEEN   When the employer or customer fails to pay the subcontracting payment for no reason, the union office should be so informed. The president shall then ask for the money in place of the injured party. Should satisfaction not be obtained such fact shall be made known to all members who shall then refuse to do business with the employer or customer involved.

ARTICLE TWENTY   The union shall always pay attention to the techniques of the craft, shall investigate the merits and demerits of such techniques, and make sure of the quality of workmanship, and shall maintain public and private trust.

Election of Officers

ARTICLE TWENTY-TWO   This union shall have the following officers: one president, one vice-president, and one assistant.

ARTICLE TWENTY-THREE   Officers shall serve for one year and may be reelected.

Rules Relating to Meetings

ARTICLE THIRTY-ONE   There shall be three types of meetings —regular meetings, emergency meetings, and officers' meetings.

ARTICLE THIRTY-TWO   Regular meetings shall be held in January and July of each year. At these meetings members shall discuss the condition of the trade, revise the constitution and consider proposals relating to revision, and elect officers. Further, a finance report shall be made concerning the funds used by the union during the previous six months.

ARTICLE THIRTY-FOUR   The officers' meeting shall be held every other month and shall consist of all officers, who shall discuss union business and deal with members who have broken the rules.

Rules Concerning Entrance and Departure

ARTICLE FORTY-ONE   The president shall urge nonmembers who are practicing the trade in the area of the union to join the union. Should the nonmember refuse to join he shall be reported to the Tokyo metropolitan government.

ARTICLE FORTY-TWO   Those who wish to join the union will be shown the constitution and asked to sign the register, and their grade shall be determined, a certificate of membership given to them, and their names made known to the union members.

ARTICLE FORTY-THREE   Those who leave the union as a result of loss of employment or a move to a different area shall inform the union office. The president shall remove the names of such persons from the register, receive their certificate of union membership, and shall make the name of that person known to the union members.

Collection and Use of Funds

ARTICLE FORTY-FIVE   The expenditures of the union are the financial responsibility of all the members. The collection and use of these funds shall follow the procedure of Article Forty-Six.

ARTICLE FORTY-SIX   In order for the union to make expenditures, funds shall be collected from the members according to their grade as follows. The assistant shall handle collection of these funds as he sees fit and payment shall be made by the twenty-fifth of each month.

Grade one members	20 sen
Grade two members	15 sen
Grade three members	10 sen

The above grades were established at a regular meeting in accordance with the amount of subcontracting fees each member collected.

Handling of Those Who Violate the Rules

ARTICLE FORTY-NINE   Those who violate Articles Eleven, Twelve, Thirteen, Fourteen, Fifteen, Sixteen, Seventeen, Nineteen or Forty-Six shall be fined between fifty sen and ten yen depending on the severity of their offense. However, the president shall only collect this fine after the violator has ignored a warning made to him by the president.

ARTICLE FIFTY   When an officer has violated an article outlined in the previous article the union shall immediately call an emergency meeting, and depending on the severity of the violation, up to 25 percent may be added to the fines of the previous article. The chairman of this emergency meeting shall be chosen appropriately from among those in attendance.

ARTICLE FIFTY-ONE   A violator of the rules still bears liability for damages after he has paid his fine.

ARTICLE FIFTY-TWO   Fines collected from offenders shall be used to defray union expenses and may be used for no other purpose.

Rules Relating to Assistance

(APPENDIX) ARTICLE ONE   When union members meet with misfortune appropriate benefits shall be paid as outlined below.

In case of death	10 yen
In case of injury	3 yen
In case of unfortunate accident	3 yen

However, this injury benefit is limited to those who were injured at work and who must recuperate for over twenty days but will recover probably in less than thirty days. In this case a certificate of medical examination must be presented.

(APPENDIX) ARTICLE TWO   Members may not receive the above benefits if they are in arrears in the payment of their monthly dues.

Source: Katayama Sen and Nishikawa Mitsujirō, *Nihon no Rōdō Undō* [The Japanese labor movement] (Tokyo: Iwanami Shoten, 1952; first published in 1901), 130–134. My translation.

"A SUMMONS TO THE WORKERS"

The year 1899 will see Japan really opened to foreign intercourse.[1] It will be a time when foreign capitalists will enter our country and attempt to amass millions in profits by exploiting our cheap labor and our clever workers. In such a situation, these foreign capitalists, who are not only different in character, manners, and customs, but who are also notorious for their cruel treatment of workers, will try to become your masters within the next three years. In the light of this situation, you workers must soon start to prepare yourselves or you cannot help suffering the same abuses as the workers of Europe and America. Considering recent development, moreover, the relations between the workers and employers of our country will in the same way as in Europe and America undergo daily changes as factories and plants increase in number.

Consideration of profit alone will prevail. The strong will be triumphant and the weak will be destroyed. Since the superior are heading for days of prosperity and the inferior for times of ruin, it will be no easy task to conquer and to flourish in the days that lie ahead. When, moreover, the foreigners do enter our country, it will be vitally necessary for you to double your resolution and to devise moderate means to protect your position on the field of struggle, without getting yourselves into scrapes on their behalf.

You workers, like others before you, are people without capital who provide a living for others than yourselves. One of your arms and one of your legs are, so to speak, devoted to the support of

[1] Because of the treaty revisions with foreign powers coming into effect in 1899, foreigners would be allowed to reside anywhere in Japan, and it was expected that this would be accompanied by the investment of foreign capital in Japan.

society. When you meet with some misfortune and are disabled or when you become infirm with age and can no longer work, you are immediately deprived of the means of earning a living and are turned out into the street. Should death overtake you, your wives and your children are hard put to stay alive. In this state of affairs you are really as helpless as a candle in the wind. Unless you workers heed the precept of the ancients and prepare for adversity while you are able, and make it your practice to provide for ways to cope with future difficulties while you are strong and sound of body, it will be hard for you to avoid transgressing the fundamental obligations of a human being, a husband, or a parent. This matter demands sober consideration.

In this day and age our country is still not enlightened. In the older days, when there were no machines, your wives and children stayed at home and worked and helped to earn a living. But with the rise of factories and mills your wives, who should be looking after the home, take themselves off to work in the factories. And since even innocent children work at the machines, the life of the home is thrown into confusion. At times the lives of children are endangered, as machines, which should be of benefit to man, function improperly and present the astounding spectacle of doing him harm. In some factories children with delicate bodies are made to work hours which would be too long even for adults. The life-blood of those who are little more than infants is squeezed out with impartiality, and for their parents this is indeed unbearable. It should be evident that you must first and foremost take vigorous action and devise ways and means of coping with the situation. You must put your homes in order and protect the lives of your women and children. Do not forget, you workers, that those who take the lives of men do not do so only with the lethal instruments of murderers and criminals.

It is evident that when wives who should be caring for the home and children who should be in school are working in factories, an extremely unnatural state of affairs exists. If we seek the reason for this, we find that because of the cheapness of labor a man with only one pair of hands cannot support a wife and children. If you are husbands, you cannot but want to give your wives a comfortable life. If you are parents, you cannot but want to see your children educated. These must of course be your feelings, and if you would only once rouse yourselves you would in the end find a way to correct this unnatural state of affairs and, by so doing, preserve your dignity.

One more matter which should be mentioned concerns your behavior. If you are an honest man earning a living by selling your labor power and if you make no mistakes in your work and conduct, you need not fear anything under the sun. But if you once do something dishonest or improper, your reputation as an upright man is thereby destroyed and your life itself is ruined. The saying that honesty prevails in the end is known to all of us. The way to protect yourselves lies in this. Furthermore, men who are in the unfortunate position that you are in find it difficult to obtain completely satisfactory results if, in attempting to improve their position, they are the least bit indiscreet in their behavior. Accordingly, it is necessary for you to strive to advance and extend your position and interests and, at the same time, to be courageous enough to follow a righteous course. Why should you workers not try to improve yourselves and mend your ways and pursue your ends in an open and above-board fashion? Know that the most heartless person will not prevail before your righteousness.

How you workers are to undertake the necessary acts of resolution and preparation, which have been indicated previously, will understandably raise questions in your minds. Some of you will say: "Matters have by now gone beyond the stage of talking. The rich are becoming richer and the poor are becoming poorer. The injustices and ruined circumstances which are the workers' lot are indeed cause for bitterness. Only by a revolution correcting this situation may the differences in wealth be equalized." This argument is truly attractive, and it would be splendid if you were able to achieve complete reform by the revolution advocated by its proponents. But the affairs of the world are not so simple as these men believe. Unexpected developments occur, making it completely impossible to realize original objectives, while great disorders are not infrequent.

You workers should think twice before accepting these arguments. The advances of society have always been at a leisurely and orderly pace. Revolutionists are opposed to the supporters of order and, when the former make haste and recklessness a prime factor, the actions of the two groups become diametrically opposed. As far as equalization of economic difference is concerned, since all men are not equally wise, inequalities in the amount of property individually possessed are inevitable. Proposals for the elimination of differences between rich and poor are more easily stated than achieved.

In view of this, you workers should firmly and resolutely reject ideas of revolution and acts of radicalism. To advance a mile one must go forward by steps. You should thus spurn the counsels of the economic levelers.

We would recommend, consequently, that you workers establish trade unions based upon the feelings common to men engaged in the same work and possessed of kindred sentiments. These trade unions, moreover, should be organized on a nationwide cooperative basis. In viewing carefully your past actions, it is evident that you have refrained from combining, that you have struggled with one another, and that you have achieved no unity. Thus, if there are some of you who have with laborious effort and after countless appeals finally secured an increase in wages, there are others who remain satisfied with their outrageously low wages. There are some who want to reprove your unworthy fellow workers but there are also those who want to protect them. The spectacle of some men building and other men destroying, of kindred people engaged in mutual strife, is really cause for regret.

Your internecine strife, the contempt in which the foreigners hold you, and the position in which you find yourselves today, all may to a large extent be attributed to the failure of you workers to act unitedly.

As has been indicated previously, attack by the foreign enemy may be expected. Today, when deplorable evils exist among you, you must stop your fratricidal struggles and see the necessity for engaging in a vast combined effort. You workers must not remain apart but should wisely combine and keep pace with the advances of society. Inwardly you should nourish wholesome thoughts and outwardly comport yourselves in sober and steady ways. Shouldn't you seek to remedy the evil practices of your heartless employers and of the foreigners? Remember that there will be others who will think as you do.

Labor is holy. Combination is strength. It is for you who are engaged in holy labor to achieve the union that is strength.[2] Just as

[2] Translation up to this point is from the partial translation by Hyman Kublin in Theodore Wm. De Bary, *Sources of Japanese Tradition* (New York, 1958), 807–811. After this point translation is my own.

feathers, if enough are piled up, can sink a ship, if the passion of you workers wells up, what couldn't you do? Once 150,000 railway workers, without wealth or property, opposed twenty-four railway companies with $800 million capital, and stopped all railway operations for three weeks. There is also the example of 30,000 dock workers who caused a food shortage in the London, England, market for three months. Even though such objectives cannot easily be realized in a short time, and even though our method is not as spectacular as that of the revolutionists, progress is solid and defense is strong. Although our method is slower, it is sure and gentle, peaceful and orderly. This is the only true method for you workers to obtain your objectives. We thus advise you again to form trade unions—but how should such trade unions be organized?

1. A local trade union should be formed whenever seven or more members of a trade gather together in a single city or county.[3]

2. A local trade union federation should be formed by uniting the various local trade unions in a city or county.

3. A national trade federation should be formed by uniting the various local trade unions in a particular trade.

4. The various national trade federations should be unified to form a national trade alliance.

For example, in Tokyo, there is a carpenters' union of 2,000, a printers' union of 2,000, and a shoemakers' union of 2,000. Together these three unions would make the Tokyo Workers' Federation. In Osaka there might be a carpenters' union of 1,000, a printers' union of 1,000, and a shoemakers' union of 1,000. Together these unions would make the Osaka Workers' Federation. Further, in Nagasaki there might be a carpenters' union of 500, a printers' union of 500, and a shoemakers' union of 500 members. Together these would make the Nagasaki Workers' Federation. The Tokyo, Osaka, and Nagasaki carpenters, printers, and shoemakers would each federate by trade, resulting in a national trade federation of 3,500 members for each trade. These three national trade federations would make a national trade alliance of 10,500 members. In addition, if there should be some

[3] The actual term used is *gun,* the administrative subdivision of a prefecture. A *gun* is actually much smaller than a country.

occurrence involving the Tokyo carpenters' union, and the help of the Tokyo Workers' Federation, when requested, is not sufficient, the help of the national carpenters' organization can be requested. With such organization, in case of need, in addition to the 6,000 workers of the Tokyo Workers' Federation, the 1,500 workers (leaving out the Tokyo carpenters' union) of the national carpenters' organization, and in addition the 3,500[4] workers (leaving out the Tokyo unions and the carpenters) of the national trade alliance, all together 10,500 workers, will work for the Tokyo carpenters' union.

The strength of trade unions is fostered in this way and its benefit is enlarged, and can sufficiently attain the workers' goals when opposing the unfairness of foreigners, and in other cases.

Also, through the fund of the trade union the members can be succored when misfortune befalls them, and when death overtakes them their wives and children can easily make ends meet. This promotes the independent spirit of the workers and helps to promote the heaven-sent responsibility of the workers. One American union of over 27,000 members[5] gave, in the fifteen[6] years from 1880 to 1893, over $225,000 to the families of union members who were overtaken by death; over $675,000 to union members who fell ill; over $150,800 to union members who were unemployed; over $534,000 to union members who were on strike; and over $506,000, as loans, to workers for traveling expenses. The expenditure of the massive sum of over $2,091,000 is an amazing fact; but that a small union of merely some 20,000 workers was able to do this can only be said to be truly wonderful. This is not that difficult to do in our country, and the method is:

Each local union and the national trade federation *builds* up a fund from the monthly dues of the union members, minus union expenses and so on.

Each union establishes rules, deciding the time to make members eligible for assistance (for example, after some number of months of payment of dues) and the lowest limit of yen in the fund beyond which the fund cannot be used to assist union members.

[4] This is an arithmetic error—the number here should be 3,000.
[5] According to a letter from Takano to Gompers, this union would be the Cigarmakers' International Union.
[6] This should read "thirteen."

Each union should expand its assistance provisions to include assistance of union members who are unemployed, wish to travel, or are old.

For example, let us say that a Tokyo carpenters' union of 2,000 members has a fund contribution of three sen[7] per month per member. In one month sixty yen, in a year 720 yen can be saved in this fund. If this is expanded to include the national carpenters' trade federation, the Tokyo, Nagasaki, and Osaka funds, collected together, would result in the massive sum of 1,260 yen per year being collected for the federation. Assistance payment would not be made for the first three or four months, and after that time assistance payments would be made according to the method outlined in the rules. When the amount in the fund falls, if payments out of the fund are stopped for a time, or a special procedure (such as a levy) is set up, then day by day the fund increases in size and the goal of assistance becomes more effective, there are few who leave the union, and mutual help in the trade, and that spirit, can be sufficiently realized.

These days, should a worker once meet with misfortune he must sometimes look to the assistance of other people, and thus cases where the workman sullies his independent honor are not few. Also, in some cases there is no one to rely upon, and the worker's situation becomes extremely difficult. In contrast, those who receive assistance from the union are truly favored, for if they receive the money they should by agreement, they do not sully in the least their independent honor. Also, in case of misfortune, not only is a method to relieve it ready in advance, but there is no need to worry, or to take base actions. Greatly heightening the spirit of self-help and the confidence of the workers should raise their dignity more than a little.

Stand up, you workers! Stand up and organize unions! Endeavor to discharge that important obligation and to preserve your honor as men! Workers, your future holds great promise—all that is needed is indomitable spirit and unyielding will. Don't they say that God helps those who help themselves? Take heart, you workers, and show that spirit of self-help.

In closing, one thing that should be said is that there may be those who say that a union cannot be formed or that there is no

[7] One sen is one one-hundredth of a yen.

case where one has been formed. But if it is left at that, when will a union be formed? It is the height of folly to degrade oneself in the face of the enemy due to petty emotional matters or internal disputes. There are those who grieve over the small number of union members in Japan. But the gathering of mere numbers, if those people do not well perceive their own responsibility, like gathering an army without fighting spirit, will end in accomplishing nothing. Rather, if a small group is gathered which realizes the insignificant nature of its position and endeavors to strive for itself and for its wives and children, that is, a band of workers sworn to fight to the death on the field of battle, a glorious movement is the result. It is our sincere desire that, from among you workers, there are those who will sally forth onto the glorious field of battle. The number, large or small, does not matter. It has been our firm belief that the number of workers who are filled with the spirit of heroism, who see themselves as part of this band of workers sworn to fight to the death certainly cannot be small.

Source: Katayama Sen and Nishikawa Mitsujirō, *Nihon no Rōdō Undō* [The Japanese labor movement] (Tokyo: Iwanami Shoten, 1952; first published in 1901), 18–26.

RULES OF THE
RŌDŌ KUMIAI KISEIKAI

General Rules

ONE   The objective of this organization is to organize unions which will promote the rights of Japanese workers, encourage good habits, eliminate old outworn customs, and promote friendship among workers in the same trades.

TWO   This organization will be called the Rōdō Kumiai Kiseikai [Association for Encouragement and Formation of Trade Unions].

THREE   The office of this organization will be at 1–12 Hongo-ku-chō, Nihombashi-ku, Tokyo.

FOUR   This organization will promote its interest in existing unions by opening communications with them, and will encourage those who attempt to organize unions among the workers.

Membership

FIVE   Those who wish to enter this organization must, according to the rules of the organization, apply to the office after having obtained introduction from two members. However, those who have obtained recognition from an officer of this organization may directly become members.

SIX   Those who wish to leave the organization should apply to the office stating their reasons.

SEVEN   Members who move to a different address are to inform the office.

EIGHT   Members are to be friendly to one another, support each other, and bring the honor of being a member to perfection.

NINE   Members who sully the honor of the organization or disobey its rules are subject to expulsion based on the decision of the officers' meeting. However, in such cases the directors should inform the membership at the next regular meeting.

TEN   Those who work for this organization but are unable to become actual members may be made honorary members by the board of directors.

Officers

ELEVEN   The officers of this organization are directors, regular officers and treasurers, and their term of office shall be one year.

TWELVE   There shall be fifteen regular officers elected from members in Tokyo by open vote. These fifteen officers shall then elect five directors and two treasurers from among themselves. However, from among the directors one[1] head director shall be chosen by the directors. The expenses of the head director will be met, as far as possible, by the funds of this organization.

THIRTEEN   Famous figures who show deep concern and friendship for this organization may be named councilors by the board of directors, and may then participate in important meetings of this organization.

FOURTEEN   Directors are to handle the finance and general affairs of this organization, while regular officers are to assist the directors and execute the affairs of this organization.

FIFTEEN   Those who are elected to office may not, barring inability to execute their duties, resign.

[1] This was revised to two in June 1899.

Meetings and Magazine

SIXTEEN   This organization will publish a monthly magazine and will deliver it to the members.

SEVENTEEN   This organization will hold a meeting every month to discuss the affairs of the organization and to give lectures on the need for labor unions. However, when necessary, emergency meetings may be called.

EIGHTEEN   In order to attain the goals of this organization, rallies with speeches by famous people or volunteers should be conducted.

Finances

NINETEEN   Each member is to contribute ten sen monthly. If there should be insufficient funds and the organization so decides, each member will be responsible for an equal share of the deficit. The board of directors can exempt members suffering from illness or accident from paying dues.

TWENTY   A monthly finance report shall be issued to the members. Members may at any time examine the accounting books of this organization.

Miscellaneous

TWENTY-ONE   Revision of or addition to the rules of this organization requires a two-thirds majority of the members regularly attending meetings.

Source: Katayama Sen and Nishikawa Mitsujirō, *Nihon no Rōdō Undō* (The Japanese labor movement) (Tokyo: Iwanami Shoten, 1952; first published in 1901), 140–143. My translation.

CONSTITUTION OF THE METALWORKERS' UNION

Chapter One—General Provisions

ARTICLE ONE   This union shall be called the Rōdō Kumiai Kiseikai Tekkō Kumiai [Metalworkers' Union of the Association for the Encouragement and Formation of Trade Unions].

ARTICLE TWO   This union shall be one of machinists, blacksmiths, boilermakers, casters, forgers, copper workers, shipbuilders, engineers, and firemen in iron works and those working in similar trades who reside in Japan.

ARTICLE THREE   The object of this union shall be to promote advancement of industrial skills, and to increase the benefits of the members and improve their status.

ARTICLE FOUR   In order to achieve the goals set forth in the previous article, this union shall undertake the following:
   1. Assistance when misfortune or disaster overtakes members;
   2. Mediation with respect to disputes involving members;
   3. Establishment of facilities for the development of knowledge among the members.
The means by which the goals outlined above shall be implemented shall not be established in this constitution but shall be decided by the committee of branch representatives.

ARTICLE FIVE   This union shall cooperate with other unions through communications set up by the Rōdō Kumiai Kiseikai and other unions.

Chapter Two—Members and Honorary Members

ARTICLE SIX   Machinists, blacksmiths, boilermakers, casters, forgers, copper workers, shipbuilders, electrical workers, engineers, and firemen at iron works, and those working in similar trades who wish to become members shall apply, under procedures established elsewhere in this constitution, for membership at headquarters or a branch and must obtain permission of the branch officers' council in order to join.

ARTICLE SEVEN   Those who have received permission to join the union shall pay the established entrance fee.

ARTICLE EIGHT   The members of this union shall obtain rights and undertake duties as established by the constitution of this union and of the Rōdō Kumiai Kiseikai.

ARTICLE NINE   Members shall pay the prescribed union dues by the fifteenth of the month to their branch or headquarters.

ARTICLE TEN   Members who, due to illness or other misfortune, are unable to pay their dues may be exempted from payment by the decision of the branch officers' council.

ARTICLE ELEVEN   Members have the right to elect their branch officers and branch representatives and to be elected to such posts.

ARTICLE TWELVE   Each member has one vote with respect to the establishment or revision of his branch's rules regarding the execution of business.

ARTICLE THIRTEEN   When funds are insufficient to cover the expenses of the union, every member may be made responsible for an equal share of the deficit by decision of the committee of branch representatives.

ARTICLE FOURTEEN   Members of this union need not go through separate procedures to become members of the Rōdō Kumiai Kiseikai as they automatically become members of that organization.

ARTICLE FIFTEEN   The Rōdō Kumiai Kiseikai dues of the union members shall be paid out of their union dues.

ARTICLE SIXTEEN   Union members who wish to leave the union shall apply for permission to the officers' council of their branch or to headquarters, stating their reasons.

ARTICLE SEVENTEEN   Members who leave the union due to military obligation and then return need not pay the entrance fee again and resume the status they held before leaving the union.

ARTICLE EIGHTEEN   Members who wish to leave the union who are in arrears with respect to dues shall pay their back dues. Members who have neglected payment of their dues, once they have done so and left, may not rejoin the union.

ARTICLE NINETEEN   Those who apply for discharge from the union need not pay that month's dues if they do so by the tenth of the month.

ARTICLE TWENTY   Members who leave the union because they are moving to a place where there are no union branches may resume their status as members without repaying the entrance fee if they return within six months after leaving.

ARTICLE TWENTY-ONE   When union members who have faithfully paid dues for over three years must leave the union due to misfortune recognized by their branch officers' council, they shall receive one-quarter of their past dues in accordance with their years as union members. However, this benefit is limited to those members who have received no mutual assistance payments.

ARTICLE TWENTY-TWO   Members who make an industrially beneficial discovery are eligible for appropriate reward approved by the committee of branch representatives. Members who withdraw from or are expelled from the union simultaneously cease to be members of the Rōdō Kumiai Kiseikai.

ARTICLE TWENTY-THREE   Those who work for the union who are not union members may be named honorary members by decision of the committee of branch representatives.

Chapter Three—Headquarters and Branches

ARTICLE TWENTY-FOUR   The headquarters of the union shall be in Tokyo and branch offices shall be located at convenient sites.

ARTICLE TWENTY-FIVE   Headquarters may establish branches with the permission of the Executive Board. Headquarters shall supervise and preside over the affairs of the branches. Branches shall supervise their members and implement the constitution and decisions of the union.

ARTICLE TWENTY-SIX   A branch shall be established when at one factory or several nearby factories there are twenty-five or more union members. A branch shall be established when twenty-five or more union members live in a relatively small area and not necessarily work at the same factory. Members who cannot set up a branch under these provisions may be attached to a nearby branch or directly to headquarters, whichever is more convenient.

ARTICLE TWENTY-SEVEN   Outside of the provisions for establishing a branch, should there emerge a need for establishing a branch, it may be so established by decision of the Executive Board.

Chapter Four—Officers

Section One—Branch Representatives

ARTICLE TWENTY-EIGHT   Branch representatives shall serve as officers at headquarters in the following capacities, as
1. Mutual assistance officers
2. General affairs officers
3. Finance officers
4. Executive Board members.
One person may not hold two or more posts.

ARTICLE TWENTY-NINE   Branch representatives shall be elected by members belonging to each branch. Branch officers may not simultaneously be branch representatives. A branch shall elect one representative for each fifty members.

ARTICLE THIRTY   A committee chairman shall be named for the committees at headquarters made up of the branch representatives serving as mutual assistance, general affairs, and finance officers, and the committee chairman shall direct and preside over his committee.

ARTICLE THIRTY-ONE   Committee chairmen and vice-chairmen shall be elected by the committee of branch representatives from among the members of the committee of branch representatives.

ARTICLE THIRTY-TWO   When the membership of a branch drops such that the number of branch representatives it elects drops, the officer from that branch to resign shall be decided by lot. This article does not apply to committee chairmen or vice-chairmen.

ARTICLE THIRTY-THREE   Each branch representative has one vote in the committee of branch representatives.

ARTICLE THIRTY-FOUR   Branch representatives maintain seats at their branch officers' councils and report to the committee of branch representatives on the situation at their branch.

ARTICLE THIRTY-FIVE   The Executive Board shall be made up of the chairman and vice-chairman of the committees of branch representatives on mutual assistance, general affairs, and finance, and the five directors of the Rōdō Kumiai Kiseikai.

ARTICLE THIRTY-SIX   The chairmen and vice-chairmen of the three committees shall elect from among themselves the chairman of the Executive Board who shall then represent the union.

ARTICLE THIRTY-SEVEN   Executive Board members are responsible for the decisions of the Executive Board and the conduct of business.

ARTICLE THIRTY-EIGHT   The term of office of branch representatives and Executive Board members shall be six months. However, officers shall remain at their posts until their replacement arrives and takes over. The term of office of Executive Board members who are directors of the Kiseikai shall be one year.

ARTICLE THIRTY-NINE   Branch representatives may be re-elected once their term is over.

ARTICLE FORTY   When the chairman of a committee is absent or such post becomes vacant the chairman's place shall be taken by the vice-chairman. A special replacement shall be elected in cases where a branch representative's or branch officer's post becomes vacant.

ARTICLE FORTY-ONE   A special replacement officer shall serve out the term of the officer replaced.

Section Two—Branch Officers

ARTICLE FORTY-TWO   At each branch of the union shall be the following officers:
1. One director
2. One finance officer
3. Three mutual assistance officers
4. Three general affairs officers.

However, should the membership of the branch exceed fifty, in addition to the above officers a vice-director, a vice-finance officer, another mutual assistance officer, and another general affairs officer shall be elected. For every additional fifty members one additional mutual assistance officer and one additional general affairs officer shall be elected.

ARTICLE FORTY-THREE   The above branch officers shall be elected from among branch members by the branch membership.

ARTICLE FORTY-FOUR   The director shall handle branch business, execute the decisions of the Executive Board and the committee of branch representatives, and supervise the membership of the branch. The vice-director shall assist the director and take charge of branch business.

ARTICLE FORTY-FIVE   The finance officer shall, under the

direction and supervision of the director, handle the financial business of the branch and the vice-finance officer shall assist the finance officer and handle the financial business of the branch.

ARTICLE FORTY-SIX   The mutual assistance officers shall, under the direction and supervision of the director, handle the mutual assistance business of the branch.

ARTICLE FORTY-SEVEN   The general affairs officers shall, under the direction and supervision of the director, handle the general affairs of the branch.

ARTICLE FORTY-EIGHT   The term of office of the director, vice-director, finance officer, and vice-finance officer shall be six months. The term of office of the mutual assistance and general affairs officers shall be three months.

ARTICLE FORTY-NINE   The provisions of Articles Forty and Forty-Two[1] also apply to this section.

Chapter Five—Proceedings

Section One—Committee of Branch Representatives

ARTICLE FIFTY   The committee of branch representatives shall meet twice a year, in June and December.

ARTICLE FIFTY-ONE   The committee of branch representatives has the power to
  1. make rules concerning the execution of union business;
  2. examine the semi-annual report of the Executive Board;
  3. hear the reports of each branch;
  4. make rules concerning the collection of union dues and levies;
  5. decide how to handle union property;
  6. judge complaints or opposition of the members or branches to decisions by the Executive Board;
  7. decide matters relating to dispute mediation.

[1] This should probably read Forty-One.

ARTICLE FIFTY-TWO   The Executive Board shall set the date for the meeting of the committee of branch representatives and shall let all branch representatives know of the date of the meeting fourteen days before the opening of the committee meeting. However, emergency committee meetings are not bound by this article.

ARTICLE FIFTY-THREE   An emergency committee meeting shall be called whenever the Executive Board sees fit or when two-thirds of the branch representatives demand it.

ARTICLE FIFTY-FOUR   The chairman of the branch representatives' committee meeting shall be the chairman of the Executive Board. Should he be unavailable, the branch representatives may elect a chairman from among themselves.

ARTICLE FIFTY-FIVE   The Executive Board shall present proposals to the committee of branch representatives. Should a branch representative wish to present a proposal it should be submitted to the chairman of the Executive Board five days before the branch representatives' committee meeting.

ARTICLE FIFTY-SIX   The branch representatives' committee meeting may not be held with less than a majority of the representatives present. In emergencies, however, the meeting may be held with one-third or more of the representatives present.

ARTICLE FIFTY-SEVEN   Passage of resolutions requires a majority vote of those present. Should there be a tie, the chairman shall decide.

ARTICLE FIFTY-EIGHT   Should a branch representative be unable to attend the committee meeting a replacement shall be elected and sent in his stead. This article and the previous two articles also apply to branch meetings.

Section Two—Branch Meetings

ARTICLE FIFTY-NINE   Each branch shall hold at least one meeting per month. At such meetings the reports of the officers shall be heard and decisions on the execution of branch business made.

ARTICLE SIXTY   An emergency branch meeting may be called at the discretion of the director or if demanded by two-thirds of the branch members.

ARTICLE SIXTY-ONE   The chairman of the branch meeting shall be the director of the branch. Should he be unavailable a chairman may be elected from among those present.

Chapter Six—The Executive Board

ARTICLE SIXTY-TWO   The Executive Board shall meet at least once a month.

ARTICLE SIXTY-THREE   The Executive Board shall select one regular officer from among Board members who shall handle headquarters business. However, the regular officer may not execute matters which are not entrusted to him by the Executive Board.

ARTICLE SIXTY-FOUR   The Executive Board has the power to
    1. execute the rules of the union and the decisions of the committee of branch representatives;
    2. call meetings of the committee of branch representatives in emergencies, and when there is no time to call such emergency meetings may promote the affairs of the union without obtaining the approval of the committee of branch representatives;
    3. judge disputes between branches;
    4. maintain and protect union property; and
    5. decide the remuneration of and employment of headquarters secretaries and other employees of the union.

Chapter Seven—Miscellaneous

ARTICLE SIXTY-FIVE   The union constitution may be revised or supplemented if two-thirds of the total membership so desire.

ARTICLE SIXTY-SIX   This union may not be dissolved without the approval of nine-tenths of the branches.

ARTICLE SIXTY-SEVEN   Points not set forth in the constitution are contained in the bylaws.

Appendix

ARTICLE ONE   The headquarters of the union shall temporarily be at 1–12 Hongoku-chō,[2] Nihombashi-ku, Tokyo.

ARTICLE TWO   For the time being chairmen and vice-chairmen of the three headquarters committees may be elected only from those living within the city of Tokyo or within two hundred kilometers of the city.

ARTICLE THREE   For the time being the entrance fee is set at thirty sen and union dues at twenty sen monthly. The entrance fee may be paid in ten-sen monthly installments over three months.

Bylaws—Mutual Assistance

PROVISION ONE   A member who has paid his dues for six months is entitled to a payment of five yen should his home burn down in a fire which started elsewhere and spread to his home. However, this payment is limited to once a year.

PROVISION TWO   A member who has paid his dues for three months is entitled to a payment of twenty sen per day, payable every ten days, should he be injured or fall ill due to causes other than his own negligence. The payment of assistance does not begin until three weeks after the occurrence of the misfortune.

PROVISION FOUR   In no case may the payments outlined in provision two continue for longer than ninety days in one year.

---

[2]In the original document this is mistakenly written as Koku-chō, a location that does not exist in Nihombashi-ku.

PROVISION FIVE   When a member is injured or falls ill he must notify the director of his branch within three days, and in cases of sickness or injury lasting longer than fifteen days, he must notify the director of his branch and present him with a medical report from a doctor.

PROVISION SIX   The director of the branch, along with three mutual assistance officers, must visit the stricken member within three days of being informed of the misfortune, and must call on him twice each ten days thereafter. If the stricken man will not see the union officers, he will not receive assistance payments, except in cases where the stricken man suffers from a contagious disease.

PROVISION NINE   When a member has paid his dues for six months and has died due to no fault of his own, and has not committed suicide, his family shall receive a funeral benefit of twenty yen. Should the deceased have no surviving relatives, the union will undertake his burial.

PROVISION ELEVEN   When a union member dies, his bereaved family will receive a sum depending on his years of membership:

From one to five years	ten yen
From five to ten years	twenty yen
Over ten years	thirty yen

Members who have been temporarily expelled from the union as punishment lose the period of expulsion when their years of membership are calculated.

PROVISION THIRTEEN   Union members who are injured or have fallen ill due to no fault of their own, and are forced to cease working for a period of over two weeks, are exempted from paying one month's dues.

PROVISION FIFTEEN   Union members who are reticent in paying dues and who are receiving assistance shall have their dues deducted from their assistance payments.

PROVISION SIXTEEN   The director of the branch of a union member who is to receive assistance payments under provisions one, two, nine, or eleven must, along with the signature of three or more mutual assistance officers of the branch, present the headquarters mutual assistance chairman with the assistance funds request, as well as any other required documents. The headquarters chairman shall inspect such documents, and if in order, shall stamp them and send them on to the finance department.

PROVISION SEVENTEEN   The finance department shall make the required payment to the appropriate branch within three days of receipt of the approved request.

PROVISION EIGHTEEN   Union members receiving assistance payments under provision two shall let the director of their branch and the headquarters mutual assistance chairman know when they have recovered their health.[3]

[3]For a complete set of by-laws including subjects other than mutual assistance, see *Labor World,* no. 51 (December 15, 1899): 6–7.
Sources: Labor World, no. 40 (July 15, 1899): 4; no. 41 (August 1, 1899): 7; no. 42 (August 15, 1899): 6–7; no. 47 (November 1, 1899): 6. My translation.

CONSTITUTION OF THE REFORM SOCIETY

Chapter One—Name

ARTICLE ONE   This organization shall be called the Kyōseikai (Reform Society).

Chapter Two—Goals

ARTICLE TWO   The members of this society shall seek only the prosperity of the company, as their future lies with it. Members will of course also work diligently and behave correctly, and will not engage in violent action.

ARTICLE THREE   This society has as its goal collective agreement, and members shall bow to the majority decision.

Chapter Three—Location

ARTICLE FOUR   The location of society headquarters shall be decided by the president of the society, and branches shall be located at each enginehouse.[1]

This constitution was considerably elaborated upon by later revisions that clarify and particularize a great deal. See Katayama Sen and Nishikawa Mitsujirō, *Nihon no Rōdō Undō* [The Japanese labor movement] (Tokyo: Iwanami Shoten, 1952; first published in 1901), 154–159. The constitution presented here is the original one, without revisions of any kind.
[1]Headquarters were located at Fukushima. See Rōdō Undō Shiryō Iinkai, ed., *Nihon Rōdō Undō Shiryō* [Collected documents on the Japanese labor movement] (Tokyo, 1962), 1:613.

Chapter Four—Organization

ARTICLE FIVE   This society is one of engineers, their assistants, enginehouse workers, and so on. In addition, engineers, their assistants, and enginehouse workers have an obligation to join. However, train janitors may join through the introduction of a member. The head of the branch shall handle this.

Chapter Five—Officers and Proceedings

ARTICLE SIX   There shall be one president, one vice-president, two directors, and two secretaries at headquarters. There shall be one branch head and two secretaries at each branch.

ARTICLE SEVEN   The president and vice-president shall be elected from among all members. Headquarters directors and secretaries shall be elected from among members employed at the enginehouse at which headquarters is located. Branch officers shall be elected at each branch. All elections will be carried out by vote.

ARTICLE EIGHT   The president shall manage the affairs of all branches. The vice-president shall represent the president. The directors shall handle finance and manage affairs under the direction of the president. The branch heads shall handle branch affairs and shall act as informants to the president and branch members.

ARTICLE NINE   The president shall become chairman during conferences and shall pass judgment on proceedings.

ARTICLE TEN   Should the president find a conference of the branch heads to be subversive, he may at once halt such a conference and refer the matter to the membership.

ARTICLE ELEVEN   Should the branch head find a branch conference to be subversive he may at once halt such a conference and submit the matter for re-decision.

ARTICLE TWELVE   The decision of a conference shall be the majority vote of the branch officers. Should the vote result in a tie, then the president's vote is cast as the tie-breaker. However, at emergency sessions decisions may be made by the majority vote of those branch officers in attendance.

ARTICLE THIRTEEN   This society shall hold a convention at a convenient location in spring and fall.

ARTICLE FOURTEEN   Branch proposals to be placed before the above conventions shall be sent to headquarters within five days of the date when the opening of the convention is made known. Headquarters shall at once send copies of all the proposals to each branch so that they may decide their stands on each proposal and present such to the conference of branch heads. However, emergency proposals are not bound by this article.

ARTICLE FIFTEEN   The branch heads shall inform the president of any definite decisions reached at branch meetings on occasional branch problems within five days of such meetings.

ARTICLE SIXTEEN   The term of all officers shall be six months, at the end of which period an election shall be held. However, there is no obstacle to reelection. Officers may not resign their posts for reasons other than illness or transfer.

Chapter Six—Members

ARTICLE SEVENTEEN   All members shall sign a branch register at their branch prepared for such purpose. The branch head shall inform the president of the contents of the branch register so that the names may be recorded at headquarters.

ARTICLE EIGHTEEN   Members who break society rules shall be expelled from membership and shall be encouraged to leave employment at the company. No communications shall be made with a rule breaker. Also, any member who advocates dissolution of the society shall be considered immoral and shall undergo punishment.

ARTICLE NINETEEN   When a member who has worked hard for the society is unfairly discharged, all members shall make a united effort. However, when a member has been severely punished for a small mistake, the situation shall be investigated and, upon the decision by all members, sufficient assistance shall be given.

ARTICLE TWENTY   Members who are transferred to other sections or leave employment at the company, although losing their status as members, are still obligated to protect the society. However, the fund for such a member is handled according to Article Twenty-Six.

Chapter Seven—Finance

ARTICLE TWENTY-ONE   Members shall make payment of one day's wages a month to the central fund for one year, and a half day's wages per month thereafter. However, in emergencies a member may make use of the fund with the approval of the branch officers. Also, members who have not received wages for more than ten days in a month are exempted from the fund payment.

ARTICLE TWENTY-TWO   Members, when entrusting their fund savings passbooks to the branch head, shall receive a receipt. When the passbook is lost or stolen the branch head should be immediately informed.

ARTICLE TWENTY-THREE   The deadline for fund payments is the third of the month. Such payments shall be made to the branch head and he shall handle such fund payments in accordance with the procedures in effect at his branch.

ARTICLE TWENTY-FOUR   The branch head, upon collecting the fund payments, shall immediately deposit such at a bank or post office savings department.

ARTICLE TWENTY-FIVE   The fund payments of each member shall be deposited in an account under his name and the passbook shall be kept by his branch head.

ARTICLE TWENTY-SIX   The fund of members who die, retire, or leave the company shall be returned to them. However, the fund of members who are expelled or who leave the society without reason shall be confiscated.

ARTICLE TWENTY-SEVEN   When members wish to leave the society they must ask the permission of the branch heads and the president shall have the final decision. Confiscated funds shall be sent to headquarters for use in defraying headquarters expenses.

ARTICLE TWENTY-EIGHT   When members are transferred they shall give their passbook to their new branch head and continue saving without interruption.

ARTICLE TWENTY-NINE   When a member misses a day's pay on account of the society he shall be given that amount by the society. When traveling on society business, if forced to stop overnight away from home, members shall receive an allowance of one yen. In such cases, if members do not stay overnight away from home they shall receive an allowance of thirty sen. However, members who receive a company overnight-stop allowance receive from the society only thirty sen.

ARTICLE THIRTY   Society expenses shall be borne as follows:
   1. Overall expenses (headquarters and conference expenses) shall be footed by each member equally.
   2. Branch expenses shall be footed by each branch member equally.

ARTICLE THIRTY-ONE   Financial reports shall be made at each convention.

Chapter Eight—Miscellaneous

ARTICLE THIRTY-TWO   All movements of members (retirement, transfer, death, promotion, demotion) shall be reported to headquarters.

ARTICLE THIRTY-THREE   When members are about to break society rules they shall be warned by the branch head. When they break the rules they shall undergo the established procedure.

ARTICLE THIRTY-FOUR The particulars necessary for the implementation of the previous articles shall be established by each branch at its convenience.

ARTICLE THIRTY-FIVE The previous articles may be revised or supplemented by a majority vote at the convention.

Source: Rōdō Undō Shiryō Iinkai, ed., *Nihon Rōdō Undō Shiryō,* [Collected documents on the Japanese labor movement] (Tokyo, 1962), 1:610–611. My translation.

PRINTERS' FRIENDLY ASSOCIATION RULES

ARTICLE ONE   This organization shall be called the Kappankō Dōshi Konwakai (Printers' Friendly Association) and shall temporarily have its offices at 7 Kaga-machi, Nihombashi-ku, Tokyo.

ARTICLE TWO   This organization is made up of anyone employed in the trade, regardless of their address or the section in which they are employed.

ARTICLE THREE   This organization seeks the development of the trade, of course the reform and improvement of the morals and actions of the members, as well as the development of good practices among the members. This organization seeks entirely to gain the trust of society.

ARTICLE FOUR   This organization shall have a president, a committee chairman, several committee members, and five directors. Their powers are as follows:

1. The president shall supervise all the affairs of this organization.

2. The committee chairman shall assist the president and supervise the committee members.

3. The committee members shall each attend to their separate business and participate in policy deliberations.

4. The directors shall handle all general matters connected with this organization.

ARTICLE FIVE   This organization shall have ten councilors who shall examine all matters relating to the establishment of this organization. However, it should be noted that when the councilors meet they must elect a chairman from among themselves.

ARTICLE SIX   The conventions of this organization shall be held in spring and fall, twice a year. However, at the president's discretion or when the councilors so demand, an emergency convention may be held.

ARTICLE SEVEN   Those who wish to join this organization shall apply to this organization through a committee member, stating their address and place of employment. Should members move or change their place of employment they must notify the organization of such change. Application for members may be made directly to this organization (at the head office or a branch) when it is convenient.

ARTICLE EIGHT   Members shall pay dues of ten sen per month. The procedure for payment of dues shall be that each member shall receive a receipt from the appropriate committee member when he pays his dues at the end of the month.

ARTICLE NINE   A financial report shall appear monthly in the organization journal. Any remaining funds shall be deposited securely in a bank by the president (or if he should be unavailable the committee chairman or the directors).

ARTICLE TEN   The term of office for councilors and officers shall be six months, and elections shall be held at the conventions. Reelection is allowed.

ARTICLE ELEVEN   In order to protect the members, this organization establishes the following procedures:
    1. When a member is unemployed he shall inform the office or his branch and the members will try to find him work.
    2. Members in the following circumstances shall receive appropriate relief on the basis of the deliberations of the committee:
    a) Death or illness of one month or more;

b) Death of parent or wife, or house burned in a fire started elsewhere;

c) Habitation (lodging, apartment) burned in a fire started elsewhere.

Payment shall be made on the basis of presentation of a doctor's examination certificate, proof, and/or investigation by the committee.

ARTICLE TWELVE   Members who have acted shamefully or otherwise sullied the honor of this organization shall be expelled from the organization if so decided by the committee on the basis of investigation.

ARTICLE THIRTEEN   Members to whom the provisions of Article Eleven apply may be temporarily exempted from payment of dues by the decision of the committee.

ARTICLE FOURTEEN   When the membership of this organization reaches fifteen hundred it shall be dissolved and a union instantly organized.

ARTICLE FIFTEEN   With the growth of membership, the number of branches and officers shall be allowed to grow.

ARTICLE SIXTEEN   The provisions of the constitution of this organization may not be revised or deleted without the consent of two-thirds of the membership.

Source: Mizunuma Tatsuo, "Insatsu Kō Rōdō Undō Shi" [The history of the printers' labor movement] *Jiyū Rengō Shimbun,* no. 29 (November 1, 1928): 3. My translation.

PROPOSED FACTORY LAW OF *1898*

Chapter One—General Provisions

ARTICLE ONE   This law applies to factories employing fifty or more workers and apprentices.

ARTICLE TWO   The scope of this law may be extended to other factories that undertake operations that are hazardous to health or of a dangerous nature, or, where it is deemed necessary, for special reasons or for the protection of the workers and apprentices. Such extension shall be by imperial decree.

Chapter Two—Factories

ARTICLE THREE   Those who wish to construct factories, or to remodel or enlarge existing factories, must apply to the appropriate government agency and obtain permission. Those who wish to make an existing building into a factory must also do the same. Factories that are to shift production to a new product or make drastic changes in the production process must also apply for permission. The rules relating to requirements, procedures, and validity of permission are to be decided by government decree.

ARTICLE FOUR   Factories are to be inspected by the appropriate government agency upon the completion of their construction, and those that do not pass inspection may not function as the site of operations for production.

ARTICLE FIVE   Factories must set up equipment necessary for safety, the protection of health, the maintenance of morals, and the protection of the public.

ARTICLE SIX   When there arise faults in equipment under the previous article, the appropriate government agency may take the following measures:

1. It may order the establishment of appropriate equipment in a specified period of time.

2. It may order the total or partial cessation of operations.

In case one, should the factory owner fail to set up the required equipment by the end of the specified period, the appropriate government agency may do so at the expense of the factory owner.

ARTICLE SEVEN   Those who wish to set up a steam engine must apply to the appropriate government agency and undergo inspection. Should the engine not pass fixed or temporary inspection it may not be used.

ARTICLE EIGHT   The provisions of this chapter and their punishments apply to company housing for workers, dormitories, clinics, and other buildings which, like factories, are for industrial purposes.

Chapter Three—Workers

ARTICLE NINE   Employment of children under ten years of age is prohibited. However, this limitation will be modified with the approval of authorities where there exist special circumstances.

ARTICLE TEN   The working hours of children under fourteen years of age are limited to ten hours per day. However, this limitation will be modified with the approval of authorities where there exist special circumstances.

ARTICLE ELEVEN   Work shall be suspended on at least two days in each month and on three national holidays, and an hour of meal time is to be given to workers every working day. These requirements will be modified with the approval of authorities where there exist special circumstances.

ARTICLE TWELVE   The employer shall provide educational facilities at his own expense for workers in his employ under the age of fourteen years who have not completed elementary school. Workers are to obey the academic rules of the employer.

ARTICLE THIRTEEN   The employer shall be liable in case of accident resulting in the injury of an employee who was discharging his duty. The employer shall pay an allowance for the recovery of the worker, or an assistance payment in cases where the worker is disabled or is permanently bedridden.[1]

ARTICLE FOURTEEN   Workers may be exempted from an employment contract when:
   1. An employer or supervisor physically attacks or abuses a worker or his family;
   2. A worker is forced to undertake particularly dangerous or unhealthy work at the request of his supervisor.

ARTICLE FIFTEEN   The employer is exempted from an employment contract in the following cases:
   1. When a worker physically attacks or abuses him or his family, or his supervisors or their families;
   2. When a worker undertakes actions injurious to the factory or its equipment.

ARTICLE SIXTEEN   The employer, in order to regulate relations with his employees, shall set down workplace regulations and have them approved by the appropriate government agency.

---

[1]Due to discrepancies between this reported version of the law and other documents, it appears that the following sentences of Article Thirteen have been left out of this version: "The employer is also liable in fatal accidents, but an exception shall be made in cases involving the intentional purpose of the victim himself or his fellow-servant, or calamity of nature." See Takano Fusatarō, "Factory Legislation in Japan," *American Federationist* 5, no. 10 (December 1898): 200; Katayama Sen and Nishikawa Mitsujirō, *Nihon no Rōdō Undō* [The Japanese labor movement] (Tokyo: Iwanami Shoten, 1952; first published in 1901), 50; *Labor World,* no. 24 (November 15, 1898): 10.

He shall also have changes in those rules approved. The appropriate government agency, when necessary, may order changes in the rules for workers, dormitories, or company housing for workers.

ARTICLE SEVENTEEN   The rules for workers shall include the following:

1. Rules relating to the employment contract;
2. Rules relating to vacations and working hours;
3. Rules relating to supervisory organization;
4. Rules relating to rewards and punishments;
5. Rules relating to wages;
6. Rules relating to the allowance and assistance payment outlined in Article Thirteen;
7. Rules relating to savings by workers with the company;
8. Prohibitions especially laid down for the avoidance of danger;
9. The academic rules outlined in Article Twelve;
10. Work rules are binding on both worker and employer.

ARTICLE EIGHTEEN   In order to clarify the movements of the workers the employer shall set up a register for workers.

ARTICLE NINETEEN   In necessary cases workers will be given an industry in which to work or an occupation, and will be given a worker certificate. In industries where the certificate system exists, employers may only employ certificate holders.

ARTICLE TWENTY   The Minister of State for Agriculture and Commerce shall grant the power to bestow workmen's certificates to those trade associations or masters' associations which have applied to receive such power and where it is deemed necessary. Such associations and their members may not employ those who do not hold the certificate.

ARTICLE TWENTY-ONE   The workmen's certificate shall include the worker's address and his native place. If issued under Article Twenty it shall include the name of the issuing association.

ARTICLE TWENTY-TWO   The employer shall hold the certificate of his workers and return them when they are discharged.

ARTICLE TWENTY-THREE   The method of keeping the register of workers and the workmen's certificates, and their contents, shall be established by government decree.

Chapter Four—Apprentices

ARTICLE TWENTY-FOUR   The factory owner who wishes to train apprentices shall lay down rules and have them approved by the appropriate government agency. The same holds true when he wishes to alter those rules.

ARTICLE TWENTY-FIVE   The rules for apprentices shall include:
1. Rules relating to the training contract;
2. Rules relating to days off and rest time;
3. Rules relating to training;
4. Rules relating to compensation;
5. Rules relating to illness, injury, and allowances;
6. Rules relating to rewards and punishments;
7. Rules relating to savings by apprentices with the company;
8. The academic rules outlined in Article Twelve.

ARTICLE TWENTY-SIX   Articles Nine through Thirteen, Fourteen, Fifteen, Sixteen, Seventeen (number 2), and Eighteen through Twenty-Two and their punishments also apply in the case of apprentices.

Chapter Five—Inspection

ARTICLE TWENTY-SEVEN   The Minister of State for Agriculture and Commerce may limit or prohibit employment where it involves women or workers under the age of fourteen, especially dangerous work for apprentices, or work which is detrimental to health or morals.

ARTICLE TWENTY-EIGHT   The factory inspection officials may inspect factories and attached buildings, documents relating to workers and apprentices, and may demand explanations from the factory owner, his representatives, or his employees. Factory inspection officials, and those acting as such, have the obligation to protect industrial secrets which they may learn in the course of their duties.

ARTICLE TWENTY-NINE   Those who have complaints about the punishments accorded them under the administration of this law have recourse to petition under the Petition Law.

ARTICLE THIRTY   Disputes between the factory owner and his workers or apprentices over work rules, apprentice rules, company housing or dormitory rules, the employment contract or the training contract may be resolved by the judgment of the factory inspection officials.

Chapter Six—Punishment

ARTICLE THIRTY-ONE   Those who disobey Articles Three, Four, Seven, Nine, Eleven, Sixteen, Eighteen, Nineteen, Twenty, or Twenty-Two, or who disobey orders and decrees issued under Articles Twenty-Six or Twenty-Seven will be subject to a fine of two hundred yen or less.

ARTICLE THIRTY-TWO   Those who tamper with registers for workers, refuse inspection or explanation demanded under Article Twenty-Eight, or who attempt to deceive the factory inspection officials shall be subject to a fine of fifty yen or less.

ARTICLE THIRTY-THREE   Should a factory owner knowingly employ the workers or apprentices of another employer while their employment contracts are in effect, or act as an intermediary agent in such employment, he shall be subject to a fine of two hundred yen or less. Anyone who attempts to deceive an *oyakata*, employer, or factory owner into breaking the employment contract in order to employ or act as an intermediary agent in the employment of workers or apprentices so obtained, shall be subject to a fine of two hundred yen or less.

ARTICLE THIRTY-FOUR   Those dealing in, using, or making tampered workmen's certificates shall be subject to a fine of two hundred yen or less.

ARTICLE THIRTY-FIVE   Those factory inspection officials who leak industrial secrets shall be subject to Article Three Hundred Sixty of the Criminal Code.

ARTICLE THIRTY-SIX   Those who break this law shall not be subject to criminal prosecution.

ARTICLE THIRTY-SEVEN   The provisions of Article Two Hundred Eight and Two Hundred Six of the Informal Case Law (Law Number Fourteen), 1898, shall apply to the fines collected under this law.

ARTICLE THIRTY-EIGHT   The representatives, family, or employees of a factory owner who break the law pertaining to factory owners shall not be exempted from punishment if the factory owner did not direct their actions.

ARTICLE THIRTY-NINE   Corporations, staff employees with managerial responsibilities, directors, and other juridical persons shall be liable to punishment described in this chapter for factory owners.

Supplement

ARTICLE FORTY   This law shall come into effect on and after July 1, 1899.

Sources: Katayama Sen and Nishikawa Mitsujirō, *Nihon no Rōdō Undō* [The Japanese labor movement] (Tokyo: Iwanami Shoten, 1952; first published in 1901), 40–47; *Labor World*, no. 22 (October 15, 1898): 6–7. My translation.

CONSTITUTION OF THE PRINTERS' UNION

Goals

ARTICLE TWO   The goals of this union are to promote and improve industrial skill, of course to reform bad practices among the workers, to support the development of morals and to raise the status of the members.

ARTICLE THREE   This union shall cooperate with the employers' association in this trade and work for mutual benefit and advantage.

ARTICLE FOUR   This union shall protect the rights and happiness of the members, relieve their sufferings in case of disaster or misfortune, and support and advance their interests.

ARTICLE FIVE   In order to achieve the goals mentioned in the previous articles a journal shall be published at least once a month. This will promote the morals, knowledge, and spirit of the members.

Unfortunately, only part of the constitution, the articles deemed to be the key ones, were recorded for posterity. They are presented here.

Members

ARTICLE SIX   The name of this organization shall be the Kappankō Kumiai (Printers' Union). Its office shall be located at _____ and branches shall be located at convenient sites.[1]

ARTICLE SEVEN   All workers employed in the printing industry should be union members.

ARTICLE EIGHT   Those who have received permission to enter the union shall pay an entrance fee of thirty sen. However, in an emergency this may be collected in ten-sen monthly installments over a period of three months.

ARTICLE NINE   Union members are obligated to respect the union constitution and the decisions of the union, and are all equally liable for union expenses.

ARTICLE TEN   Members who wish to leave the union shall apply for permission, stating their reason, to their branch officers' council.

Headquarters and Branches

ARTICLE SEVENTEEN   Headquarters of this union shall establish branches and supervise and preside over their affairs. Each branch shall supervise its membership and execute the provisions of the constitution and the decisions of the union.

ARTICLE TWENTY-ONE   This union shall establish a branch when there are one hundred or more union members in a single location or area, which will handle the affairs of union members belonging to it. However, when there are less than one hundred members in one locality they may be federated with a different branch.

[1]The exact location of headquarters was left blank in the original constitution, later to be filled in. The location was never in fact filled in.

Officers

ARTICLE TWENTY-FIVE   There shall be one president of this union.

ARTICLE TWENTY-SIX   The following officers shall be at union headquarters:
1. Head director
2. Directors
3. Secretaries
4. Messengers
5. Head of Finance
6. Head of Mutual Assistance
7. Head of General Affairs
8. Editor-in-Chief

ARTICLE TWENTY-NINE   There shall be one head director at headquarters, whose term of office shall be one year.

ARTICLE THIRTY   The term of office of the head director, the heads of the different departments,[2] and directors shall be one year, with one-half of these officers undergoing election every six months. The terms of messengers and secretaries are not fixed.

Duties of Officers

ARTICLE FIFTY-SEVEN   The powers of the directors are as follows:
1. To execute the provisions of the constitution and the decisions of the committee;
2. To maintain and protect union property;
3. To represent the union and carry out external union negotiations under the direction of the head director;
4. To set the remuneration and terms of the secretaries and other headquarters employees.

[2] These departments were finance, mutual assistance, and general affairs.

Proceedings

ARTICLE FIFTY-SIX   There are five types of meetings:
1. Conventions
2. Directors' meetings
3. Deliberations
4. Committee meetings
5. Emergency meetings

ARTICLE SIXTY-SIX   The convention shall be held on January third of every year.

ARTICLE SIXTY-SEVEN   The chairman of the convention shall be the president, or if he is not available the head director or one elected from among the membership shall serve as chairman.

ARTICLE SIXTY-EIGHT   Committee meetings shall be held in January, April, July, and October of every year.

ARTICLE SIXTY-NINE   The committee shall handle the following matters:
1. The reelection of officers;
2. Revisions, decisions, or rules relating to the handling of union business;
3. Examination of the directors' report;
4. Establishment of rules relating to the collection of union dues and levies;
5. Establishment of rules relating to the handling of union property;
6. Establishment of rules relating to mediation of disputes.

ARTICLE SEVENTY   The exact date and time of the committee meetings shall be decided near the time when such meetings are to be held. However, emergency meetings are not so limited.

ARTICLE SEVENTY-THREE   Proposals are made to the committee by the directors. Should a committee member wish to present a proposal to the committee he must submit it to the head director five days before the committee meeting is to be held.

ARTICLE SEVENTY-FIVE   The majority of union members may demand an emergency meeting with respect to a matter relating to their immediate interest.

ARTICLE SEVENTY-SIX   Emergency branch meetings may be held at the request of two-thirds of the branch membership or the directors of the union.

By-Laws—Mutual Assistance

ARTICLE FIFTEEN   Those members who have faithfully paid their dues for three months are eligible to receive a mutual assistance payment of ten sen per day payable every ten days starting on the twenty-first day of an illness that has prevented them from working and that at that time shows no signs of abatement.

ARTICLE SIXTEEN   Members who are injured on the job such that they are unable to work are eligible to receive a mutual assistance payment of ten sen per day payable every ten days starting on the first day of their injury. However, those who were injured as a result of their own carelessness or misconduct are not eligible to receive the above payments.

ARTICLE SEVENTEEN   Those who have paid their dues faithfully for three months are eligible for a relief payment of five yen if their house burns down and three yen if it is partially burned. However, this is limited to home owners with a family.

ARTICLE EIGHTEEN   Lodgers whose lodging burns down are entitled to a two-yen relief payment.

ARTICLE TWENTY   The families of members who have paid their dues for six months who die as a result of illness, injury, or natural disaster, shall receive a funeral benefit of ten yen. Should the deceased have no living relatives the union shall handle the funeral, using the above sum.

ARTICLE TWENTY-TWO   When a union member dies his family shall receive a benefit in accordance with his years of service as follows:

Members for a period of from one to five years   five yen
Members for a period of five to ten years   ten yen
Members for over ten years   twenty yen

Members who are punished with temporary expulsion from the union are not considered to be members for the above benefit for the period of their expulsion.

ARTICLE THIRTY-FOUR   Union members may not receive benefits for over ninety days in any one year.

Expenditures and Rights of Members

ARTICLE THIRTY-NINE   Every member shall pay fifteen sen a month to cover union expenditures.

ARTICLE FORTY-THREE   Union members who, due to sickness or other misfortune, are unable to pay their dues may be exempted from such payment by decision of the officers' council.

ARTICLE FORTY-FOUR   Members may elect committee members and officers and may be elected to such posts.

ARTICLE FORTY-FIVE   Each member has one vote with respect to revision of his branch constitution or rules relating to the execution of union business at his branch.

ARTICLE FORTY-SIX   Should union funds be insufficient the officers' council may make each member liable for an equal share of the deficit.

ARTICLE FORTY-SEVEN   Members have the right to protection under the constitution and decisions of the union.

Dispute Mediation

ARTICLE FORTY-EIGHT   When a dispute arises between a member and his employer the member's branch head shall investigate the facts and report to headquarters as well as attempt to mediate the dispute. Should the mediation be refused or not go smoothly this also should be reported to headquarters.

ARTICLE FORTY-NINE   Should such a report be received at headquarters, the head director or a director shall investigate the facts, open a directors' meeting, and work for harmony between the two parties.

ARTICLE FIFTY   Should the employer refuse the mediation of the directors without reason and make an unfair reply, and in cases where there is no progress, this shall be taken up by the directors with the Printers' Employers' Association and a suitable result obtained through discussion.

Relations with Employers' Association and Employers

ARTICLE FIFTY-ONE   The union recognizes the Printers' Employers' Association and will cooperate with it.

ARTICLE FIFTY-TWO   When a member of the Printers' Employers' Association seeks to employ a union member, the two shall be tied together with a contract the terms of which have been worked out between the union and the employers' association.

ARTICLE FIFTY-FIVE   When a union member is laid off at the convenience of the employer, the employer shall pay the wages of the union member during the period of lay-off.

ARTICLE FIFTY-SIX   If it is recognized that it has become difficult to make ends meet on the established wages due to inflation, this situation shall be taken care of by petitioning the Printers' Employers' Association and conducting mutual negotiations.

ARTICLE FIFTY-SEVEN   The union, in addition to other business, should make efforts to provide a supply of workmen to the various plants where union men are employed and to guarantee all workmen so employed. However, costs so incurred shall be born by the Printers' Employers' Association.

ARTICLE FIFTY-EIGHT   When an employer employs a worker the employer shall inform the union.

ARTICLE FIFTY-NINE   The ten-hour day with thirty minutes for rest shall be observed at all plants where union members are employed.

ARTICLE SIXTY   There shall be a 20 percent night shift allowance.

ARTICLE SIXTY-TWO   Should a union member without reason leave the employ of a member of the Printers' Employers' Association before his contract term is up, or make unfair demands or act threateningly, on the basis of a report from the plant owner the union shall send a director to investigate the facts and punish the offender appropriately.

ARTICLE SIXTY-THREE   Should an employer act unfairly toward a union member in his employ the union shall dispatch a director to investigate and shall negotiate with the employer. If the employer does not respond to such negotiation the procedures of Article Fifty shall be undertaken.

Punishment

ARTICLE SIXTY-FIVE   Members who act improperly, harm friendship between members, or who are violent toward employers shall be suspended from the union for up to two months.

ARTICLE SIXTY-SIX   Members who sully the honor of the union shall be subject to suspension or expulsion depending on the circumstances.

ARTICLE SIXTY-SEVEN   Union members who break the law and are convicted shall be expelled from the union.

ARTICLE SIXTY-EIGHT   Suspension shall be for up to one month.

Source: Katayama Sen and Nishikawa Mitsujirō, *Nihon no Rōdō Undō* [The Japanese labor movement] (Tokyo: Iwanami Shoten, 1952; first published in 1901), 160–167. The source for articles 55, 58, and 60 of the bylaws is ibid., 283. My translation.

REFERENCE TABLES

Table J-1. Metalworkers' Union Branches, Date and Place Established

BRANCH NO.	FORMATION DATE	LOCATION
1	December 1, 1897	Tokyo Armaments Works
2	December 1, 1897	Ōmiya Factory (Japan Railways Co.)
3	December 1, 1897	Yokohama
4	December 1, 1897	Ministry of Posts and Communications Factory (lighthouse equipment)
5	December 1, 1897	Tokyo Armaments Works
6	December 1, 1897	Honjo Ward, Tokyo
7	December 1, 1897	Tokyo Armaments Works
8	December 1, 1897	Tokyo Armaments Works
9	December 1, 1897	Tokyo Armaments Works
10	December 1, 1897	Tokyo Armaments Works
11	December 1, 1897	Tokyo Armaments Works
12	December 1, 1897	Tokyo Armaments Works
13	December 1, 1897	Shimbashi Railway Factory (Tokyo)
14	February 11, 1898	Shibaura Engineering Works (Tokyo)
15	February 11, 1898	Shimbashi Railway Dept. (Tokyo)
16	March 1, 1898	Ishikawajima Shipyards
17	March 2, 1898	Yokosuka Navy Shipyards
18	March 13, 1898	Kōbu Railway Factory
19	March 20, 1898	Tokyo Armaments Works
20	May 1, 1898	Ishikawajima Shipyards
21	May 1, 1898	Ishikawajima Shipyards
22	May 10, 1898	Akabane Navy Shipyards
23	May 25, 1898	Japan Railway Co. workshops at Fukushima, Kuroiso, and Sendai
24	July 9, 1898	Tokyo Harbor Steamship Company
25	August 5, 1898	Japan Railway Co. at Aomori
26	August 6, 1898	Japan Railway Co. at Morioka

continued

220

Table J-1. Continued

BRANCH NO.	FORMATION DATE	LOCATION
27	August 13, 1898	Fitters of Branch 19 at the Tokyo Armaments Works
28	October 1, 1898	Tokyo Armaments Works[a]
29	October 1, 1898	Hokkaidō Ishikarinokuni Takikawa Government Railway Factory
30	October 15, 1898	Tokyo Armaments Works
31	October 28, 1898	Ishikawajima Shipyards
32	October 29, 1898	Ishikawajima Shipyards
33	February 25, 1899	Ōji Paper Co. (Tokyo)
34	March 19, 1899	Hokkaidō Ishikarinokuni Asahikawa
35	May 30, 1899	Hokkaidō Sapporo Hemp Co.
36	July 15, 1899[b]	Kyōbashi-ku Electric Works (Tokyo)
37	July 15, 1899[c]	Tokyo Armaments Works
38	September 10, 1899	Ōji Paper Co. (Tokyo)
39	November 1, 1899	Woodworkers at Branch 2, the Ōmiya Factory of the Japan Railway Co.
40	November 22, 1899	Japan Railway Co. at Mito
41	July 1900	Yokohama Western Furniture Makers
42	September 1900	Ishikawajima Shipyards

Source: Katayama Sen and Nishikawa Mitsuhirō, *Nihon no Rōdō Undō* [The Japanese labor movement] (Tokyo: Iwanami Shoten, 1952; first published in 1901), 79–80.

[a] This branch was dissolved in February 1899. See *Labor World,* no. 40 (July 15, 1899): 5.

[b] This is the date this branch is first mentioned in *Labor World.* The formation date is not given. See *Labor World,* no. 40 (July 15, 1899): 7.

[c] This is the date this branch is first mentioned in *Labor World.* The formation date is not given. See *Labor World,* no. 40 (July 15, 1899): 7.

Table J-2. Dues-Paying Membership of the Metalworkers' Union, 1898–1900, by branch

	MEMBERSHIP				
BRANCH NO.	SEPT.–NOV. 1898	MAR.–MAY 1899	JUNE–AUG. 1899	SEPT.–NOV. 1899	DEC.–FEB. 1899/1900
1	36	112	98	74	37
2	69	175	222	158	62
3	132	177	393	225	12
4	10	12	8	15	7
5	27	25	29	31	13
6	68	54	69	50	18
7	43	24	21	20	18
8	84	79	72	62	30

continued

	MEMBERSHIP				
BRANCH NO.	SEPT.–NOV. 1898	MAR.–MAY 1899	JUNE–AUG. 1899	SEPT.–NOV. 1899	DEC.–FEB. 1899/1900
9	91	113	142	116	49
10	55	121	89	88	22
11	63	153	75	59	50
12	14	9	10	13	11
13	26	18	38	17	—
14	70	—	75	34	22
15	—	—	—	—	—
16	298	90	68	70	52
17	353[a]	241	222	228	93
18	22	39	—	—	—
19	37	14	—	—	—
20	68	91	64	68	54
21	94	51	52	37	14
22	76	54	30	24	14
23	83	74	74	72	58
24	27	21	12	11	11
25	52[b]	49	114	59	36
26	59	50[c]	43	14	8
27	39	21	42	26	9
28	49	—	—	—	—
29	55	34	—	—	—
30	24	60	32	39	15
31	—	40	51	50	40
32	38	—	72	21	14
33	—	20	39	51	—
34	—	—	45	68	19
35	—	—	21	45	—
36	—	—	21	52	43
37	—	—	34	38	21
38	—	—	—	22	17
39	—	—	—	38	49
40	—	—	—	29	46
41	—	—	—	—	—
42	—	—	—	—	—

Source: Quarterly fiscal reports in *Labor World,* no. 27 (January 1, 1899): 10–11; no. 40 (July 15, 1899): 5; no. 46 (October 15, 1899): 8; no. 55, supplement (February 15, 1900): 5; no. 62 (June 1, 1900): 5–6. *Note:* Monthly dues payments show fantastic variation—from 3 to 394 to 0 for the period September to November 1898 (branch 3), for example—so averages are given.

[a] The September figure in this quarterly period is incorrectly listed as 38 in *Labor World* instead of 380 as subtotals and money figures indicate.
[b] The November figure in this quarterly period is listed as 35 in *Labor World* instead of 69, as subtotals and money figures indicate.
[c] The quarterly subtotal in *Labor World* for this period is incorrectly listed as 109 members instead of 150, as money figures and monthly figures indicate.

Table J-3. Metalworkers' Union Membership at Major Unionized Plants, September 1898–February 1900

	TOKYO ARMAMENTS WORKS		YOKOSUKA NAVY SHIPYARDS		ISHIKAWAJIMA SHIPYARDS		ŌMIYA FACTORY		TOTAL	
	MEM	%	MEM	%	MEM	%	MEM	%	MEM	%
Sept.–Nov. 1898	454	30	236	16	243	16	46	3	939	65
Dec.–Feb. 1898/1899										
Mar.–May 1899	631	37	241	14	139	8	175	10	1186	69
June–Aug. 1899	509	24	222	11	286	14	148	7	1165	56
Sept.–Nov. 1899	530	29	228	13	247	14	158	9	1163	65
Dec.–Feb. 1899/1900	218	24	94	10	176	19	62	7	550	60

Sources: Quarterly fiscal reports in *Labor World,* no. 27 (January 1, 1899): 10–11; no. 40 (July 15, 1899): 5; no. 46, supplement (October 15, 1900): 5; no. 55, supplement (February 15, 1900): 5; no. 62 (June 1, 1900): 5–6.

Note: Membership figures are based on dues-paying members and averaged for time periods listed. Percentages are of total union members paying dues in that time period.

NOTES

CHAPTER I

1. Ōtsu Jun'ichirō, *Dai Nihon Kensei Shi* [A constitutional history of greater Japan], 11 vols. (Tokyo: Hōbunkan, 1927–1928), 1:635–636; Fujii Jintarō, *Outline of Japanese History in the Meiji Era,* translated and adapted by Hattie K. Colton and Kenneth E. Colton (Tokyo: Ōbunsha, 1958), 108.

2. See "Memorial on the Establishment of a Representative Assembly," January 17, 1874, in Walter W. McLaren, ed., "Japanese Government Documents, 1867–1889," part 1 of *Transactions of the Asiatic Society of Japan* (Tokyo: Asiatic Society of Japan, 1914), 42: 427–430. See also Fujii, *Outline of Japanese History,* 109–110.

3. Fujii, *Outline of Japanese History,* 134.

4. Robert A. Scalapino, *Democracy and the Party Movement in Prewar Japan* (Berkeley: University of California Press, 1962), 60–61.

5. G. M. Beckmann, *The Making of the Meiji Constitution* (Lawrence, Kansas: University Press of Kansas, 1957), 126–149.

6. Scalapino, *Democracy,* 82–83.

7. Osatake Takeshi, *Nihon Kensei Shi Taimō* [An outline of Japanese constitutional history], 2 vols. (Tokyo: Nihon Hyōronsha, 1939), 2:832–833.

8. McLaren, "Documents," 136–144.

9. Fukaya Hakuji, *Shoki Gikai Jōyaku Kaisei* [The first Diets: Treaty revision], Kindai Nihon Rekishi Kōza [Modern Japanese History Series] (Tokyo: Hakuyōsha, 1940), 207. Also Hayashida Kametarō, *Nihon Seitō Shi* [History of Japanese political parties], 2 vols. (Tokyo: Dai Nihon Yūben Kaikōdansha, 1927), 1:309–312.

10. Scalapino, *Democracy,* 160–162.

11. Ibid., 163–165.

12. Ibid., 166–172.

13. Ibid., 173–178.

14. Ishii Ryōsuke, *Japanese Legislation in the Meiji Era,* translated and adapted by William J. Chambliss (Tokyo: Pan-Pacific Press, 1958), 257–259.

15. Ibid., 260–261; Scalapino, *Democracy,* 60.

16. Ishii, *Japanese Legislation*, 465–467.

17. Ibid., 467.

18. Ibid., 263.

19. Ibid., 467–470.

20. Ibid., 471.

21. Sumiya Mikio, *Nihon Chin Rōdō Shiron* [An historical treatise on Japanese wage labor] (Tokyo: Tokyo Daigaku Shuppankai, 1955), 302–304. For the text of these proposals, see Nōshōmushō [Ministry of Agriculture and Commerce], "Kōgyō Iken" [View of industry] (1884), in Tsuchiya Takao and Ōuchi Hyōei, *Meiji Zenki Zaisei Keizai Shiryō Shūsei* [Collected documents on economics and finance in the early Meiji period] (Tokyo: Meiji Bunken Shiryō Kankōkai, 1933), 20:691.

22. Sumiya, *Nihon Chin Rōdō Shiron*, 307–308, 316–318.

23. Ibid., 321–324.

24. Ibid., 324.

25. Silk-reeling data from Takahashi Keizai Kenkyūjo, *Nihon Sanshigyō Hattatsu Shi* [The history of the development of the Japanese silk industry] (Tokyo: Seikatsusha, 1941), 1:384; precious metals output from Nihon Kōgakukai, *Meiji Kōgyō Shi: Kōgyō Hen* [History of industry in the Meiji period: Mining edition] (Tokyo: Nihon Kōgakukai, 1930), 162–163; coal output from G. C. Allen, *A Short Economic History of Modern Japan, 1867–1937* (London: Allen and Unwin, 1972), 80–81; domestic-built shipping tonnage from Shibusawa Keizō, *Japanese Society in the Meiji Era*, translated and adapted by Aora H. Culbertson and Kimura Michiko (Tokyo: Pan-Pacific Press, 1958), 306, 326; cotton-spinning data from W. A. Graham Clark, *Cotton Goods in Japan* (Washington: U.S. Department of Commerce, 1914), 40, and Sumiya, *Nihon Chin Rōdō Shiron*, 181.

26. Clark, *Cotton Goods*, 40.

27. Sumiya, *Nihon Chin Rōdō Shiron*, 211; Hyōdō Tsutomu, *Nihon ni Okeru Rōshi Kankei no Tenkai* [The development of labor relations in Japan] (Tokyo: Tokyo Daigaku Shuppankai, 1971), 89–90; Sumiya Mikio, *Nihon Rōdō Undō Shi* [Japanese labor movement history] (Tokyo: Yūshindō, 1966), 9.

28. Telegraph data from Thomas C. Smith, *Political Change and Industrial Development in Japan: Government Enterprise 1868–1880* (Stanford: Stanford University Press, 1955), 45; railroad data from Nihon Kōgakukai, *Meiji Kōgyō Shi: Tetsudō Hen* [History of industry in the Meiji period: Railroad edition] (Tokyo: Nihon Kōgakukai, 1930), 121–154, 190–196, 280–281, and Tōyō Keizai Shimpōsha, ed., *Meiji Taishō Kokusei Sōran* [All about Japan in the Meiji and Taishō eras] (Tokyo: Tōyō Keizai Shimpōsha, 1927), 617–618.

29. Allen, *Economic History*, 48, 82.

30. Sōrifu Tōkeikyoku Hen [Bureau of Statistics, Office of the Prime Minister], *Dai Nanakai Nihon Tōkei Nenkan* [Seventh annual statistical handbook of Japan] (Tokyo: Sōrifu Tōkeikyoku, 1955), 10; Namiki Masayoshi, *Nōson wa Kawaru* [The changing farm villages] (Tokyo: Iwanami Shoten, 1960), 85; Inegaki Yasuhiro, Kawamura Zenjirō, Murai Masuo, and Amagasu Ken, *Nihon Shi* [Japanese history] (Tokyo: Sanshōdō, 1979), 210.

31. This is distinctly different from the West, where all peasants were regarded

as tenants of the feudal lord, who collected rents. In Japan it is estimated that only some 30 percent of the land was worked by tenant farmers in the early Meiji years. See Hirano Yoshitarō, *Nihon Shihonshugi no Kikō to Hōritsu* [The structures and Laws of Japanese capitalism] (Tokyo: Meizenshobō, 1948), 54.

32. Sumiya, *Nihon Chin Rōdō Shiron,* 15.

33. Ibid., 23, 32, 88.

34. Okurashō Kokusai Kyoku, *Zokuroku Shobunroku* [Record of the elimination of the samurai stipends] (1882), in Tsuchiya Takao and Ōuchi Hyōei, eds., *Meiji Zenki Zaisei Keizai Shiryō Shūsei* [Collected documents on economics and finance in the early Meiji period] (Tokyo: Kaizōsha, 1933), 8:13, 15, 24.

35. Sumiya, *Nihon Chin Rōdō Shiron,* 54–64.

36. This pattern is still very much evident in Japan today, although housewives now sometimes return to the work force on a part-time basis after their children are mature.

37. Naimushō Sōmu Kyoku [Bureau of Administration, Home Ministry], *Nihon Teikoku Kokusei Ippan* [All about imperial Japan], no. 10 (Tokyo: Naimushō Sōmu Kyoku, 1891), 52–54; Tōkeikyoku [Bureau of Statistics], *Nihon Teikoku Tōkei Nenkan* [Imperial Japanese statistical yearbook], no. 13 (Tokyo: Tōkeikyoku, 1894), 62; Thomas O. Wilkinson, *The Urbanization of Japanese Labor, 1868–1955* (Amherst, Mass.: University of Massachusetts, 1965).

38. Umemura Mataji, "Sangyōbetsu Koyō no Hendō 1800–1940" [Change in employment by industry: 1800–1940], *Keizai Kenkyū* [Hitotsubashi University], 24, no. 2 (April 1973): 112–113, 116.

39. Nōshōmushō Shōkō Kyoku [Bureau of Commerce and Industry, Ministry of Agriculture and Commerce], *Shokukō Jijō* [The condition of industrial workers], edited by Tsuchiya Takao, 3 vols. (Tokyo: Seikatsusha, 1947; first published in 1903), 1:69–70, 187, and 2:11. Hereinafter cited *Shokukō Jijō.*

40. Hazama Hiroshi, *Nihon Rōmu Kanri Shi Kenkyū* [A study of the history of Japanese labor management] (Tokyo: Daiyamondosha, 1974), 18–19.

41. Yasui Jirō, *Sen'i Rōshi Kankei no Shiteki Bunseki* [Historical analysis of labor relations in textiles] (Tokyo: Ocha no Mizu Shobō, 1967), 40–85; Hyōdō Tsutomu, *Tenkai,* 55–66.

42. Yasui, *Sen'i,* 85–131.

43. Ibid., 40–65.

44. Kinugawa Taiichi, *Hompō Menshi Bōseki Shi* [History of cotton-spinning in Japan] (Osaka: Nihon Mengyō Kurabu, 1938–1939), 3:423–424; Seki Keizō, *The Cotton Industry of Japan* (Tokyo: Japan Society for the Promotion of Science, 1956), 15–16. For a detailed description of the life of Japan's most famous entrepreneur, see Johannes Hirschmeier, "Shibusawa Eiichi: Industrial Pioneer," in William H. Lockwood, ed., *The State and Economic Enterprise in Japan* (Princeton N.J.: Princeton University Press, 1965), 209–248.

45. Yasui, *Sen'i,* 99–114.

46. Ibid., 115.

47. *Shokukō Jijō* 1:74–90.

48. Yasui, *Sen'i,* 118–131.

49. Hyōdō, *Tenkai,* 55–66.

50. Ibid., 67.

51. Ikeda Makoto, _Nihon Kikaikō Kumiai Seiritsu Shiron_ [An historical treatise on the formation of the machinists' unions in Japan] (Tokyo: Nihon Hyōronsha, 1970), 24.

52. Ibid., 25–26.

53. Ibid., 22–23, 27; Hyōdō, _Tenkai_, 92–93. Professor Hyōdō Tsutomu has analyzed the _oyakata_ of the period in terms of a transition from "apprentice" to "subcontracting" _oyakata_ combined with a strengthening of direct management supervision systems and management control over subcontracting profits. See Hyōdō Tsutomu, "Tekkō Kumiai no Seiritsu to Sono Hōkai—Nisshin Sensōgo ni Okeru Jūkōgyō no Rōshi Kankei" [The rise and fall of the Metalworkers' Union —Labor relations in heavy industry after the Sino-Japanese War], in three parts, _Keizaigaku Ronshū_ (Tokyo University), 31, no. 4 (January 1966): 14–31; 32, no. 2 (July 1966): 89–113; and 32, no. 3 (October 1966): 63–94. Also Hyōdō Tsutomu, _Tenkai_, 55–213. Professor Sumiya Mikio sees labor relations in this period as a process of restriction of type two ("subcontracting") _oyakata_ by management. See Sumiya Mikio, Kobayashi Ken'ichi, and Hyōdō Tsutomu, _Nihon Shihonshugi to Rōdō Mondai_ [Japanese capitalism and labor problems] (Tokyo: Tokyo Daigaku Shuppankai, 1967), 108–112.

54. Hyōdō, _Tenkai_, 110.

55. _Shokukō Jijō_ 2:15–29.

56. Ōyama Shikitarō, _Kōgyō Rōdō to Oyakata Seido_ [Mine labor and the _oyakata_ system] (Tokyo: Yūhikaku, 1964), 31–32.

57. Ōkōchi Kazuo and Matsuo Hiroshi, _Nihon Rōdō Kumiai Monogatari, Meiji_ [The tale of the Japanese trade unions] (Tokyo: Chikuma Shobō, 1965), 1:30–32.

58. Ibid., 1:30–32.

59. _Kōfu Taigū Jirei_ [Condition of miners] (1908) (includes surveys and data from 1906), 39–52.

60. Ōkōchi and Matsuo, _Monogatari_ 1:27.

61. Ibid., 1:27–28.

62. Several published sources give the wrong date for this dispute. Ōkōchi and Matsuo (_Monogatari_ 1:29) give the date as October 1893. According to Murayama Shigetada in his _Nihon Rōdō Sōgi Shi_ [History of Japanese labor disputes] (Tokyo: Tokyo Kasumigaseki Shobō, 1946), 8, it took place on January 26, 1893. Murayama's original source, Suzuki Jun'ichirō's "Waga Kuni ni Okeru Dōmei Hikō no Senrei" in _Kokuka Gakukai Zasshi_, no. 116 (October 1896): 1127–1145, supports the January 26, 1894, date. For several newspaper articles dated January 1894 that also confirm that date, see Rōdō Undō Shiryō Iinkai [The Committee on Japanese Labor Movement Documents], ed., _Nihon Rōdō Undō Shiryō_ [Collected documents on the Japanese labor movement] (Tokyo, 1962), 1: 134–135.

63. Sumiya, _Nihon Rōdō Undō Shi_, 17.

64. Chapter VIII, Article 270 of the Criminal Code. Translated and quoted in Takano Fusatarō, "Strikes in Japan," _Far East_ 2, no. 6 (June 20, 1897): 238. For the Japanese text of this section, see Sumiya, _Nihon Chin Rōdō Shiron_, 314.

65. Yamamoto Shirō, "Meiji Zenki no Kōzan Rōdō Oyobi Rōdō Undō" [Min-

ing labor and the labor movement in the early Meiji period], in Meiji Shiryō
Kenkyū Renrakukai [Contact Committee on Meiji Period Research Documents],
ed., *Meiji Zenki no Rōdō Mondai* [Labor problems in the early Meiji period]
(Tokyo: Ocha no Mizu Shobō, 1960), 178–192.

66. Matsushima Shizuo, *Rōdō Shakaigaku Josetsu* [An introduction to labor
sociology] (Tokyo: Fukumura Shoten, 1951), 223–380.

67. Yamamoto, "Meiji," 184–185, 189–192.

68. Katayama Sen and Nishikawa Mitsujirō, *Nihon no Rōdō Undō* [The Japanese labor movement] (Tokyo: Iwanami Shoten, 1952; first published in 1901),
138–140.

69. Sumiya, *Nihon Chin Rōdō Shiron,* 283–284.

70. Ibid., 284–285; Katayama and Nishikawa, *Nihon no Rōdō Undō,* 277.

71. Sumiya, *Nihon Chin Rōdō Shiron,* 287–288.

72. Ōkōchi Kazuo, *Reimeiki no Nihon Rōdō Undō* [The early Japanese labor
movement] (Tokyo: Iwanami Shoten, 1952), 29–31; Ōkōchi and Matsuo,
Monogatari 1:25; Takano Fusatarō, "Typical Japanese Workers," *Far East* 20,
no. 4 (April 20, 1897): 172.

73. Ōkōchi and Matsuo, *Monogatari* 1:36; Taira Kōji, "Factory Legislation
and Management Modernization during Japan's Industrialization, 1886–1916,"
Business History Review 44, no. 1 (Spring 1970): 99–101; Katayama and Nishikawa, *Nihon no Rōdō Undō,* 14.

74. For the complete text of the constitution, see Katayama and Nishikawa,
Nihon no Rōdō Undō, 125–129.

75. Katayama Sen, "Aida Kichigorō ni Tou" [Questions to Aida Kichigorō],
Labor World, no. 67 (September 1, 1900): 3. My translation.

76. Katayama and Nishikawa, *Nihon no Rōdō Undō,* 14, 16.

77. "Rōdōsha no Koe" [Voice of the workers], *Kokumin no Tomo* [Friend of
the People], 7, no. 95 (September 23, 1890), quoted in Sumiya, *Nihon Chin
Rōdō Shiron,* 282. My translation.

78. Quoted in Ōkōchi and Matsuo, *Monogatari* 1:39. My translation.

79. Ibid.

80. For the rules of this organization, see "Ōmiya Kōjō Kumitate Senbankō
Kyōkyūkai Kisoku" [Rules of the Ōmiya Factory fitters' and lathe operators'
mutual assistance society], *Labor World* no. 30 (February 15, 1899): 4. It was
actually two separate mutual assistance societies, one for fitters and the other for
lathe operators, but they were jointly administered. Shin's subcontracting transactions are outlined in "Nittetsu Ōmiya Kōjō no Fuhai" [The rot at the Japan
Railway Company's Ōmiya Factory], *Labor World* no. 47 (December 1,
1899): 5.

81. Katayama and Nishikawa, *Nihon no Rōdō Undō,* 205. My translation.
For the complete constitution of the Alliance for Industrial Organization, see
appendix A.

82. Katayama and Nishikawa, *Nihon no Rōdō Undō,* 211.

83. For the key provisions of the constitution of the Tokyo Ship Carpenters'
Union, which was very similar to the Yokohama constitution, see appendix B.

84. Takano Fusatarō, "A Remarkable Strike in Japan," *American Federationist*
4, no. 7 (September 1897): 144–145.

CHAPTER 2

1. Komatsu Ryūji, "Waga Kuni ni Okeru Rōdō Kumiai Shisō no Seisei: Sakuma Teiichi to Takano Fusatarō wo Chūshin ni" [The formation of labor union ideology in Japan: Centering on Sakuma Teiichi and Takano Fusatarō], in Institute of Management and Labor Studies, ed., *Management and Labor Studies Series*, no. 272 (Tokyo: Keiō University, 1969–1970), 161.

2. Komatsu, "Waga Kuni," 161; Hyman Kublin, *Meiji Rōdō Undō Shi no Hitokoma—Takano Fusatarō no Shōgai to Shisō* [One aspect of the history of the Meiji period labor movement—The life and thought of Takano Fusatarō] (Tokyo: Yūhikaku, 1959), 24, 53; Shimoide Shunkichi, *Meiji Shakai Shisō Kenkyū* [Studies in Meiji period social thought] (Tokyo: Asano Shoten, 1932), 244–246. Note that Kublin incorrectly dates several of these events on page 53 of his book.

3. Nishida Nagatoshi, "Takano Fusatarō Rōdō Mondai Ronshū" [The collected works of Takano Fusatarō on labor problems], in Meiji Bunka Kenkyūkai, ed., *Meiji Bunka Zenshū* [Collected materials on Meiji period culture], 15:24 (Tokyo: Nihon Hyōronsha, 1955).

4. Kublin, *Meiji*, 24; Sumiya Mikio, "Takano Fusatarō to Rōdō Undō—Gompers to no Kankei wo Chūshin ni" [Takano Fusatarō and the labor movement—Centering on his relationship with Gompers], *Keizaigaku Ronshū* (Tokyo University), 29, no. 1 (April 1963): 64. Although the documents in Shimoide (*Kenkyū*, 244–246) give the date for Takano's uncle's death as 1885, Professor Ōshima Kiyoshi, who has access to the most complete collection of documents on Takano's life, has indicated that the actual date was 1886. See Komatsu, "Waga Kuni," 161, and Ōshima Kiyoshi, *Takano Iwasaburō Den* [A biography of Takano Iwasaburō] (Tokyo: Iwanami Shoten, 1968), 8. This chapter relies heavily on the data and interpretation provided in Sumiya Mikio's article on Takano's relationship with Gompers. Little would be known of Takano's doings and whereabouts in the United States were it not for the preservation of many of his letters by his younger brother. This collection was later kept intact by Professor Uno Kōzō, and was brought to light by the diligent efforts of Professor Sumiya. Those involved in research in this field must thank Professor Sumiya for his unceasing efforts to extend knowledge of Japanese labor history.

5. In the short biography of Takano written by his brother, Takano Iwasaburō, in *Kappa no He* [Wind of whimsy], edited by Suzuki Kōichirō (Tokyo: Hōsei Daigaku Shuppankyoku, 1961), 291–292, Takano Iwasaburō wrote: "with his free time my brother entered the municipal Commercial School of San Francisco, and finished the course of the school." There is also a statement that Takano "opened a small store." With respect to this there are several documents dated in the last half of 1888, addressed to Takano at 10 Stockton St., San Francisco, which deal mostly with trade in cigarettes (Sumiya, "Takano," 64). My translation.

6. Takano's move to Washington is indicated by a letter from a friend of his, Albert Brayton, addressed to him in Seattle. This letter was dated October 24, 1889, and stated: "I am glad to hear that you got work. $45 is good wages and you had better stay with it." Virtually all the letters sent to Takano from April

1890 to September 1892 are addressed to him in Tacoma. Two articles written by Takano indicated that he was in Tacoma when they were published: "Hoku Bei Gasshūkoku no Rōeki Shakai no Arisama wo Josu" [On American working-class society], which appeared serially in the *Yomiuri Shimbun,* a Tokyo daily, in May and June of 1890; and " 'Aikoku' Kisha ni Tsugu—Rōdō Mondai no Ittan" [To the "patriotic" journalist—One aspect of labor problems], which appeared in *Ensei,* a Japanese-language magazine published by Japanese living in San Francisco, in November 1892. See Sumiya, "Takano," 64.

7. See Takano Fusatarō, "Hoku Bei Gasshūkoku no Rōeki Shakai no Arisama wo Josu" [On American working-class society], *Yomiuri Shimbun,* no. 4651 (May 31, 1890); no. 4658 (June 7, 1890); no 4661, supplement (June 10, 1890); no. 4664, supplement (June 13, 1890); no. 4669 (June 18, 1890); no. 4670 (June 19, 1890); no. 4674 (June 23, 1890); no. 4675 (June 24, 1890); no 4676 (June 25, 1890); no. 4677 (June 26, 1890); no. 4678, supplement (June 27, 1890).

8. Three receipts from the New York office of G. P. Putnam's Sons give a hint as to what Takano was studying. A receipt dated June 8, 1892, carries books by Jevans, McCulloch, and other noted economists of the period. On a receipt dated September 27, 1892, the following books appear: Rogers, *Industrial and Commercial History of England;* Bawerk, *The Positive Theory of Capital;* Marshall, *Principles of Economics;* Fawcett, *The Manual of Political Economy;* Clark, *The Distribution of Wealth;* and Blanqui, *History of Political Economy.* Takano also asked Putnam's Sons for a way to obtain a copy of the "Journal of the Knights of Labor." Sumiya, "Takano," 65.

9. "Shokukō Giyūkai" was a direct translation into Japanese of the "Knights of Labor," an organization that must have had an impact on the Japanese in San Francisco in 1890, as it had recently finished its period of rapid growth and was only beginning to decline. See Hyman Kublin, *Meiji,* 54. Takano tactfully refers to this organization as the "Friends of Labor" in his correspondence with Samuel Gompers.

10. Sumiya, "Takano," 64. According to *Labor World,* no. 15 (July 1, 1898): 3, Takano was a founding member of the San Francisco "Knights of Labor," but this is inaccurate. It is clear from the October 16, 1891, article in *Keisei Shimpō,* "Beikoku San Francisco ni Waga Rōdō Giyūkai Okoru" [Our Knights of Labor arises in San Francisco, the United States], that Takano was not a founding member. This is reinforced by the fact that Takano was living in Tacoma at the time the San Francisco "Knights of Labor" was founded. There is no question about the fact that Takano became intimately involved with the group upon his return to San Francisco, and became its most prominent member.

Jō Tsunetarō was born in Kumamoto, Japan, in 1863, became a cobbler in Kobe, and went to America to help develop Japanese shoemaking as a representative of his trade. He worked as a cobbler in San Francisco and set up a shoemakers' association in 1893 upon his return to Japan. He moved to Kobe after Takano set up his union organizing body in Tokyo in 1897. In 1901 Jō set up a shoemaking company in Tientsin, China, but succumbed to illness in 1904.

Sawada Hannosuke was born at Sukagawa in Fukushima Prefecture in Japan in 1868. He went to America in 1890 and set up a tailor's shop at Jō Tsunetarō's shoemaking shop. He returned to Japan when the Sino-Japanese War broke out in 1894 and opened up a tailor's shop at Ginza, Tokyo. Sawada served as a director in Takano's union organizing body and attempted to set up a union of tailors of Western-style clothing.

Hirano Eitarō was a cobbler. From Rōdō Undō Shiryō Iinkai, ed., *Nihon Rōdō Undō Shiryō* [Collected documents on the Japanese labor movement] (Tokyo, 1962), 11:394, 408–409.

11. Sumiya, "Takano," 64.

12. Ibid., 65.

13. Ibid., 65–66. This is a rough draft of the letter; the letter itself has been lost.

14. Ibid., 66–68.

15. Ibid., 69.

16. Ibid., 71.

17. Ibid., 71–72.

18. Samuel Gompers, *Seventy Years of Life and Labor* (New York: E. P. Dutton and Co., 1925), 2:59. In this passage, Gompers indicated that Takano was a student at Columbia and went home to serve in the Sino-Japanese War. Both of Gompers' assertions are in error. No evidence can be found that Takano studied formally at Columbia. Either Takano was attending informally or Gompers was mistaken about the name of the college. Kublin, *Meiji,* 26.

19. Sumiya, "Takano," 72.

20. Hyman Kublin, *Asian Revolutionary: The Life of Sen Katayama* (Princeton, 1964), 136. Unfortunately for Western scholarship, Western authors who deal with this topic skip over it in a few sentences. The concept of social policy not only has been very important in the consideration of labor problems in Japan, it has had considerable impact on other related fields as well.

21. Stephen S. Large, *The Yūaikai: The Rise of Labor in Japan, 1912–1919* (Tokyo, 1972), 17. Takano Iwasaburō was born in 1871 and attended Japan's most prestigious university, Tokyo Imperial University. Takano Iwasaburō graduated from Tokyo Imperial University's Law Department in 1895 and went on to do graduate work at the same university in the fields of industrial economics and labor problems. He supported his brother's efforts at union organization. Later, he became Japan's most famous social scientist and founded the famous Ōhara Social Sciences Research Institute. Ikeda Makoto, "Nisshin Sensō-go no Shakai Seisaku Shisō" [Social policy ideology after the Sino-Japanese War], *Shakai Kagaku Ronshū* (Saitama University), no. 31 (January 1973): 74–75.

22. The complete name of the organization was Nihon Shakai Seisaku Gakukai [Social Policy School of Japan]. The circumstances of its founding are well presented in Sumiya Etsuji, *Nihon Keizaigaku Shi no Hitokoma: Shakai Seisaku Gakukai wo Chūshin to Shite* [One aspect of the history of Japanese economics study—Centering on the Social Policy School] (Tokyo: Nihon Hyōronsha, 1948), 262–263. The text of the objectives of the association, from which this translation was made, will be found on pages 263–264 of the same work. Translation is from Kublin, *Asian Revolutionary,* 187.

23. Ōkōchi Kazuo, *Shakai Seisaku Genri* [The basis of social policy] (Tokyo: Keisō Shobō, 1951), 7.

24. Ibid., 7–8.

25. Ibid., 163–164.

26. Ibid., 14, 18, 165, 167–170.

27. Ikeda, "Nisshin," 74–75.

28. Ibid., 74–75.

29. Takano wrote to his brother in a letter dated March 7, 1892: ". . . I have translated this work, which is a brilliant original economic treatise. It is George Gunton's *Wealth and Progress*." Quoted in Ōshima Kiyoshi, *Hito ni Kokorozashi Ari* [Man is ambitious] (Tokyo: Iwanami Shoten, 1974), 40–41. My translation.

George Gunton was born in Cambridgeshire, England, on September 8, 1845 or 1847 (sources conflict). Gunton came to the United States in 1874 and worked at the cotton mills at Fall River, Massachusetts, as a machinist. In 1875 he became a secretary of the machinists' union and became acquainted with Aira Steward.

Gunton took an active part in the textile workers' strike in 1876, was blacklisted by the mill owners, and turned from work in the mills to journalism. Gunton became the owner of the *Labor Standard,* a Fall River weekly paper.

In 1883 Gunton began work on a manuscript left by Aira Steward, and in 1887 published his most famous and influential work: *Wealth and Progress*. Gunton subsequently moved to New York City, where he devoted himself to scientific, economic, and sociological work. In 1899 he was appointed international examiner and director of the economic and sociological work of the Young Men's Christian Association of North America. *Gunton's Magazine* ceased publication in 1904. Gunton died on September 11, 1919.

For more information on Gunton see John W. Leonard, ed., *Who's Who in America, 1901–1902* (Chicago, 1901), 473; Albert Nelson Marquis, ed., *Who's Who in America, 1914–1915* (Chicago, 1914), 984–985; *New York Times* (Saturday, September 13, 1919), 11.

30. Joan Robinson and John Eatwell, *An Introduction to Modern Economics* (Maidenhead, England, 1973), 34–39.

31. George Gunton, *Wealth and Progress* (New York: Appleton, 1887), 23–31.

32. Ibid.

33. Takano Fusatarō, " 'Aikoku' Kisha ni Tsugu—Rōdō Mondai no Ittan" [To the "patriotic" journalist—One aspect of labor problems], *Ensei*, no. 19 (November 1, 1892). My translation. Reprinted in Hyman Kublin, *Meiji Rōdō Undō Shi no Hitokoma, 101.*

34. *Takano Fusatarō, "Labor Movement in Japan," American Federationist* 1, no. 8 (October 1894): 164.

35. Ibid.

36. Letter by Takano dated August 16, 1894, to the Grand International Brotherhood of Locomotive Engineers, in Sumiya, "Takano," 70.

37. Takano Fusatarō, "Nihon ni Okeru Rōdō Mondai" [Labor problems in Japan], *Yomiuri Shimbun,* August 9, 1891. My translation.

38. Ibid. My translation.

39. Takano Fusatarō, "Labor Problem in Japan," *Taiyō* 2, no. 14 (July 5, 1896): 75.

40. Takano left San Francisco in late 1894 on a small American warship and, while working as a hand on the ship, observed various American ports. He returned to Tokyo in the spring of 1895 in time to attend his brother's graduation from Tokyo University. Takano's brother Iwasaburō promptly embarked upon graduate studies at Tokyo University. Takano's presence in Tokyo in the spring of 1895 is confirmed by his article "The War and Labor in Japan," *Social Economist,* no. 9 (July 1895): 30–33. This article is postscripted "Tokio, Japan, March, 1895."

Takano continued his cruise for the next year in an effort to broaden his experience and knowledge. He signed on the USS *Machias,* probably the same warship in which he crossed the Pacific, as a deckhand. Takano's first stop was at Kyūshū, Japan's southernmost major island, in late April 1895. He then went on to Chefoo, China, in May, and saw a number of Chinese ports, including Shanghai where he stopped in October 1895. The *Machias* steamed on to Korea in late 1895 and returned to Tokyo in early 1896. Takano's stop in Kyūshū can be deduced from an extant letter by Takano's younger sister Kiwa, who lived in Karatsu, Kyūshū, Japan. See Sumiya, "Takano," 73; an article by Takano—"Chinese Tailors' Strike in Shanghai," *American Federationist* 3, no. 1 (March 1896): 5–6—which places Takano in Shanghai in October 1895; a February 18, 1896, letter from Gompers, which states: "I am in receipt of your favor of December 15 dated Chelempo, Corea" (Sumiya, "Takano," 73).

41. This scholar is sometimes referred to as Kanai Noburu.

42. Ikeda, "Nisshin," 38, 42, 62.

43. For a well-balanced analysis and comparison of the ideologies of Takano and the Social Policy School, see Ikeda Makoto, "Takano Fusatarō to Shakai Seisaku Shisō" [Takano Fusatarō and the ideology of social policy], *Shakai Kagaku Ronshū* (Saitama University) no. 30 (March 1972): 159–182.

CHAPTER 3

1. It has often been asserted that Takano only left his job at the *Advertiser* when persuaded to do so by Sawada Hannosuke in the spring of 1897. This is the view forwarded in Katayama Sen and Nishikawa Mitsujirō, *Nihon no Rōdō Undō* [The Japanese labor movement] (Tokyo: Iwanami Shoten, 1952; first published in 1901), 27. This assertion is in error, however, as is clear from the December letter from Takano to Gompers, which indicates that Takano began efforts to organize the workers on his own initiative much earlier.

2. Sumiya Mikio, "Takano Fusatarō to Rōdō Undō—Gompers to no Kankei wo Chūshin ni" [Takano Fusatarō and the labor movement—Centering on his relationship with Gompers], *Keizaigaku Ronshū* (Tokyo University), 29, no. 1 (April 1963): 75–76.

3. Ikeda Makoto, "Takano Fusatarō to Shakai Seisaku Shisō" [Takano Fusatarō and the ideology of social policy], *Shakai Kagaku Ronshū* (Saitama University), no. 30 (March 1972): 163.

4. Sumiya, "Takano," 76–77.

5. See Takano's diary entry for March 22, 1897, in Ōshima Kiyoshi, "Rōdō

Kumiai no Soshisha—Takano Fusatarō" [Takano Fusatarō—Founder of labor unions], *Sekai,* no. 277 (December 1968), 209–210. Quotation from Article VI of the rules of the Industrial Institute. For the rules of the Institute and information about it and Sakuma Teiichi, see Toyohara Matao, *Sakuma Teiichi Shoden* [The biography of Sakuma Teiichi] (Tokyo: Shūeisha, 1932; first published in 1904), 105–109.

6. Ōshima, "Rōdō Kumiai," 210; Katayama and Nishikawa, *Nihon no Rōdō Undō,* 18. The Japanese title of "A Summons to the Workers" has been incorrectly introduced to the West as "Shokkō Shokun ni Yokosu" by Hyman Kublin in his book *Asian Revolutionary: The Life of Sen Katayama* (Princeton, N.J.; Princeton University Press, 1964), 105.

Until recently it was believed by labor scholars that "A Summons to the Workers" was written by Sawada Hannosuke and Jō Tsunetarō. Some sources seemed to indicate this, although they did not state so outright. Newly discovered documents have conclusively established the fact that this important document was written by Takano Fusatarō. Three separate facts confirm Takano's authorship. First, Takano was a journalist and had published several articles, while Sawada and Jō had no such training or experience. Second, Takano's first public speech—given at the meeting of the Industrial Institute on April 6, 1897—is on the very same subject discussed in the pamphlet. Third, Takano refers to "a pamphlet written by me" being distributed at the meeting of the Industrial Institute in a letter to Gompers. This pamphlet, according to Takano's description, is identical in content to that of "To My Fellow Workers." It was Takano, not Jō and Sawada, who wrote the pamphlet. See Hyman Kublin, *Meiji Rōdō Undō Shi no Hitokoma —Takano Fusatarō no Shōgai to Shisō* [One aspect of the history of the Meiji period labor movement—The life and thought of Takano Fusatarō] (Tokyo: Yūhikaku, 1959), 36–37. See also Takano Fusatarō, "Our Organizer in Japan," *American Federationist* 4, no. 4 (June 1897): 78.

7. A complete translation of "A Summons to the Workers" appears in appendix C.

8. Katayama and Nishikawa, *Nihon no Rōdō Undō,* 18–26. My translation.

9. Takano Fusatarō, "Our Organizer in Japan," 77–78. The speakers at this meeting were Takano, Sakuma Teiichi, Tajima Kinji, and T. Takeuchi. Tajima Kinji was the author of *Nihon Genji no Shakai Mondai* [Current social problems in Japan] (Tokyo, 1897). See Rōdō Undō Shiryō Iinkai, *Nihon Rōdō Undō Shiryō* [Collected documents on the Japanese labor movement] (Tokyo: Rōdō Undō Shiryō Kankō Iinkai, 1962), 1:403 (hereinafter cited *Nihon Rōdō Undō Shiryō*). Although Takano in his letter to Gompers indicates the meeting was sponsored by the "friends of labor"—the Knights of Labor of San Francisco, which had returned to Japan—it is clear that it was in fact the general meeting of the Industrial Institute. See Takano's diary entry for April 6, 1897, which states: "From 1:00 P.M. I attended the general meeting of the Industrial Institute at the Kinkikan. Takeuchi Tsunetarō advocated thrift and diligence, I talked on the condition of workers in America. . . . " Quoted in Ōshima, "Rōdō Kumiai," 210. My translation.

Hyman Kublin in *Asian Revolutionary* (p. 112) states that this meeting on April 6, "which was attended by 'several hundred workers,' has unfortunately been overlooked by almost all Japanese labor historians, yet the event marked the real opening of the labor movement in Japan." This goes a little far, as the meeting was not actually sponsored by the Knights of Labor.

10. Takano, "Our Organizer in Japan," 78. Katayama and Nishikawa, *Nihon no Rōdō Undō,* 28–30. Suzuki financed the July 5 rally, which was estimated to have cost some forty yen.

11. Diary entries by Takano on June 12, 17, 21, and 24, 1897, in Ōshima, "Rōdō Kumiai," 210–211. See also *Labor World,* no. 15 (July 1, 1898): 3.

12. The *Mainichi Shimbun* (July 27, 1897) indicates that there were 1,500 people in the audience, while Katayama and Nishikawa, *Nihon no Rōdō Undō,* 27, and *Labor World,* no. 15 (July 1, 1898): 3, give the figure as 1,200. One reason for such large audiences was the lack of recreation available to the workers, who saw such meetings as a chance for some free entertainment.

13. *Mainichi Shimbun* (July 27, 1897), in *Nihon Rōdō Undō Shiryō* 1:405–406; Katayama and Nishikawa, *Nihon no Rōdō Undō,* 27; Ōshima, "Rōdō Kumiai," 211.

The number "forty-seven" should not be passed over lightly. It harkens back to the most popular legend in Japanese history, that of the forty-seven samurai. In order to avenge the unfair action that led to the death of their lord, these forty-seven samurai pretended to lead separate and dissolute lives to escape surveillance and suspicion. Then, one night, they banded together and wiped out the family that had caused the death of their lord. They then committed ritual suicide in the true fashion of the samurai. It is clear that the Kiseikai attempted to take advantage of this legend by trying to make its members feel like loyal and courageous warriors. See, for example, the wording in *Labor World,* no. 15 (July 1, 1898): 3, which refers to these men as *gishi* ("virtuous warriors").

14. See William C. Birdsall, "The Problem of Structure in the Knights of Labor," *Industrial and Labor Relations Review* 6, no. 4 (July 1958): 532–546, for an analysis of the structure of the Knights.

15. Ibid.

16. American Federation of Labor, *History, Encyclopedia Reference Book* (Washington: American Federation of Labor, 1919), 230.

17. Philip Taft, *The American Federation of Labor in the Time of Gompers* (New York: Harper and Row, 1957), 97.

18. Original documents and contemporary secondary sources conflict as to the actual date of the inaugural ceremony of the Kiseikai. The most conclusive evidence is Takano's diary entry for July 5, 1897, which makes it clear that the Kiseikai's organization date was the 5th. Up to this time the date of this inaugural ceremony has been given as July 3, 4, 5, and even 7. For example: Yokoyama Gennosuke's article "Rōdō Undō no Shomaku" [The birth of the labor movement], *Chūō Kōron* 14, no. 8 (August 1899): 8, gives the date as July 3; Katayama and Nishikawa, *Nihon no Rōdō Undō,* 27, give the date as July 5; *Labor World,* no. 15 (July 1, 1898): 3, gives the date as July 4; *Nihon Rōdō Undō Shiryō* 1:408, as July 4; and Kublin's *Asian Revolutionary,* 115, as July 7. Whether the Kiseikai was founded on July 4 or 5 is important as Takano and the other members of the Knights of Labor, who had been to America, might have seen fit to begin the Japanese labor movement on the U.S. Independence Day,

July 4. They did not, so they did not consider this symbol of the American tradition important in their organizing efforts.

19. *Labor World,* no. 15 (July 1, 1898): 3. The constitution of the Kiseikai appears in appendix D.

20. Katayama and Nishikawa, *Nihon no Rōdō Undō,* 28–30.

21. Takano Fusatarō, "Prospects of the Japanese Labor Movement," *American Federationist* 4, no. 9 (November 1897): 210. Among Japanese labor historians, Professor Ōkōchi has been almost alone in noting this essential point. See his *Reimeiki no Nihon Rōdō Undō* [The early Japanese labor movement] (Tokyo: Iwanami Shoten, 1952), 148–149.

CHAPTER 4

1. Rōdō Undō Shiryō Iinkai, *Nihon Rōdō Undō Shiryō* [Collected documents on the Japanese labor movement] (Tokyo: Rōdō Undō Shiryō Kankō Iinkai, 1962), 1:406, hereinafter cited *Nihon Rōdō Undō Shiryō;* Takano Fusatarō, "Prospects of the Japanese Labor Movement," *American Federationist* 4, no. 9 (November 1897): 210; *Labor World,* no. 16 (July 15, 1898): 3.

The organization of these three labor bodies can hardly be attributed to Kiseikai activity, and no reputable primary source does so. Yet they are occasionally listed as the product of Kiseikai agitation. See Hyman Kublin, *Asian Revolutionary: The Life of Sen Katayama* (Princeton, N.J.: Princeton University Press, 1964), 120. Very little information is available on these three "unions," but what information exists indicates they were *oyakata*-dominated organizations for the benefit of master craftsmen.

2. See chapter 1.

3. *Labor World,* no. 9 (April 1, 1898): 10.

4. Ikeda Makoto, *Nihon Kikaikō Kumiai Seiritsu Shiron* [An historical treatise on the formation of the Machinists' Unions in Japan] (Tokyo: Nihon Hyōronsha, 1970), 37.

5. Ibid., 22; Katō Hirō, "Kōsaku Kikai Kōgyō no Kōzō to Kadai" [The structure and problems of the machine and manufacturing industries], in Arisawa Hiromi, ed., *Gendai Nihon Sangyō Kōza* [Modern Japanese industry series] (Tokyo: Iwanami Shoten, 1960), 6:325.

6. Nihon Kōgakukai, *Meiji Kōgyō Shi: Kahei-hen Tekko-hen* [History of industry in the Meiji period: Armaments and steel edition] (Tokyo: Nihon Kōgakukai, 1929), 301; Ikeda, *Nihon,* 22.

7. Of 2,717 members of the Kiseikai in October, 1898, 2,620 were metalworkers. See *Nihon Rōdō Undō Shiryō* 1:415.

8. *Labor World,* no. 16 (July 15, 1898): 3.

9. Katayama Sen and Nishikawa Mitsujirō, *Nihon no Rōdō Undō* [The Japanese labor movement] (Tokyo: Iwanami Shoten, 1952; first published in 1901), 28–29; *Labor World,* no. 3 (January 1, 1898): 8. Mamie is mentioned as a fitter and Takahashi as a smith in Katayama Sen, *Jiden* [Autobiography] (Tokyo: Iwanami Shoten, 1954), 222.

10. Takano Fusatarō, "A New Trade Union in Japan," *American Federationist,*

4, no. 12 (February 1898): 272–273. Takano refers to Katayama as having an M.A. from Wisconsin University, but actually Katayama had received his M.A. degree *pro mento* from Grinnell College. See Kublin, *Asian Revolutionary*, 74.

11. Katayama and Nishikawa, *Nihon no Rōdō Undō*, 76.

12. Uttered by Captain John Smith in slightly different language ("he that shall not work shall not eat") in reference to idlers at Jamestown. See Richard T. Ely, *The Labor Movement in America* (New York: Macmillan, 1905), 7.

13. Quoted in the concluding introductory paragraph of the preamble to the constitution of the Employers' General Association of Michigan, which was singled out and highly recommended by the editor of the *Detroit Tribune:* "We cordially accept the principle that 'the laborer is worthy of his hire'—that he should be remunerated for his labour and so treated and provided for in general arrangement of society and of the body politic, as to enable him by diligence and fair economy to place himself and those dependent on him on a footing of intellectual and social equality with others." From the *Detroit Tribune,* (July 25, 1864), quoted in Fincher's, August 13, 1864. See also John R. Commons et al., *History of Labor in the United States* (New York, 1918), 2:26–28.

14. Sumiya Mikio, *Nihon Rōdō Undō Shi* [Japanese labor movement history] (Tokyo: Yūshindō, 1966), 35.

15. This representation was in proportion to membership. Branches of twenty-five to fifty members had one representative, and branches of over fifty members had one representative per fifty members. Katayama and Nishikawa, *Nihon no Rōdō Undō*, 145.

16. *Labor World*, no. 42 (August 15, 1899): 6–7.

17. Ikeda, *Nihon*, 56–57.

18. Original member definition per *Nihon Rōdō Undō Shiryō* 1:474. Constitution revision per article six of the constitution of the Metalworkers' Union, in *Labor World*, no. 40 (July 15, 1899): 4, and no. 42 (August 15, 1899): 6–7. The term "engineers" applies to railway engineers and workers in engineering jobs, not to industrial or technical engineers. The absence of an age restriction was determined at the fifth officers' meeting (December 18, 1898) "It was decided that there would be no lower age limit and that the upper age limit for membership would be 60 years." *Labor World*, no. 27 (January 1, 1899): 8 (English).

19. *Labor World*, no. 42 (August 15, 1899): 6.

20. Ikeda, *Nihon* 57.

21. Ibid., 58.

22. *Labor World*, no. 40 (July 15, 1899): 4; ibid., no. 42 (August 15, 1899): 6–7.

23. The Ōmiya branch, branch two, was another example of a branch covering a workplace with sub-branches for each shop. When it was founded it had no sub-branches, but as it grew it set up assembly, lathe, forger, and woodworker sub-branches. Later, the woodworker sub-branch grew so large that it became the thirty-ninth branch of the union. Again at Ōmiya, sub-branches were formed on a shop basis, grouping union members who shared the same occupation and worked in the same building. *Labor World*, no. 15 (July 15, 1899): 9; ibid., no. 20 (October 15, 1898): 6.

24. Katayama and Nishikawa, *Nihon no Rōdō Undō*, 79–80.

25. *Labor World*, no. 5 (February 1, 1898): 4.

26. Ikeda, *Nihon,* 58.

27. See Andrew Gordon, *The Evolution of Labor Relations in Japan: Heavy Industry, 1853–1955* (Cambridge, Mass.: Council on East Asian Studies, Harvard University, 1985), 18–50.

28. Takano Fusatarō, "New Trade Union," 272.

29. *Labor World,* no. 51 (December 15, 1899): 6–7.

30. For a translation of the mutual assistance provisions of the Metalworkers' Union, see the bylaws to the constitution of the Metalworkers' Union in appendix E.

31. *Labor World,* no. 14 (June 15, 1898): 4.

32. *Labor World,* no. 32 (March 15, 1899): 2. My translation.

33. *Nihon Rōdō Undō Shiryō* 1:516; *Labor World,* no. 42 (August 15, 1899): 2; ibid., no. 54 (February 1, 1900): 2.

CHAPTER 5

1. W. G. Beasley, *The Modern History of Japan* (New York: Praeger, 1963), 164–165.

2. Royama Masamichi, *Seiji Shi* [Political history], *Gendai Nihon Bunmei Shi* [History of contemporary Japanese civilization series] (Tokyo: Tōyō Keizai Shimpōsha, 1940), 334–335.

3. Robert A. Scalapino, *Democracy and the Party Movement in Prewar Japan* (Berkeley: University of California Press, 1962), 171–172.

4. It was during this period that Germany got a lease on Kiaochow, England leased Weihaiwei, Russia received Port Arthur and Dairen, and France was active in Kwangsi Province. Even the Liberty Party demanded that Japan either take part in this imperialistic plunder or take steps to curtail it. Beasley, *Modern History of Japan,* 166–167.

5. Scalapino, *Democracy,* 172–173.

6. Ibid., 173.

7. Beasley, *Modern History of Japan,* 164–165.

8. Rōdō Undō Shiryō Iinkai, ed., *Nihon Rōdō Undō Shiryō* [Collected documents on the Japanese labor movement] (Tokyo: Rōdō Undō Shiryō Kankō Iinkai, 1965), 2:45–46, hereinafter cited *Nihon Rōdō Undō Shiryō.*

9. Sumiya Mikio, "The Emergence of Modern Japan," in Ōkōchi Kazuo, Bernard Karsh, and Solomon B. Levine, eds., *Workers and Employers in Japan* (Tokyo: University of Tokyo Press, 1974), 39.

10. Distribution date from Ishida Rokujirō, "Taigū Kisei Dōmeikai Ichinoseki Shibu Kiji" [The story of the Ichinoseki branch of the Treatment Improvement Association] (1898), in *Nihon Rōdō Undō Shiryō* 2:17, 35. This pamphlet was written directly after the strike by one of its leaders and deals with the happenings at the Ichinoseki station. Note that Sumiya Mikio in his *Nihon Rōdō Undō Shi* [Japanese labor movement history] (Tokyo: Yūshindō, 1966), 27, incorrectly dates the distribution of this pamphlet as February 1897. Text of pamphlet from Ishida, "Taigū," 17, 19–20. My translation.

11. Sumiya, *Nihon Rōdō Undō Shi,* 29; *Nihon Rōdō Undō Shiryō* 2:45.

12. Ikeda Makoto, *Nihon Kikaikō Kumiai Seiritsu Shiron* [An historical trea-

tise on the formation of the machinists' unions in Japan] (Tokyo: Nihon Hyōron-sha, 1970), 70.

13. Ishida, "Taigū," 20. My translation.

14. Ibid., 20–21.

15. Sumiya, *Nihon Rōdō Undō Shi,* 29.

16. *Nihon Rōdō Undō Shiryō* 2:48. My translation.

17. Ishida, "Taigū," 24.

18. Ibid., 27–32.

19. Katayama Sen, "Great Strike in Japan," *Labor World,* no. 8 (March 15, 1898): 10.

20. Takano Fusatarō, "Great Railway Strike in Japan," *American Federationist* 5, no. 3 (May 1898): 48–50.

21. *Nihon Rōdō Undō Shiryō* 2:49–51; *Labor World,* no. 12 (May 15, 1898): 10; ibid., no. 15 (July 1, 1898): 3; ibid., no. 45 (October 1, 1899): 4–5; Kata-yama Sen, *Waga Kaisō* [My recollections] (Tokyo: Tokuma Shoten, 1967), 1:324.

22. Note that Hyman Kublin incorrectly translates the name of the union as Treatment Improvement Association in his book *Asian Revolutionary: The Life of Sen Katayama* (Princeton, 1964), 120. He also incorrectly gives the impression that the Kiseikai had a part in the organization of the engineers (ibid.).

23. *Nihon Rōdō Undō Shiryō* 1:610. My translation.

24. For a translation of the Reform Society constitution, see appendix F.

25. *Nihon Rōdō Undō Shiryō* 1:610. My translation.

26. Katayama Sen and Nishikawa Mitsujirō, *Nihon no Rōdō Undō* [The Jap-anese labor movement] (Tokyo: Iwanami Shoten, 1952; first published in 1901), 97.

27. *Labor World,* no. 69 (January 1, 1901): 4. My translation.

28. Sumiya, *Nihon Rōdō Undō Shi,* 37; *Labor World,* no. 33 (April 1, 1899): 1.

29. *Labor World,* no. 17 (August 1, 1898): 4.

30. *Labor World,* no. 17 (August 1, 1898): 4–5; ibid., no. 18 (August 15, 1898): 6; ibid., no. 19 (September 1, 1898): 3–4.

31. Katayama and Nishikawa, *Nihon no Rōdō Undō,* 79–80.

32. Ibid.; *Labor World,* no. 19 (September 1, 1898): 4. Katayama Sen toured the north again in 1899 from July 10 to July 31, speaking at all the major railway stops and also visiting Hokkaidō. *Labor World,* no. 41 (August 1, 1899): 4–6; ibid., no. 42 (August 15, 1899): 3–5; ibid., no. 43 (September 1, 1899): 4–5.

The concentration of Metalworkers' Union branches in the north was also due to the lack of Kiseikai efforts to organize metalworkers in southern Japan. Despite the fact that several activists of the Kiseikai and Metalworkers' Union moved to the Kobe-Osaka area prior to 1900, no efforts were made to organize workers there. The only time a Kiseikai leader spoke in southern Japan was when Takano spoke at a meeting sponsored by an organization of workers opposing immigration of Chinese workers in Kobe on July 31, 1899. See *Labor World,* no. 42 (August 15, 1899): 5.

33. *Labor World,* no. 6 (March 1, 1898): 5, 9.

34. *Labor World,* no. 10 (April 15, 1898): 5, 10; ibid., no. 11 (May 1, 1898): 5, 10; *Nihon Rōdō Undō Shiryō,* 633. One hundred eight men refused to go back

to work for the company and earned the name "Suikoden Gumi" ("The Suikoden Group"). Suikoden is the name of a very old Chinese story that was very popular in Japan in the feudal period. It dealt with a group of 108 men who had been imprisoned. They were all experts in the martial arts, and when they were released from prison they went their separate ways and all turned over a new leaf. Oppression of the people by a corrupt government officer caused them to reassemble, however, and oppose the government. When the government sought to suppress them it was defeated in open battle and, realizing its error, made the 108 men officers in its army, which was then attempting to hold back the northern barbarians. The 108 men successfully defended their country, but many were killed in battle. The remainder became heroes, but the chief minister, an evil, ambitious character, feared their popularity and poisoned them. They then became gods for their good deeds. Mizunuma Tatsuo, "Insatsukō Rōdō Undō Shi" [The history of the labor movement of the printers], *Jiyū Rengō Shimbun,* no. 27 (September 1, 1928): 2; Sekai Daihyakka Jiten [World encyclopedia] (Tokyo, 1957), 15:503–504.

35. One of these eleven had been fired and blacklisted in the earlier unionization attempt. See Katayama and Nishikawa, *Nihon no Rōdō Undō,* 98, 100.

36. For a translation of the rules of this organization, see appendix G.

37. Katayama and Nishikawa, *Nihon no Rōdō Undō,* 99, 100; *Nihon Rōdō Undō Shiryō* 1:631, 634. Katayama and Nishikawa give the date of the first issue of the association newspaper as September 28, but this is incorrect. See Mizunuma, "Insatsukō," no. 29:3.

38. Mizunuma, "Insatsukō," no. 29:3. My translation.

39. Katayama and Nishikawa, *Nihon no Rōdō Undō,* 101. Takeuchi Shinji, originally a director of the Workers' Life Insurance Company, was one of the mediators of the 1898 strike against the Japan Railway Company. See *Nihon Rōdō Undō Shiryō* 1:635.

40. For a review of the Japanese government's concern with factory legislation before 1897, see Ishii Ryōsuke, *Japanese Legislation in the Meiji Era* (Tokyo: Pan-Pacific Press, 1958), 559, translated and adapted by William J. Chambliss.

41. Kublin, *Asian Revolutionary,* 125.

42. This clause is not listed in the text of the factory law, which appears in *Labor World,* no. 22 (October 15, 1898): 6–7. However, there is evidence of its existence in Katayama and Nishikawa, *Nihon no Rōdō Undō,* 50, and later on in the same work by Takano. Thus it appears that the text of the law was abbreviated in *Labor World* and this clause was lost.

43. Takano Fusatarō, "Factory Legislation in Japan," *American Federationist* 5, no. 10 (December 1898): 200. For the complete text of the proposed factory act, see appendix H.

44. Takano, "Factory Legislation," 200–201.

45. There are four primary sources on these decisions: Takano, "Factory Legislation," 201; *Labor World,* no. 22 (October 15, 1898): 10; ibid., no. 21 (October 1, 1898): 8; and Katayama and Nishikawa, *Nihon no Rōdō Undō,* 48–50. These sources conflict as to what decisions were actually made. This list has been prepared by comparing and reconciling these four sources.

46. Henry Pelling, *A History of British Trade Unionism* (London: Macmillan and Co., 1963), 71, 80, 103; Helga Grebing, *The History of the German Labor*

Movement (London: Oswald Wolff, 1969), 55; Val R. Lorwin, *The French Labor Movement* (Cambridge, Mass.: Harvard University Press, 1954), 7, 27–28.

47. Don D. Leschohier and Elizabeth Brandeis, *History of Labor in the United States, 1896–1932* (New York, 1935), 3:403–405, 457, 540–542, 564, 611.

48. *Labor World,* no. 22 (October 15, 1898): 10.

49. *Labor World,* no. 24 (November 15, 1898): 6. Katayama and Nishikawa, *Nihon no Rōdō Undō,* 50, list the date of this occasion as November 5, but *Labor World* goes into detail on the problems caused by the religious festival so it is probably correct.

50. *Labor World,* no. 23 (November 1, 1898): 3; ibid., no. 24 (November 15, 1898): 6; also Katayama and Nishikawa, *Nihon no Rōdō Undō,* 52.

51. *Labor World,* no. 22 (October 15, 1898): 2, 10; also Katayama and Nishikawa, *Nihon no Rōdō Undō,* 50–51.

52. The third set of interviews started on October 22. Of the five calls made, two were refused and three were made when the members were away. *Labor World,* no. 22 (October 15, 1898): 2; ibid., no. 23 (November 1, 1898): 2; also Katayama and Nishikawa, *Nihon no Rōdō Undō,* 51.

53. See *Labor World,* no. 23 (November 1, 1898): 3–4, for the text of the petition.

54. Takano Fusatarō, "Japanese Factory Legislation," *American Federationist* 5, no. 11 (January 1899): 216.

55. Ibid.

56. Ibid.

57. Scalapino, *Democracy,* 175–176.

58. *Labor World,* no. 24 (November 15, 1898): 10. For an analysis of Sakuma Teiichi's writings and his thought, see Komatsu Ryūji, "Waga Kuni ni Okeru Rōdō Kumiai Shisō no Seisei: Sakuma Teiichi to Takano Fusatarō wo Chūshin ni" [The formation of labor union ideology in Japan: Centering on Sakuma Teiichi and Takano Fusatarō], in Institute of Management and Labor Studies, ed., *Management and Labor Studies Series,* no. 272 (Tokyo: Keiō University, 1969–1970), 137–159. For a description of work at Sakuma's company, the Shūeisha, see Takano Fusatarō, "Prospects of the Japanese Labor Movement," *American Federationist* 4, no. 9 (November 1897): 211.

59. Although Kublin states that the bill was presented to the Diet and "rejected with dispatch" (*Asian Revolutionary,* 127) it is clear that the bill was never brought before the Diet. See Katayama and Nishikawa, *Nihon no Rōdō Undō,* 52, who state: "The government . . . did not present it to the Diet . . . and again this year [1901] it will not be presented." My translation. See also *Labor World,* no. 26 (December 15, 1898): 10, for confirmation that the bill was never brought before the Diet.

CHAPTER 6

1. Takano Fusatarō, "Rodo Kumiai Kisei Kwai," *American Federationist* 6, no. 8 (October 1899): 188–189; Ikeda Makoto, "Nisshin Sensō-go no Shakai Seisaku Shisō" [Social policy ideology after the Sino-Japanese War], *Shakai Kagaku Ronshū* (Saitama University), no. 31 (January 1973): 74–75.

2. Takano Fusatarō, "Experience of a Labor Agitator in Japan," *American Federationist 5*, no. 1 (March 1898): 4.

3. Hyman Kublin, in his *Asian Revolutionary: The Life of Sen Katayama* (Princeton, N.J.: Princeton University Press, 1964), 121, gives the impression the date was changed before the police intervened, when actually it was done so only afterward.

4. *Labor World,* no. 10 (April 15, 1898): 4.

5. *Labor World,* no. 10 (April 15, 1898): 4, 10.

6. Kublin (*Asian Revolutionary,* 121) gives the number of participants as three hundred, which is incorrect. Contemporary accounts put the number of participants at eight hundred, although not all of these were union members. See *Labor World,* no. 11 (May 1, 1898): 5; Katayama Sen and Nishikawa Mitsujirō, *Nihon no Rōdō Undō* [The Japanese labor movement] (Tokyo: Iwanami Shoten, 1952; first published in 1901), 36. In any case, 488 adults and 114 children paid the attendance fee, and 508 lunches and 487 bottles of rice wine were provided by the union. See Rōdō Undō Shiryō Iinkai, ed., *Nihon Rōdō Undō Shiryō* [Collected documents on the Japanese labor movement] (Tokyo: Rōdō Undō Shiryō Kaukō Iinkai, 1962), 1:429, hereinafter cited *Nihon Rōdō Undō Shiryō.* Note that a typographical error appears in *Labor World,* no. 11 (May 1, 1898): 5, which indicates the festival took place on April 15 rather than April 10. The correct date is April 10. See Katayama and Nishikawa, *Nihon no Rōdō Undō,* 35.

7. See Hyman Kublin, *Asian Revolutionary: The Life of Sen Katayama* (Princeton, N.J.: Princeton University Press, 1964), 122, 129–156, 235–260.

8. Kublin (*Asian Revolutionary,* 129) states that the organization was founded in November 1898. Actually, its first meeting was held on October 18, 1898. See Akamatsu Katsumarō, *Nihon Shakai Undō Shi* [The history of Japanese social movements] (Tokyo: Iwanami Shoten, 1952), 69.

9. Akamatsu, *Nihon Shakai Undō Shi,* 70; also Hayashi Shigeru, "Nihon ni Okeru Shakaishugi Kenkyū Soshiki no Tanjō: Meiji 31-nen no Shakaishugi Kenkyūkai ni Tsuite" [The birth of an organization to study socialism in Japan: About the Society for the Study of Socialism of 1898], *Shakai Kagaku Kenkyū* (Tokyo University), no. 1 (February 1948): 59.

10. Of course, because Christianity represented the West and progressive thought to the Japanese, many intellectuals at the time were nominally Christians. Christianity shared with socialism certain basic points, thus making it easy to simultaneously advocate both. On this, see Abe Isō, "Shakaishugi to Kirisuto-kyō" [Socialism and Christianity], *Shinkigen,* no. 5 (March 1906), reprinted in Kishimoto Eitarō, ed., *Meiji Shakaishugi Shiron* [A treatise on the history of socialism in the Meiji period] (Tokyo, 1955), 172–180. Although the members of the Society for the Study of Socialism were all Christians, some, such as Murai, were only nominally Christians. Only Katayama was a true Christian, the rest of the members covering a broad spectrum between Buddhism and Unitarianism. Ishikawa Kyokuzan and Kōtoku Shūsui, "Nihon Shakaishugi Shi" [The history of Japanese socialism], serially in *Heimin Shimbun,* nos. 2–7, 9–14, 17–19, 25, 29–30, 36–37, 46–57 (January–March 1907), reprinted in Kishimoto, *Meiji Shakaishugi Shiron,* 9–84.

11. Abe Isō, one of the outstanding socialists of modern Japan, was born in 1865. After graduating from Dōshisha University in Kyoto, he studied at Hart-

ford Theological Seminary in the United States, as well as in Europe. He served as a Christian minister in Okayama for several years after he returned to Japan, and thereafter was a professor on the staff of Waseda University. Kublin, *Asian Revolutionary,* 133.

Born in 1871, Kōtoku Shūsui, as he came to be known [Shūsui was his pen name, Denjirō his actual name], became a socialist early on, and then an anarchist. He was an important leftist leader until 1911, when he was arrested and executed on charges of conspiring to assassinate the Emperor. See Kublin, *Asian Revolutionary,* 143–144, 152–153, 194, 207–208. At this time Kōtoku was a journalist for the *Yorozu Chōhō,* a popular newspaper.

12. Ishikawa and Kōtoku, "Nihon Shakaishugi Shi," 70; Hayashi, "Nihon ni Okeru Shakaishugi," 60; Akamatsu, *Nihon Shakai Undō Shi,* 70.

13. Article Two of the rules. See Akamatsu, *Nihon Shakai Undō Shi,* 69. Translation from Kublin, *Asian Revolutionary,* 129.

14. Article Four of the rules. See Akamatsu, *Nihon Shakai Undō Shi,* 69. Translation from Kublin, *Asian Revolutionary,* 129.

15. Ishikawa and Kōtoku, "Nihon Shakaishugi Shi," 72, 80–81; Akamatsu, *Nihon Shakai Undō Shi,* 69. For Katayama's articles in *Labor World,* see no. 27 (January 1, 1899): 5, and each subsequent issue.

16. Shin undertook the construction of an engine under the subcontracting system. He received 78 yen in payment, of which 9 yen 48 sen went to pay the regular wages of the workers, with another 7 yen 58 sen paid as a bonus. Shin kept the remainder. *Labor World,* no. 50 (December 1, 1899): 5.

17. Saitama-Ken Rōdōbu Rōseika, *Saitama-Ken Rōdō Undō Shi* [History of the labor movement in Saitama Prefecture], prewar volume (Tokyo: Saitama-Ken Rōdōbu Rōseika, 1965), 19–23; also *Labor World,* no. 16 (July 15, 1898): 3.

18. Ikeda Makoto, *Nihon Kikaikō Kumiai Seiritsu Shiron* [An historical treatise on the formation of the machinists' unions in Japan] (Tokyo: Nihon Hyōronsha, 1970), 88; Katayama and Nishikawa, *Nihon no Rōdō Undō,* 82.

19. *Labor World,* no. 25 (December 1, 1898): 8–9; ibid., no. 30 (February 15, 1899): 3–4.

20. *Labor World,* no. 30 (February 15, 1899): 4. My translation.

21. *Labor World,* no. 31 (March 1, 1899): 10 (English). What Katayama meant to say was that the membership doubled. Of interest here is the comment that "at the Ōmiya Factory . . . there are Christians. . . . " This would make Sunday holidays particularly important. See ibid., no. 3. My translation.

22. *Labor World,* no. 33 (April 1, 1899): 4; ibid., no. 34 (April 15, 1899): 4. There had been two separate but affiliated mutual assistance organizations, one for fitters and the other for lathe operators. See Ikeda, *Nihon Kikaikō Kumiai Seiritsu Shiron,* 38, 41.

23. Katayama and Nishikawa, *Nihon no Rōdō Undō,* 101.

24. Ibid.; *Nihon Rōdō Undō Shiryō* 1:636–639.

25. *Labor World,* no. 34 (April 15, 1899): 4.

26. *Nihon Rōdō Undō Shiryo* 1:638.

27. Shimada was ex-vice-president of the lower house of the Diet. *Labor World,* no. 19 (September 1, 1898): 10. He was also a liberal journalist and became a Christian. See Kublin, *Asian Revolutionary,* 113; *Labor World,* no. 52 (January 1, 1900): 10.

28. *Labor World,* no. 46 (October 15, 1899): 4. This is a transcript of the speech Katayama gave at the July 9 meeting. My translation.

29. *Labor World,* no. 46 (October 15, 1899): 4–5. This is a transcript of the speech Professor Kanai gave at the rally. My translation.

30. Ikeda Makoto, "Nisshin Sengoki no Shakai Seisaku Shisō" [Social policy ideology after the Sino-Japanese War], *Shakai Kagaku Ronshū* (Saitama University), no. 31 (January 1973): 38, 42, 62.

31. *Labor World,* no. 34 (April 15, 1899): 7. My translation.

32. Katayama Sen, "Kongo no Rōdō Undō" [The future labor movement], *Rikugō Zasshi,* no. 225 (September 1899): 15. My translation.

33. The employers wanted changes due to the fact that minors could not be treated as workers under the law. See *Nihon Rōdō Undō Shiryō* 1:651–652. See also Katayama and Nishikawa, *Nihon no Rōdō Undō,* 106.

34. *Nihon Rōdō Undō Shiryō* 1:652; Katayama and Nishikawa, *Nihon no Rōdō Undō,* 106.

35. Katayama and Nishikawa, *Nihon no Rōdō Undō,* 283. My translation.

36. Sumiya Mikio, *Nihon Rōdō Undō Shi* [Japanese labor movement history] (Tokyo: Yūshindō, 1966), 55; Katayama and Nishikawa, *Nihon no Rōdō Undō,* 106.

37. Katayama and Nishikawa, *Nihon no Rōdō Undō,* 107.

38. Quote is from *Labor World,* no. 47 (November 1, 1899): 8. Emphasis as in original.

See appendix I for a translation of the Printers' Union constitution. "Excluding non-members" probably refers to a clause reported to have been in the constitution of the Printers' Union in an article in *Labor World* on September 15, 1899. Since this article was published prior to the October 10 revision of the constitution, it is conceivable that this clause was revised or dropped. The clause is reproduced here: "Each printing workshop owned by members of the employers' association shall, as a policy, employ workers who are union members, now that the Printers' Union has been formed." *Labor World,* no. 44 (September 15, 1899): 2. My translation.

39. Takano Fusatarō, "Rōdō Kumiai Kisei Kwai," *American Federationist* 6, no. 8 (October 1899): 189. The role of the Kiseikai in the formation of the Printers' Union has often been exaggerated by Japanese scholars. See Sumiya, *Nihon Rōdō Undō Shi,* 37–38, 46–48, 55–56.

CHAPTER 7

1. My summary. See *Labor World,* no. 43 (September 1, 1899): 7 for detailed provisions.

2. *Labor World,* no. 3 (January 1, 1898): 8; ibid., no. 15 (July 1, 1898): 8; ibid., no. 27 (January 1, 1899): 8; ibid., no. 40 (July 15, 1899): 6.

3. *Labor World,* no. 3 (January 1, 1898): 8; ibid., no. 10 (April 15, 1898): 8; ibid., no. 14 (June 15, 1898): 8; ibid., no. 15 (July 1, 1898): 6; ibid., no. 40 (July 15, 1899): 6. For turnover in membership see table 11.

4. *Labor World,* no. 46, supplement (October 15, 1899): 2.

5. Whether Sawano had learned of their attempts to rectify his behavior is not

clear. *Labor World,* no. 48 (November 15, 1899): 2; ibid., no. 51 (December 15, 1899): 6.

6. *Labor World,* no. 48 (November 15, 1899): 2; Katayama Sen and Nishikawa Mitsujirō, *Nihon no Rōdō Undō* [The Japanese labor movement] (Tokyo: Iwanami Shoten, 1952; first published in 1901), 84–85.

7. *Labor World,* no. 48 (November 15, 1899): 2–3.

8. This is clear from the uninformed nature of the articles in *Labor World* on the Ōmiya affair, which appeared directly after its occurrence. See *Labor World,* no. 48 (November 15, 1899): 2–3.

9. Katayama and Nishikawa, *Nihon no Rōdō Undō,* 85.

10. Ibid.

11. The full text of this petition can be found in *Labor World,* no. 51 (December 15, 1899): 6. The entire text of the bills posted by the company can be found in Katayama and Nishikawa, *Nihon no Rōdō Undō,* 85–86. My translation.

12. *Labor World,* no. 51 (December 15, 1899): 4, 10; Katayama and Nishikawa, *Nihon no Rōdō Undō,* 86; Saitama-Ken Rōdōbu Rōseika, *Saitama-Ken Rōdō Undō Shi* [History of the labor movement in Saitama Prefecture], prewar volume (Tokyo: Saitama-Ken Rōdōbu Rōseika, 1965), 23–29, hereinafter cited *Saitama.*

13. *Labor World,* no. 55, supplement (February 15, 1900): 3.

14. *Labor World,* no. 62 (June 1, 1900): 5.

15. *Labor World,* no. 51 (December 15, 1899): 10; ibid., no. 52 (January 1, 1900): 10.

16. Shōji Kichinosuke, "Nittetsu Kikangata—Shokukō Dōmei Higyō no Igi" [The engineers of the Japan Railway Company—The significance of the strike], *Shōgaku Ronshū* 36, no. 4 (March 1968): 119–125.

17. See *Labor World,* no. 57 (March 15, 1900): 2; ibid., no. 58 (April 1, 1900): 4.

18. *Labor World,* no. 59 (April 15, 1900): 2. The petition has been abbreviated here. Under each request there appears explanation and clarification. My translation.

19. Shōji, "Nittetsu Kikangata—Shokukō Dōmei Higyō no Igi," 125.

20. *Labor World,* no. 58 (April 1, 1900): 4; ibid., no. 59 (April 15, 1900): 1–2; ibid., no. 60 (May 1, 1900): 3.

21. George E. Uyehara, *The Political Development of Japan, 1867–1909* (London: London School of Economics, 1910), 182. For a description of the provisions of the Peace Preservation Regulations, see Ishii Ryōsuke, *Japanese Legislation in the Meiji Era* (Tokyo: Pan-Pacific Press, 1958), 468–470.

22. Ishii, *Japanese Legislation,* 467–468, 556.

23. This translation, with minor grammatical corrections, is from Ayusawa Iwao, *A History of Labor in Modern Japan* (Honolulu: East-West Center Press, 1966), 71. The complete text of the Peace Police Act (March 10, 1900, Law No. 36), known in Japanese as the Chian Keisatsu Hō, can be found in Hioki Norio et al., *Nihon Hanrei Taisei* [A compendium of the laws of Japan], 24 vols. (Tokyo: Hibonkaku, 1935–1937), 22: 37–52.

24. This is from a presentation by a government official before the Tenth Diet Special Committee for the Investigation of Proposed Laws on February 16, 1900.

Quote from Rōdō Undō Shiryō Iinkai, ed., *Nihon Rōdō Undō Shiryō* [Collected documents on the Japanese labor movement] (Tokyo: Rōdō Undō Shiryō Kankō Iinkai, 1962), 1:746, hereinafter cited *Nihon Rōdō Undō Shiryō*. My translation.

25. Hyman Kublin, *Asian Revolutionary: The Life of Sen Katayama* (Princeton, N.J.: Princeton University Press, 1964), 140.

26. *Nihon Rōdō Undō Shiryō* 1:652.

27. *Insatsu Zasshi* 9, no. 12 (February 28, 1900), in *Nihon Rōdō Undō Shiryō* 1:653.

28. *Mainichi Shimbun* (February 25, 1900), in *Nihon Rōdō Undō Shiryō* 1:653. My translation.

29. *Labor World*, no. 55 (February 15, 1900): 2.

30. Katayama and Nishikawa, *Nihon no Rōdō Undō*, 107–108.

31. What was actually meant was adult manhood suffrage, but Katayama Sen in English refers to this as "universal suffrage" in all his writings, so his usage has been adopted.

32. *Labor World*, no. 57 (March 15, 1900): 6.

33. *Labor World*, no. 58 (April 1, 1900): 6; ibid., no. 59 (April 15, 1900): 8.

34. *Labor World*, no. 63 (July 1, 1900): 6; also Katayama and Nishikawa, *Nihon no Rōdō Undō*, 59.

35. *Labor World*, no. 59 (April 15, 1900): 4.

36. Katayama Sen, *Waga Kaisō* [My recollections], (Tokyo: Tokuma Shoten, 1967), 1:59.

37. *Saitama*, prewar volume, 33–34.

38. Sumiya Mikio, *Nihon Rōdō Undō Shi* [Japanese labor movement history] (Tokyo: Yūshindō, 1966), 62.

39. *Labor World*, no. 65 (September 1, 1900): 6, 8 (on Takano); ibid., no. 63 (July 1, 1900): 6 (on Ozawa). See ibid., no. 57 (March 15, 1900): 8, for a description of Shimada's many activities.

40. *Labor World*, no. 68 (December 1, 1900): 8.

41. Katayama and Nishikawa, *Nihon no Rōdō Undō*, 117–120.

42. *Labor World*, no. 75 (April 3, 1901): 4; ibid., no. 77 (May 1, 1901): 8.

43. Sakai Toshihiko, born in 1870, was a schoolteacher turned journalist. Strongly affected by the radical philosophical currents of the late nineteenth century, he became a well-known social critic and one of the first systematic students of Western socialism. He founded the Japanese Communist Party in 1922. Kublin, *Asian Revolutionary*, 143.

44. Kublin dates the start of such plans from the spring of 1900 (ibid., 144) but Japanese scholars date plans for the new party from the spring of 1901. See Akamatsu Katsumarō, *Nihon Shakai Undō Shi* [The history of Japanese social movements] (Tokyo: Iwanami Shoten, 1952), 69.

45. Kublin, *Asian Revolutionary*, 76.

46. "It [the platform] contains a long preliminary discussion on the defects of the present social regime . . . modelled on the manifesto of the Communist Party as formulated by Karl Marx and Frederick Engels in 1848." Karl Kiyoshi Kawakami, *The Political Ideas of Modern Japan* (Iowa City, 1903), 187. Kawakami also gives an English translation of the text of the manifesto (564–565). The Jap-

anese text of the program appears in Kishimoto Eitarō, ed., *Meiji Shakai Undō Shisō* [The ideology of social movements in the Meiji period] (Tokyo: Aoki Shoten, 1955), 155–159.

47. Kublin, *Asian Revolutionary,* 144–145.

48. Ibid., 145–146.

49. Ibid., 146.

50. Ibid., 146–148.

51. *Labor World,* no. 66 (October 1, 1900): 2; see *Nihon Rōdō Undō Shiryō* 1:609–610, for an analysis that puts weight on the Peace Police Act of 1900 as an important factor in the change in the attitude of the Japan Railway Company.

52. *Nihon Rōdō Undō Shiryō* 1:621, 626–627.

53. The events of this affair are clearly set forth in a series of articles in the *Mainichi Shimbun,* which appear in *Nihon Rōdō Undō Shiryō* 1:625–628.

CHAPTER 8

1. *Labor World,* no. 65 (September 1, 1900): 6, 8; ibid., no. 69 (January 1, 1901): 16; ibid., no. 75 (April 3, 1901): 8; Hyman Kublin, *Meiji Rōdō Undō Shi no Hitokoma—Takano Fusatarō no Shōgai to Shisō* [One aspect of the history of the Meiji period labor movement—The life and thought of Takano Fusatarō] (Tokyo: Yūhikaku, 1959), 52; Shimoide Shunkichi, *Meiji Shakai Shisō Kenkyū* [Studies in Meiji period social thought] (Tokyo: Asano Shoten, 1932), 245.

2. Previously *Labor World.*

3. Yokoyama Gennosuke (under the pen name Tenshō Bōbōsei), "Takano Fusatarō wo Omou" [Thinking of Takano Fusatarō], *Tōyō Dōtetsu Zasshi* 1, no. 1 (June 1904).

4. Hyman Kublin, *Asian Revolutionary: The Life of Sen Katayama* (Princeton, N.J.: Princeton University Press, 1964), 157–243.

5. Ibid., 249–336.

6. Ibid., 337–338.

7. The curious reader will find a history of the Yūaikai and Suzuki Bunji in Stephen S. Large, *The Yūaikai: The Rise of Labor in Japan, 1912–1919* (Tokyo: Sophia University, 1972).

8. Suzuki Bunji, *Rōdō Undō Nijū-nen* [Twenty years of the labor movement] (Tokyo: Sōdōmei Gojūnenshi Kankō Iinkai, 1931), 22.

9. Ibid., 70. My translation.

10. Ibid., 30.

11. Ibid., 65.

12. Ibid., 66.

13. Large, *Yūaikai,* 15.

14. Ibid., 44–49.

BIBLIOGRAPHY

English Sources

Abegglen, James, C. *The Japanese Factory: Aspects of Its Social Organization.* Glencoe, Ill.: Free Press, 1958.

Allen, George Cyril. *A Short Economic History of Modern Japan, 1867–1937.* London: Allen and Unwin, 1972.

American Federation of Labor. *History, Encyclopedia Reference Book.* Washington: American Federation of Labor, 1919.

Ayusawa, Iwao. *A History of Labor in Modern Japan.* Honolulu: East-West Center Press, 1966.

Beasley, W. G. *The Modern History of Japan.* New York: Praeger, 1963.

Beckmann, George M. *The Making of the Meiji Constitution.* Lawrence, Kans.: University Press of Kansas, 1957.

Birdsall, William C. "The Problem of Structure in the Knights of Labor." *Industrial and Labor Relations Review* 6, no. 4 (July 1958): 532–536.

Brody, David. *Steelworkers in America: The Nonunion Era.* Cambridge, Mass.: Harvard University Press, 1960.

Clark, Rodney. *Social Relations in a Japanese Company,* Ph.D. diss., University of London, 1972.

Clark, W. A. Graham. *Cotton Goods in Japan.* Washington: U.S. Department of Commerce, 1914.

Clegg, H. A., Alan Fox, and A. F. Thompson. *A History of British Trade Unions since 1889,* vol. 1. Oxford: Clarendon Press, 1964.

Cole, G. D. H. *An Introduction to Trade Unionism.* London: George Allen and Unwin, 1953.

———. *A Short History of the British Working-Class Movement.* London: George Allen and Unwin, 1947.

Cole, Robert E. *Japanese Blue Collar.* Berkeley: University of California Press, 1971.

249

Commons, John R., et al. *History of Labor in the United States,* 2 vols. New York: Macmillan, 1918.

Conroy, Hilary. "*Chōsen Mondai*: The Korean Problem in Meiji Japan." *American Philosophical Society, Proceedings* 100 (October 1956): 443–454.

Cook, Alice Hanson. *An Introduction to Japanese Trade Unionism.* Ithaca, N.Y.: New York State School of Industrial and Labor Relations, 1966.

De Bary, Theodore, Tsunoda Ryusaku, and Donald Keene. *Sources of Japanese Tradition.* New York: Columbia University Press, 1958.

Den, Kenjirō. "Japanese Communications: The Post, Telegraph and Telephone." In Ōkuma, Shigenobu, *Fifty Years of New Japan* 1: 408–423. London: Smith, Elder, 1909.

Department of State. *Commercial Relations of the United States with Foreign Countries during the Years 1895 and 1896,* vol. 1. Washington: Department of State, 1897.

Dobb, Maurice Herbert. *Wages.* Cambridge: Cambridge University Press, 1960.

Dore, Ronald. *City Life in Japan: A Study of a Tokyo Ward.* London: Routledge and Paul, 1958.

———. *Land Reform in Japan.* London: Oxford University Press, 1959.

———. *British Factory—Japanese Factory: The Origins of National Diversity in Industrial Relations.* Berkeley: University of California Press, 1973.

Ely, Richard T. *The Labor Movement in America.* New York: Macmillan, 1905.

Evans, Robert, Jr. "Evolution of the Japanese System of Employer—Employee Relations, 1868–1945." *Business History Review* 44, no. 1 (Spring 1970): 1101–1125.

Feldman, Horace Z. "The Meiji Political Novel: A Brief Survey." *The Far East Quarterly* 9, no. 3 (May 1950): 245–255.

Fujii, Jintarō. *Outline of Japanese History in the Meiji Era,* translated and adapted by Hattie K. Colton and Kenneth E. Colton. Tokyo: Ōbunsha, 1958.

Galenson, Walter, and Seymour Martin Lipset, eds. *Labor and Trade Unionism: An Interdisciplinary Reader.* New York, 1960.

Gompers, Samuel. *Seventy Years of Life and Labor,* 2 vols. New York: E. P. Dutton and Co., 1925.

Gordon, Andrew. *The Evolution of Labor Relations in Japan: Heavy Industry, 1853–1955.* Cambridge, Mass.: Council on East Asian Studies, Harvard University, 1985.

Grebing, Helga. *The History of the German Labor Movement.* London: Oswald Wolff, 1969.

Gunton, George. *Wealth and Progress.* New York: Appleton, 1887.

Harrison, Martin. *Trade Unions and the Labour Party since 1945.* London: Allen and Unwin, 1960.

Hirschmeier, Johannes. "Shibusawa Eiichi: Industrial Pioneer." In William W. Lockwood, ed., *The State and Economic Enterprise in Japan,* 208–248. 1965.

———. "The Japanese Spirit of Enterprise, 1867–1970." *Business History Review* 44, no. 1 (Spring 1970): 13–38.

Horie, Yasuzō. "Modern Entrepreneurship in Meiji Japan." In William W. Lockwood, ed., *The State and Economic Enterprise in Japan,* 183–208. 1965.

———. "The Role of the *Ie* (House) in the Economic Modernization of Japan." *Kyoto University Economic Review* 36, no. 80 (April 1966): 1–16.

Hovell, Mark. *The Chartist Movement.* Manchester: Manchester University Press, 1918.

Hoxie, Robert Franklin. *Trade Unionism in the United States.* New York: D. Appleton and Co., 1920.

Iddittie, Junesay. *The Life of Marquis Shigenobu Ōkuma: A Biographical Study in the Rise of Democratic Japan.* Tokyo: Hokuseido Press, 1956.

Ike, Nobutaka. "Triumph of the Peace Party in Japan in 1873." *Far Eastern Quarterly* 2, no. 3 (May 1942): 286–295.

Inoue, Masaru. "Japanese Communications: Railroads." In Ōkuma, Shigenobu, *Fifty Years of New Japan,* vol. 1: 424–446. 1909.

Ishii, Ryōsuke. *Japanese Legislation in the Meiji Era,* translated and adapted by William J. Chambliss. Tokyo: Pan-Pacific Press, 1958.

Jansen, Marius B. *Sakamoto Ryōma and the Meiji Restoration.* Princeton, N.J.: Princeton University Press, 1961.

Jeakes, John, and E. M. Gray. *Wages and Labour in the Lancashire Cotton Spinning Industry.* Manchester, 1935.

Kahn, Herman. "Some Problems in the Writing of Labor History." In Industrial Relations Research Assoc., *Proceedings of the Eighteenth Annual Winter Meeting,* 324–332. New York: Industrial Relations Research Assoc., 1965.

Katayama, Sen. "The Labor Movement and Socialism in Japan." *International Socialist Review* 2, no. 3 (September 1901): 188–191.

———. *The Labour Movement in Japan.* Chicago: C. H. Kerr and Co., 1918.

Kawakami, Karl Kiyoshi. "Socialism in Japan." *International Socialist Review* 2, no. 8 (February 1902): 561–569.

———. *The Political Ideas of Modern Japan.* Iowa City: University of Iowa, 1903.

Kerr, Clark, John T. Dunlop, Frederick H. Harbison, and Charles A. Myers. *Industrialism and Industrial Man: The Problems of Labor and Management in Economic Growth.* Cambridge, Mass.: Harvard University Press, 1960.

Kishimoto, Eitarō. "The Characteristics of Labor-Management Relations in Japan and Their Historical Formation." In two parts, *Kyoto University*

Economic Review 35, no. 79 (October 1965–1966): 33–55 and 36, no. 80 (April): 17–38.

Knox, John Ballenger. *The Sociology of Industrial Relations: An Introduction to Industrial Sociology.* New York: Random House, 1955.

Kō, Sung Jae. *Stages of Industrial Development in Asia; A Comparative History of the Cotton Industry in Japan, India, China and Korea.* Philadelphia: University of Pennsylvania Press, 1966.

Kōsaka, Masaaki. *Japanese Thought in the Meiji Era,* translated and adapted by David Abosch. Tokyo: Pan-Pacific Press, 1958.

Kublin, Hyman. "Takano Fusataro: A Study in Early Japanese Trades-Unionism." *American Philosophical Society, Proceedings* 103 (August 1959): 571–583.
———. *Asian Revolutionary: The Life of Sen Katayama.* Princeton, N.J.: Princeton University Press, 1964.

Landes, David S. "Japan and Europe: Contrast in Industrialization." In William W. Lockwood, ed., *The State and Economic Enterprise in Japan,* 93–182. 1965.

Large, Stephen S. *The Yūaikai: The Rise of Labor in Japan, 1912–1919.* Tokyo: Sophia University, 1972.

Lebra, Joyce C. "Ōkuma Shigenobu and the 1881 Political Crisis." *Journal of Asian Studies* 18, no. 4 (August 1959): 475–487.

Leschohier, Don D., and Elizabeth Brandeis. *History of Labor in the United States, 1896–1932.* New York, 1935.

Levine, Solomon Bernard. *Industrial Relations in Japan.* Urbana, Ill.: University of Illinois Press, 1958.
———. "Labor Markets and Collective Bargaining in Japan." In William W. Lockwood, ed., *The State and Economic Enterprise in Japan,* 633–667. 1965.

Lockwood, William W. *The Economic Development of Japan: Growth and Structural Change.* Princeton, N.J.: Princeton University Press, 1968.

Lockwood, William W., ed. *The State and Economic Enterprise in Japan: Essays in the Political Economy of Growth.* Princeton, N.J.: Princeton University Press, 1965.

Lorwin, Val R. *The French Labor Movement.* Cambridge, Mass.: Harvard University Press, 1954.

McLaren, Walter Wallace, ed. "Japanese Government Documents, 1867–1889," part 1 of *Transactions of the Asiatic Society of Japan,* vol. 42. Tokyo: Asiatic Society of Japan, 1914.

Ministry of Labor. *Labour Administration in Japan.* Tokyo: Rōdō Hōrei Kyōkai Foundation, 1980.

Musson, A. E. *The Typographical Association: Origins and History up to 1949.* London, 1954.

Nakane, Chie. *Japanese Society.* London: Wiedenfeld and Nicolson, 1970.

Ōkōchi, Kazuo. *Labor in Modern Japan.* Tokyo: The Science Council of Japan, Division of Economics, Commerce and Business Administration, 1958.
———. "Traditionalism of Industrial Relations in Japan." In Japan Institute of Labour, ed., *The Changing Patterns of Industrial Relations,* 126–141. Tokyo, Japan Institute of Labour, 1965.

Ōkōchi, Kazuo, Bernard Karsh, and Solomon B. Levine, eds. *Workers and Employers in Japan.* Tokyo: University of Tokyo Press, 1974.

Ōkuma, Shigenobu. "The Industrial Revolution in Japan." *North American Review* 171 (November 1900): 677–691.
———. *Fifty Years of New Japan,* ed. Marcus B. Huish, vol. 1. London: Smith, Elder, 1909.

Pelling, Henry. *A History of British Trade Unionism.* London: Macmillan and Co., 1963.

Reed, Louis S. *The Labor Philosophy of Samuel Gompers.* Port Washington, N.Y.: Kennikat Press, 1930.

Robbins, Lionel. *The Theory of Economic Policy.* London: Macmillan and Co., 1953.

Robinson, Joan, and John Eatwell. *An Introduction to Modern Economics.* Maidenhead, England, 1973.

Rosovsky, Henry. "Japan's Transition to Modern Economic Growth, 1868–1885." In Henry Rosovsky, ed., *Industrialization in Two Systems,* 91–139. New York: J. Wiley, 1966.

Sait, Edward M. *American Parties and Elections.* New York, 1927.

Sakurabayashi, Makoto, and Robert Ballon, Jr. "Labor Management Relations in Modern Japan: A Historical Survey of Personnel Administration." In Joseph Roggendorf, ed., *Studies in Japanese Culture,* 245–266. Tokyo: Sophia University, 1963.

Sansom, Sir George. *Japan—A Short Cultural History.* London: Cresset Press, 1931.

Scalapino, Robert A. *Democracy and the Party Movement in Prewar Japan.* Berkeley: University of California Press, 1962.
———. "Labor and Politics in Postwar Japan." In William W. Lockwood, ed., *The State and Economic Enterprise in Japan,* 669–720. 1965.

Seki, Keizō. *The Cotton Industry of Japan.* Tokyo: Japan Society for the Promotion of Science, 1956.

Shibusawa, Keizō. *Japanese Society in the Meiji Era,* translated and adapted by Aora H. Culbertson and Kimura Michiko. Tokyo: Pan-Pacific Press, 1958.

Smith, Thomas C. *Political Change and Industrial Development in Japan: Government Enterprise 1868–1880.* Stanford: Stanford University Press, 1955.

Taft, Phillip. *The American Federation of Labor in the Time of Gompers.* New York: Harper and Row, 1957.

Taira, Kōji. "The Characteristics of Japanese Labor Markets." *Economic Development and Cultural Change* 10, no. 2, part 1 (January 1962): 150–168.
———. "Factory Legislation and Management Modernization during Japan's Industrialization 1886–1916." *Business History Review* 44, no. 1 (Spring 1970): 84–109.

Tweney, C. F., and I. P. Shirshov, eds. *Hutchinson's Technical and Scientific Encyclopedia,* vol. 4. London: Hutchinson, 1935.

Uyehara, George E. *The Political Development of Japan, 1867–1909.* In Studies in Economics and Political Science Series, ed. W. A. S. Hewins, vol. 19. London: London School of Economics, 1910.

Webb, Sidney, and Beatrice Webb. *The History of Trade Unions.* London: Longmans, Green, 1920.
———. *Industrial Democracy.* London: Longmans, Green, 1920.

Wilkinson, Thomas O. *The Urbanization of Japanese Labor, 1868–1955.* Amherst, Mass.: University of Massachusetts, 1965.

Yanaga, Chitoshi. *Japan Since Perry.* New York: McGraw-Hill, 1949.

Yoshino, M. Y. *Japan's Managerial System.* Cambridge, Mass.: MIT Press, 1968.

Japanese Sources

Abe Isō. "Shakaishugi to Kirisutokyō" [Socialism and Christianity]. *Shinkigen,* no. 5 (March 1906). Reprinted in Kishimoto Eitarō, ed., *Meiji Shakaishugi Shiron* [A treatise on the history of socialism in the Meiji period], 172–180. Tokyo: Aoki Shoten, 1955.

Akamatsu Katsumarō. *Nihon Shakai Undō Shi* [The history of Japanese social movements]. Tokyo: Iwanami Shoten, 1952.

Aono Gon'emon. *Nihon Seitō Hensen Shi* [A history of changes in Japanese parties]. Tokyo: Ankyūsha, 1935.

Asahi Shinbunsha. *Meiji Taishō Shi* [History of the Meiji and Taisho eras], 6 vols. Tokyo: Asahi Shinbunsha, 1930.

Dai Ikkai Naikoku Kangyō Hakurankai Tokyo-fu Iin. *Meiji Jyūnen Fuken Kangyō Chakushu Gaikyō* [The overview of the early attempts to stimulate industry in the prefectures in 1877]. In Tsuchiya Takao, ed., *Gendai Nihon Kōgyō Shi Shiryō* [Documents on the history of modern Japanese industry], 1: 1–214. Tokyo: Rōdōbunkasha, 1949.

Dai Nippon Bōseki Kabushiki Kaisha. *Dai Nippon Bōseki Kabushiki Kaisha Gojūnen Shi* [Fifty years history of the Dai Nippon Spinning Company]. Osaka: Dai Nippon Bōseki Kabushiki Kaisha, 1941.

Endō Masao. *Nihon Kinsei Shogyō Shihon Hattatsu Shiron* [An historical treatise on the development of modern commerical capital in Japan]. Tokyo:
Nihon Hyōronsha, 1936.

————. "Meiji Shoki ni Okeru Rōdōsha no Jōtai—Gunjuteki Sho Sangyō ni
Okeru Rōdō Jijō" [The conditions of workers in the early Meiji period—
Conditions of labor in the various military industries]. In Meiji Shiryō
Kenkyū Renrakukai, ed., *Meiji Zenki no Rōdō Mondai,* Meiji-shi
Kenkyū Gyōsho series, second period, supplemental vol. a, 43–95. 1960.

Etō Tsuneharu. "Koyū no Mengyō to Yōshiki no Ishoku" [The traditional cotton
industry and the importation of the Western cotton industry]. *Keizai Shi
Kenkyū* 19, no. 6 (June 1938): 1–16.

Fujibayashi Keizō. "Meiji Nijū Nendai ni Okeru Waga Bōsekigyō Rōdōsha no
Idō Genshō ni Tsuite" [On the phenomenon of labor turnover among cot-
ton spinning workers in the Meiji twenties]. In Meiji Shiryō Kenkyū
Renrakukai, ed., *Meiji Zenki no Rōdō Mondai,* Meiji-shi Kenkyū
Gyōsho series, second period, supplemental vol. 1, 137–176. 1960.

Fukaya Hakuji. *Shoki Gikai Jōyaku Kaisei* [The first Diets: Treaty revision], Kindai Nihon Rekishi Kōza [Modern Japanese History Series]. Tokyo:
Hakuyōsha, 1940.

"Gumma Ken Shanshigyō Enkaku Shōsa Hōkoku Sho" [Investigation of and
information on the course of the development of the silk-reeling industry
in Gumma Prefecture]. In Yasuoka Shinshi, *Maebashi Hanjōki* [Chroni-
cle of the prosperity of Maebashi]. Tokyo: Miyama Bunko, 1891.

Hayashi Shigeru. "Nihon ni Okeru Shakaishugi Kenkyū Soshiki no Tanjō: Meiji
31-nen no Shakaishugi Kenkyūkai ni Tsuite" [The birth of an organization to study socialism in Japan: About the Society for the Study of
Socialism of 1898], *Shakai Kagaku Kenkyū* (Tokyo University), no. 1:
58–100 (February 1948).

Hayashida Kametarō. *Nihon Seitō Shi* [History of Japanese political parties], vol.
1. Tokyo: Dai Nihon Yūben Kaikōdansha, 1927.

Hazama Hiroshi. *Nihon Rōmu Kanri Shi Kenkyū* [A study of the history of Japanese labor administration]. Tokyo: Daiyamondosha, 1974.

Hioki Norio, et al. *Nihon Hanrei Taisei* [A compendium of the laws of Japan], 24
vols. Tokyo: Hibonkaku, 1935–1937.

Hirano Yoshitarō. *Nihon Shihonshugi no Kikō to Hōritsu* [The structures and
laws of Japanese capitalism]. Tokyo: Meizenshobō, 1948.

Honjō Eitarō, ed. *Meiji Ishin Keizai Shi Kenkyū* [Studies of the economic history
of the Meiji restoration period]. Tokyo: Kaizōsha, 1930.

Horie Yasuzō. *Nihon Shihonshugi no Seiritsu* [The formation of Japanese capital-
ism]. Osaka: Taidōshoin, 1939.

Hozumi Yatsuka. *Ie no Hōri-teki Kannen* [The juridical concept of the family].
Tokyo, 1898. In Ineseki Shigemasa, ed., *Hozumi Yatsuka Hakushi Ron-*

bunshū [Collected works of Dr. Hozumi Yatsuka]. Tokyo: Yūhikaku, 1943.

Hyōdō Tsutomu. "Tekkō Kumiai no Seiritsu to Sono Hōkai—Nisshin Sensōgo ni Okeru Jūkōgyō no Rōshi Kankei" [The rise and fall of the Metalworkers' Union—Labor relations in heavy industry after the Sino-Japanese War], in three parts, *Keizaigaku Ronshū* (Tokyo University), 31, no. 4 (January 1966): 14–31; 32, no. 2 (July 1966): 89–113; and 32, no. 3 (October 1966): 63–94.

———. *Nihon ni Okeru Rōshi Kankei no Tenkai* [The development of labor relations in Japan]. Tokyo: Tokyo Daigaku Shuppankai, 1971.

Iida Kanae. *Igirisu Rōdō Undō no Seisei: Reimeiki no Rōdō Undō to Kakumeiteki Minshushugi* [The development of the British labor movement: The early labor movement and revolutionary democratism]. Tokyo: Yūhikaku, 1958.

Iijima Manji. *Nihon Bōseki Shi* [History of the Japanese Spinning Industry]. Tokyo: Sōgensha, 1949.

Ikeda Makoto. *Nihon Kikaikō Kumiai Seiritsu Shiron* [An historical treatise on the formation of the machinists' unions in Japan]. Tokyo: Nihon Hyōronsha, 1970.

———. "Takano Fusatarō to Shakai Seisaku Shisō" [Takano Fusatarō and the ideology of social policy]. *Shakai Kagaku Ronshū* (Saitama University), no. 30 (March 1972): 154–182.

———. "Nisshin Sensō-go no Shakai Seisaku Shisō" [Social policy ideology after the Sino-Japanese War]. *Shakai Kagaku Ronshū* (Saitama University), no. 31 (January 1973): 27–82.

Inegaki Yasuhiro, Kawamura Zenjirō, Murai Masuo, and Amagasu Ken. *Nihon Shi* [Japanese history]. Tokyo: Sanshōdō, 1979.

Ishida Rokujirō. "Taigū Kisei Dōmeikai Ichinoseki Shibu Kiji" [The story of the Ichinoseki branch of the Treatment Improvement Association]. 1898. In Rōdō Undō Shiryō Iinkai, ed., *Nihon Rōdō Undō Shiryō*, vol. 2: 16–38. 1963.

Ishikawa Kyokuzan and Kōtoku Shūsui. "Nihon Shakaishugi Shi" [The history of Japanese socialism], serially in *Heimin Shimbun*, nos. 2–7, 9–14, 17–19, 25, 29–30, 36–37, 46–57 (January–March 1907). Reprinted in Kishimoto Eitarō, ed., *Meiji Shakaishugi Shiron* [A treatise on the history of socialism in the Meiji period], 9–84. Tokyo: Aoki Shoten, 1955.

Itō Tadajirō. "Naigai Sekitan no Gaikyō" [General view of coal production]. *Nihon Kōgyō Kaishi 5*, no. 47 (February 1890): 6–24.

Kanai En. "Kanai En Shi no Shakaishugi" [The socialism of Kanai En]. *Rōdō Sekai*, no. 44 (October 15, 1899): 4–5.

Katayama Sen. "Dōmei Hikō wo Ronzu" [On strikes]. *Rōdō Sekai*, no. 8 (March 15, 1898): 2.

———. "Katayama Sen Shi no Shakaishugi" [The socialism of Katayama Sen]. *Rōdō Sekai*, no. 44 (October 15, 1899): 4.

————. "Kongo no Rōdō Undō" [The future labor movement]. *Rikugō Zasshi*, no. 225 (September 1899): 10–18.

————. "Nihon ni Okeru Rōdō" [Labor in Japan]. *Shakai* 1, no. 5 (July 1899): 33–43.

————. "Aida Kichigorō ni Tou" [Questions to Aida Kichigorō]. *Rōdō Seikai*, no. 67 (September 1, 1900): 3–4.

————. "Nijū Seiki ni Okeru Rōdō Undō no Hōshin" [The policy of the labor movement in the twentieth century]. *Rōdō Sekai*, no. 69 (January 1, 1901): 2–3.

————. *Jiden* [Autobiography]. Tokyo: Iwanami Shoten, 1954.

————. *Waga Kaisō* [My recollections], vol. 1. Tokyo: Tokuma Shoten, 1967.

Katayama Sen and Nishikawa Mitsujirō. *Nihon no Rōdō Undō* [The Japanese labor movement]. 1901. Reprinted. Tokyo: Iwanami Shoten, 1952.

Katō Hirō. "Kōsaku Kikai Kōgyō no Kōzō to Kadai" [The structure and problems of the machine and manufacturing industries]. In Arisawa Hiromi, ed., *Gendai Nihon Sangyō Kōza* [Modern Japanese industry series], vol. 6: 307–402. Tokyo: Iwanami Shoten, 1960.

Katsu Masanori. *Nihon Zaisei Kaikaku Shi* [A history of the changes in Japanese taxation]. Tokyo: Chikura Shobō, 1948.

Kinugawa Taiichi. *Hompō Menshi Bōseki Shi* [History of cotton-spinning in Japan], vols. 2, 3, and 11. Osaka: Nihon Mengyō Kurabu, 1938–1939.

Kishimoto Eitarō. *Nihon Rōdō Undō Shi* [The history of the Japanese labor movement]. Tokyo: Kōbundō, 1953.

————. *Katayama Sen Tazoe Tetsuji Shū* [Collected works of Katayama Sen and Tazoe Tetsuji]. Tokyo: Aoki Shoten, 1955.

Kishimoto Eitarō, ed. *Meiji Shakai Undō Shisō* [The ideology of social movements in the Meiji period], two vols. Tokyo: Aoki Shoten, 1955.

————. *Meiji Shakaishugi Shiron* [A treatise on the history of socialism in the Meiji period]. Tokyo: Aoki Shoten, 1955.

Kobayashi Tango. *Kōjōhō to Rōdō Undō* [The factory law and the labor movement]. Tokyo: Aoki Shoten, 1965.

Komatsu Hirotake. *Nihon Gunji Kōgyō no Shiteki Bunseki* [Historical analysis of Japanese military industries]. Tokyo: Ocha no Mizu Shobō, 1972.

Komatsu Ryūji. "Waga Kuni ni Okeru Rōdō Kumiai Shisō no Seisei: Sakuma Teiichi to Takano Fusatarō wo Chūshin ni" [The formation of labor union ideology in Japan: Centering on Sakuma Teiichi and Takano Fusatarō]. In Institute of Management and Labor Studies, ed., *Management and Labor Studies Series*, no. 272: 131–181. Tokyo: Keiō University, 1969–1970.

————. *Kigyōbetsu Kumiai no Seisei* [The formation of enterprise unionism]. Tokyo: Ocha no Mizu Shobō, 1971.

————. *Shakai Seisaku Ron* [A treatise on social policy]. Tokyo: Aoki Shoin Shinsha, 1974.

Kublin, Hyman. *Meiji Rōdō Undō Shi no Hitokoma—Takano Fusatarō no Shō-gai to Shisō* [One aspect of the history of the Meiji period labor movement—The life and thought of Takano Fusatarō]. Tokyo: Yūhikaku, 1959.

Kyoto Daigaku Bungakubu Kokushi Kenkyūshitsu. *Nihon Kindai Shi Jiten* [Encyclopedia of modern Japanese history]. Tokyo: Tōyō Keizai Shinpōsha, 1958.

Levine, Solomon B. "Nihon ni Okeru Rōshi Kankei Kenkyū ni Kansuru Hitotsu no Kōsatsu" [An assessment of industrial relations research by Japanese scholars]. *Nihon Rōdō Kyōkai Zasshi* 17, nos. 11–12 (combined issue) (November and December 1975): 4–13.

Matsushima Shizuo. *Rōdō Shakaigaku Josetsu* [An introduction to labor sociology]. Tokyo: Fukumura Shoten, 1951.

Mayett, P. "Nihon Nōmin no Hihei Oyobi Sono Kyūji Saku" [The grief of the Japanese farmers and policies to relieve it]. 1893. In Takimoto Seiichi and Mukai Shikamatsu, eds., *Nihon Sangyō Shiryō Taikei* [General data on Japanese industry], vol. 2: 323–522. Tokyo: Naigaishōgyō Shinpōsha, 1926.

Meiji Shiryō Kenkyū Renrakukai, ed. *Meiji Zenki no Rōdō Mondai* [Labor problems in the early Meiji period]. In the Meiji-shi Kenkyū Gyōsho series, second period, supplemental vol. 1. Tokyo: Ocha no Mizu Shobō, 1960.

Mizuno Gorō. "Horonai Tankō no Kan'ei to Sono Haraisage" [The government operation and sale of the Horonai mine]. *Keizaigaku Kenkyū* (Hokkaidō University) 9 (1955): 65–119.

Mizunuma Tatsuo. "Insatsukō Rōdō Undō Shi" [The history of the labor movement of the printers], *Jiyū Rengō Shimbun*, no. 27 (September 1, 1928): 2; no. 29 (November 1, 1928): 3; no. 30 (December 1, 1928): 3; no. 31 (January 1, 1929): 3; no. 32 (February 1, 1929): 3; no. 33 (March 1, 1929): 2; no. 34 (April 1, 1929): 3; no. 36 (June 1, 1929): 3; and no. 37 (July 1, 1929): 2.

Mombushō. *Nihon no Kyōiku Tōkei: Meiji—Shōwa* [Education statistics of Japan from the Meiji era to the Shōwa era]. Tokyo: Mombushō, 1971.

Moriyasu Kichirō. *Sanshigyō Shihonshugi Shi* [The history of capitalism in the silk industry]. Tokyo: Moriyama Shoten, 1931.

Murayama Shigetada. *Nihon Rōdō Sōgi Shi Gaikan* [Overview of the history of Japanese labor disputes]. Tokyo: Dōkai Hakkō, 1930.

———. *Nihon Rōdō Sōgi Shi* [History of Japanese labor disputes]. Tokyo: Tokyo Kasumigaseki Shobō, 1946.

Naimushō Sōmu Kyoku [Bureau of Administration, Home Ministry]. *Nihon Teikoku Kokusei Ippan* [All about imperial Japan], no. 10. Tokyo: Naimushō Sōmu Kyoku, 1891.

Namiki Masayoshi. *Nōson wa Kawaru* [The changing farm villages]. Tokyo: Iwanami Shoten, 1960.

Nihon Kōgakukai. *Meiji Kōgyō Shi: Zōsen Hen* [History of industry in the Meiji period: Shipbuilding edition]. Tokyo: Nihon Kōgakukai, 1925.

————. *Meiji Kōgyō Shi: Tetsudō Hen* [History of industry in the Meiji period: Railroad edition]. Tokyo: Nihon Kōgakukai, 1926.

————. *Meiji Kōgyō Shi: Kahei-hen Tekkō-hen* [The history of industry in the Meiji period: Armaments and steel edition]. Tokyo: Nihon Kōgakukai, 1929.

————. *Meiji Kōgyō Shi: Kōgyō Hen* [History of industry in the Meiji period: Mining edition]. Tokyo: Nihon Kōgakukai, 1930.

————. *Meiji Kōgyō Shi: Kikai Hen Chigaku Hen* [History of industry in the Meiji period: Machinery and geology edition]. Tokyo: Nihon Kōgakukai, 1931.

Nihon Rōdō Undō Shiryō. *See* Rōdō Undō Shiryō Iinkai, ed.

Nishida Nagatoshi. "Takano Fusatarō Rōdō Mondai Ronshū" [The collected works of Takano Fusatarō on labor problems]. In Meiji Bunka Kenkyū-kai, ed., *Meiji Bunka Zenshū* [Collected materials on Meiji period culture] 15: 361–379. Tokyo: Nihon Hyōronsha, 1955.

Nishikawa Shunsaku. *Chiiki Kan Rōdō Idō to Rōdō Shijō* [The labor market and inter-district labor mobility]. Tokyo: Keiō Gijuku Daigaku Shōgakukai, 1966.

Nōshōmushō [Ministry of Agriculture and Commerce]. "Kōgyō Iken [View of industry]. 1884. In Tsuchiya Takao and Ōuchi Hyōei, *Meiji Zenki Zaisei Keizai Shiryō Shūsei* [Collected documents on economics and finance in the early Meiji period], vols. 18–20. Tokyo: Meiji Bunken Shiryō Kankō-kai, 1963–1965.

————. "Meiji Jūhachinen Kōgyō Gaikyō" [Overview of industry in 1885]. In *Meiji Jūshichinen Dō Jūhachinen Nōshōkō Gaikyō* [Overview of agriculture, commerce and industry in 1884 and 1885]. Tokyo: Nōshōmushō, 1885. Published in *Nōshōkō Kōhō Gogai* in Tsuchiya Takao, ed., *Gendai Nihon Kōgyō Shi Shiryō* [Documents on the history of modern Japanese industry], vol. 1: 215–436. Tokyo: Rōdō Bunkasha, 1949.

Nōshōmushō Shōkō Kyoku [Bureau of Commerce and Industry, Ministry of Agriculture and Commerce]. *Shokukō Jijō* [The condition of industrial workers], 1903. Reprinted in three vols. Tsuchiya Takao, ed. Tokyo: Seikatsusha, 1947.

Oka Yoshitake. *Kindai Nihon no Kensei* [The formation of modern Japan]. Tokyo: Kōbundō, 1949.

Ōkawa Kazushi, Shinohara Miyōei, and Umemura Mataji. *Chōki Keizai Tōkei* [Estimates of long-term economic statistics of Japan since 1868], vol. 12 [Railroad and electric utilities]. Tokyo: Tōyō Keizai Shinpōsha, 1965.

Ōkōchi Kazuo. *Shakai Seisaku Genri* [The basis of social policy]. Tokyo: Keisō Shobō, 1951.

————. *Reimeiki no Nihon Rōdō Undō* [The early Japanese labor movement]. Tokyo: Iwanami Shoten, 1952.

————. "Nihonteki Rōshi Kankei to Sono Dentō" [Traditionalism in Japanese labor relations]. *Keizaigaku Ronshuu* (Tokyo University) 29, no. 1 (April 1963): 1–13.

Ōkōchi Kazuo and Matsuo Hiroshi. *Nihon Rōdō Kumiai Monogatari, Meiji* [The tale of the Japanese trade unions], vol. 1. Tokyo: Chikuma Shobō, 1965.

Ōkurashō. "Kōbunshō Enkaku Hōkoku" [Report on the history of the Department of Industry]. 1888. In Tsuchiya Takao and Ōuchi Hyōei, eds., *Meiji Zenki Zaisei Keizai Shiryō Shūsei* 17: 3–503. 1931.

Ōkurashō Kokusai Kyoku. *Zokuroku Shobunroku* [Record of the Delimination of the samurai stipends]. Tokyo: Ōkurashō Kokusai Kyoku, 1882. In Tsuchiya Takao and Ōuchi Hyōei, eds., *Meiji Zenki Zaisei Keizai Shiryō Shūsei* 8: 1–268. 1933.

Ono Takeo. *Nōson Shi* [A history of the agricultural village]. Tokyo: Genmatsu-dō Shoten, 1941.

Osatake Takeshi. *Meiji Seiji Shi Tembyō* [Sketches in Meiji political history]. Tokyo: Ikuseisha, 1938.
————. *Nihon Kensei Shi Taimō* [An outline of Japanese constitutional history], vol. 2. Tokyo: Nihon Hyōronsha, 1939.
————. *Nihon Kensei Shi no Kenkyū* [A study of Japanese constitutional history]. Tokyo: Ichigensha, 1943.

Ōshima Kiyoshi. "Takano Fusatarō to Rōdō Kumiai no Tanjō" [Takano Fusatarō and the birth of the labor unions]. In Ōkōchi Kazuo and Ōtaku Shoichi, eds., *Kindai Nihon wo Tsukutta Hyakunin* [The hundred people who made modern Japan], vol. 1: 378–385. Tokyo: Mainichi Shinbunsha, 1965.
————. "Rōdō Kumiai no Soshisha—Takano Fusatarō" [Takano Fusatarō— Founder of labor unions]. *Sekai*, no. 277 (December 1968): 208–218.
————. *Takano Iwasaburō Den* [A biography of Takano Iwasaburō]. Tokyo: Iwanami Shoten, 1968.
————. *Hito ni Kokorozashi Ari* [Man Is Ambitious]. Tokyo: Iwanami Shoten, 1974.

Ōtsu Jun'ichirō. *Dai Nihon Kensei Shi* [A constitutional history of greater Japan], vols. 1–4. Tokyo: Hōbunkan, 1927.

Ōyama Shikitarō. *Kōgyō Rōdō to Oyakata Seido* [Mine labor and the *oyakata* system]. Tokyo: Yūhikaku, 1964.

Rōdō Kumiai Keiseikai. *Kōjōhōan ni Taisuru Ikensho* [Opinion with respect to the proposed factory law]. October 1898. In Rōdō Undō Shiryō Iinkai, ed., *Nihon Rōdō Undō Shiryō*, vol. 1: 415. 1962.

Rōdō Undō Shiryō Iinkai, ed. *Nihon Rōdō Undō Shiryō* [Collected documents on the Japanese labor movement], vols. 1–3. Tokyo: Rōdō Undō Shiryō Kankō Iinkai, 1962–1968.

Royama Masamichi. *Seiji Shi* [Political history]. *Gendai Nihon Bunmei Shi* [History of contemporary Japanese civilization series]. Tokyo: Tōyō Keizai Shimpōsha, 1940.

Royama Masamichi, ed. *Musan Seitō Ron* [Treatises on proletarian parties], vol. 11 of *Gendai Seijigaku Zenshū* [Collected works on modern political science]. Tokyo: Nihon Hyōronsha, 1930.

Saitama. See Saitama-Ken Rōdōbu Rōseika.

Saitama-Ken Rōdōbu Rōseika. *Saitama-Ken Rōdō Undō Shi* [History of the labor movement in Saitama Prefecture], prewar vol. Tokyo: Saitama-Ken Rōdōbu Rōseika, 1965.

Sekiyama Naotarō. *Nihon Jinkōshi* [History of Japanese population]. Tokyo: Shikai Shobō, 1942.

Shimoide Shunkichi. *Meiji Shakai Shisō Kenkyū* [Studies in Meiji period social thought]. Tokyo: Asano Shoten, 1932.

Shisō Hattori, ed. *Kindai Nihon Jimbutsu Keizaishi* [A biographical economic history of modern Japan]. Tokyo: Tōyō Keizai Shimpōsha, 1955.

Shōji Kinnosuke. "Nittetsu Kikangata—Shokukō Dōmei Higyō no Igi" [The engineers of the Japan Railway Company—The significance of the strike]. *Shōgaku Ronshū* 36, no. 4 (March 1968): 76–126.

Shokukō Jijō. See Nōshōmushō Shōkō Kyoku.

Sōrifu Tōkeikyoku Hen [Bureau of Statistics, Office of the Prime Minister], ed. *Dai Nanakai Nihon Tōkei Nenkan* [Seventh annual statistical handbook of Japan]. Tokyo: Sōrifu Tōkeikyoku, 1955.

Sumiya Etsuji. *Nihon Keizaigaku Shi no Hitokoma: Shakai Seisaku Gakukai wo Chūshin to Shite* [One aspect of the history of Japanese economics study —centering on the Social Policy School]. Tokyo: Nihon Hyōronsha, 1948.

Sumiya Mikio. *Nihon Chin Rōdō Shiron* [An historical treatise on Japanese wage labor]. Tokyo: Tokyo Daigaku Shuppankai, 1955.

———. *Katayama Sen.* Tokyo: Tokyo Daigaku Shuppankai, 1960.

———. "Naya Seido no Seiritsu to Hōkai" [The rise and fall of the *Naya* system]. *Shisō* no. 434 (August 1960): 102–112.

———. "Takano Fusatarō to Rōdō Undō—Gompers to no Kankei wo Chūshin ni" [Takano Fusatarō and the labor movement—Centering on his relationship with Gompers]. *Keizaigaku Ronshū* (Tokyo University) 29, no. 1 (April 1963): 63–82.

———. "Meiji Zenki Sekitan Shijō no Kōzō" [The structure of the coal market in the early Meiji period]. *Keizaigaku Ronshū* (Tokyo University) 31, no. 1 (April 1965): 9–22.

———. *Nihon Rōdō Undō Shi* [Japanese labor movement history]. Tokyo: Yūshindō, 1966.

———. *Nihon Shokugyō Kunren Hattatsu Shi* [The history of the development of occupational training in Japan], vol. 1. Tokyo: Nihon Rōdō Kyōkai, 1970.

Sumiya Mikio, Kobayashi Ken'ichi, and Hyōdō Tsutomu. *Nihon Shihonshugi to Rōdō Mondai* [Japanese capitalism and labor problems]. Tokyo: Tokyo Daigaku Shuppankai, 1967.

Suzuki Bunji. *Rōdō Undō Nijū-nen* [Twenty years of the labor movement]. Tokyo: Sōdōmei Gojū Nenshi Kankō Iinkai, 1931.

Suzuki Jun'ichirō. "Waga Kuni ni Okeru Dōmei Hikō no Senrei" [The precedents of concerted work stoppages in our country]. In *Kokuka Gakukai Zasshi* no. 116 (October 1896): 1127–1145.

Suzuki Kōichirō, ed. *Kappa no He* [Winds of whimsy]. Tokyo: Hōsei Daigaku Shuppankyoku, 1961.

Suzuki Yasuzō. *Jiyūminken Kempō Happu* [Civil rights and the promulgation of the constitution]. In *Kindai Nihon Rekishi Kōza* [Modern Japanese history series]. Tokyo: Hakuyōsha, 1939.

Tajima Kinji. *Nihon Genji no Shakai Mondai* [Current social problems in Japan]. Tokyo: Shūeisha, 1897.

Takahashi Kamekichi. *Nihon Kindai Keizai Keisei Shi* [The history of the formation of the modern Japanese economy], vol. 2. Tokyo: Tōyō Keizai Shimpōsha, 1968.

Takahashi Keizai Kenkyūjo. *Nihon Sanshigyō Hattatsu Shi* [The history of the development of the Japanese silk industry], vol. 1. Tokyo: Seikatsusha, 1941.

Takano Iwasaburō. "Torawaretaru Minshū" [The captured people]. *Shinsei* 2, no. 2 (February 1946): 2–6.

Teishin Shō. *Tsūshin Jigyō Gojū Nenshi* [The fifty year history of communications]. Tokyo: Teishin Shō, 1921.

Tōkeikyoku [Bureau of Statistics]. *Nihon Teikoku Tōkei Nenkan* [Imperial Japanese statistical yearbook], nos. 1–19. Tokyo: Tōkeikyoku, 1882–1900.

———. *Nihon Teikoku Tōkei Zensho* [A volume of complete statistics on imperial Japan]. Tokyo: Tōkeikyoku, 1902.

Toyohara Matao. *Sakuma Teiichi Shoden* [The biography of Sakuma Teiichi]. Tokyo: Shūeisha, 1904. Reprinted 1932.

Tōyō Keizai Shimpōsha, ed. *Meiji Taishō Kokusei Sōran* [All about Japan in the Meiji and Taishō eras]. Tokyo: Tōyō Keizai Shimpōsha, 1927.

Tsuchiya Takao. *Zoku Nihon Keizaishi Gaiyō* [Overview of Japanese economic history, continued]. Tokyo: Iwanami Shoten, 1953.

Tsuchiya Takao and Okazaki Saburō. *Nihon Shihonshugi Hattatsu Shi Gaisetsu* [An outline history of Japanese capitalist development]. Tokyo: Yūhikaku, 1948.

Tsuchiya Takao and Ōuchi Hyōei, eds. *Meiji Zenki Zaisei Keizai Shiryō Shūsei* [Collected documents on economics and finance in the early Meiji period], 21 vols. Tokyo: Kaizōsha, 1931–1936.

Tsuda Masumi. *America Rōdō Kumiai no Kōzō* [The structure of American unions]. Tokyo: Nihon Hyōronsha, 1967.

———. *Nenkōteki Rōshi Kankei Ron* [A treatise on nenkō-type labor relations]. Kyoto: Minerva Shobō, 1968.

Umemura Mataji. "Sangyōbetsu Koyō no Hendō 1800–1940" [Change in employment by industry: 1800–1940]. *Keizai Kenkyū* [Hitotsubashi University], 24, no. 2 (April 1973).

Watanabe Kango. *Nihon Shakai Undō Shi* [The history of Japanese social movements]. Tokyo: Tachibana Shobō, 1955.

Watanabe Tōru. "Meiji Zenki no Rōdō Shijō Keisei wo Megutte" [On the structure of the labor market in the early Meiji period]. In Meiji Shiryō Kenkyū Renrakukai, ed., *Meiji Zenki no Rōdō Mondai,* Meiji-shi Kenkyū Gyōsho series, second period, supplemental vol. a, 96–136. 1960.

Yagi Ayao. *Meiji no Kure Oyobi Kure Kaigun* [The Navy at Kure and Kure in the Meiji period]. Tokyo: Kure Zōsensho, 1957.

Yajima Tahachi. *Kairaku Sangyō Sōdan* [Interesting tales of industry]. Tokyo: Shūeisha, 1909.

Yamamoto Itsuji. "Tomioka Seishijo Setsuritsu to Shoki no Jōtai" [The establishment and early condition of the Tomioka silk mill]. *Rekishigaku Kenkyuu* 6, no. 11 (November 1936): 2–38.

Yamamoto Shirō. "Meiji Zenki no Kōzan Rōdō Oyobi Rōdō Undō" [Mining labor and the labor movement in the early Meiji period]. In Meiji Shiryō Kenkyū Renrakukai, ed., *Meiji Zenki no Rōdō Mondai,* Meiji-shi Kenkyū Gyōsho series, second period, supplemental vol. 1: 177–230. 1960.

Yasui Jirō. *Sen'i Rōshi Kankei no Shiteki Bunseki* [Historical analysis of labor relations in textiles]. Tokyo: Ocha no Mizu Shobō, 1967.

Yokoi Tokifuyu. *Nihon Kōgyō Shi* [History of Japanese industry]. Tokyo: Kaizōsha, 1927.

Yokosuka Kaigun Senshō. *Yokosuka Kaigun Senshō Shi* [History of the Yokosuka Navy shipyards], vol. 1. Tokyo: Yokosuka Kaigun Senshō, 1915. In *Meiji Zenki Sangyō Hattatsu Shiryō* [Historical documents on the development of industry in the early Meiji period], vol. 8. Tokyo: Meiji Bunken Shiryō Kankōkai, 1966.

Yokoyama Gennosuke. "Tekkō Kumiai Seiritsu wo Yorokobu" [The fortunate founding of the metalworkers' union]. *Mainichi Shimbun* (December 4, 1897). In Rōdō Undō Shiryō Iinkai, ed., *Nihon Rōdō Undō Shiryō,* vol. 1: 473–474. 1962.

———. *Nihon no Kasō Shakai* [Japanese lower-class society]. 1898. In Sumiya Mikio, ed., *Yokoyama Gennosuke Zenshū* [The collected works of Yokoyama Gennosuke], 1–339. Tokyo: Meiji Bunken, 1972.

———. "Rōdō Undō no Shomaku" [The birth of the labor movement]. *Chūō Kōron* 14, no. 8 (August 1899): 5–12.

————. [Tenshō Bōbōsei, pseud.] "Takano Fusatarō wo Omou" [Thinking of Takano Fusatarō]. *Tōyō Dōtetsu Zasshi* 1, no. 1 (June 1904).

————. "Tokyo no Kōjōchi Oyobi Kōjō Seikatsu no Panorama" [The panorama of the Tokyo factory districts and factory life]. *Shinkōron* (September 1910). Reprinted in Rōdō Undō Shiryō Iinkai, ed., *Nihon Rōdō Shiryō*, vol. 3: 11–16. 1968.

Works by Takano Fusatarō

"Hoku Bei Gasshūkoku no Rōeki Shakai no Arisama wo Josu" [On American working-class society]. *Yomiuri Shimbun*, 1890, no. 4651 (May 31); no. 4658 (June 7); no. 4661, supplement (June 10); no. 4664, supplement (June 13); no. 4669 (June 18); no. 4670 (June 19); no. 4674 (June 23); no. 4675 (June 24); no. 4676 (June 25); no. 4677 (June 26); and no. 4678, supplement (June 27). In Hyman Kublin, *Meiji Rōdō Undō Shi no Hitokoma*, 65–87. 1959.

"Nihon ni Okeru Rōdō Mondai" [Labor problems in Japan]. *Yomiuri Shimbun*, 1891, no. 5084 (August 7); no. 5085 (August 8); no. 5086 (August 9); and no. 5087 (August 10). In Hyman Kublin, *Meiji Rōdō Undō Shi no Hitokima*, 88–95. 1959.

"Kanai Hakase Oyobi Soeda Gakushi ni Teisu" [To Professor Kanai and Scholar Soeda]. *Kokumin Shimbun* no. 717 (May 20, 1892). In Hyman Kublin, *Meiji Rōdō Undō Shi no Hitokoma*, 96–99. 1959.

" 'Aikoku' Kisha ni Tsugu—Rōdō Mondai no Ittan" [To the "patriotic" journalist —One aspect of labor problems]. *Ensei*, 1892, no. 19 (November 1) and no. 20 (November 15). In Hyman Kublin, *Meiji Rōdō Undō Shi no Hitokoma*, 100–104. 1959.

"Fukoku no Saku wo Ronjite Nihon ni Okeru Rōdō Mondai ni Oyobu" [The policy of a wealthy nation and its effects on Japanese labor problems]. *Tokyo Keizai Zasshi*, 1893, no. 661 (February 11) and no. 662 (February 18). In Hyman Kublin, *Meiji Rōdō Undō Shi no Hitokoma*, 105–113. 1959.

"Labor Movement in Japan." *American Federationist* 1, no. 8 (October 1894): 163–166.

"The War and Labor in Japan." *Social Economist* 9 (July 1895): 30–33.

"The Japanese Workers' Condition." *American Federationist* 2, no. 7 (September 1895): 119–120.

"Chinese Tailors' Strike in Shanghai." *American Federationist* 3, no. 1 (March 1896): 5–6.

"Labor Problem in Japan." *Taiyō* 2, no. 14 (July 15, 1896): 73–78.

"Typical Japanese Workers." *Far East* 2, no. 4 (April 20, 1897): 168–173.

"Nihon ni Okeru Rōdō Mondai" [Labor problems in Japan]. *Shakai Zasshi* 1, no. 2 (May 15, 1897): 1–6.

"Our Organizer in Japan." *American Federationist* 4, no. 4 (June 1897): 77–78.

"Strikes in Japan." *Far East* 2, no. 6 (June 20, 1897): 235–239.

"Jisatsuteki Nihon no Kōgyō" [Suicidal Japanese industry]. *Shakai Zasshi* 1, no. 4 (July 15, 1897): 9–11.

"A Remarkable Strike in Japan." *American Federationist* 4, no. 7 (September 1897): 144–145.

"From Our Organizer in Japan." *American Federationist* 4, no. 8 (October 1897): 196–197.

"Prospects of the Japanese Labor Movement." *American Federationist* 4, no. 9 (November 1897): 210–211.

"Female Labor in Japan." *American Federationist* 4, no. 10 (December 1897): 231–232.

"Proposed Factory Act in Japan." *American Federationist* 4, no. 11 (January 1898): 250–252.

"A New Trade Union in Japan." *American Federationist* 4, no. 12 (February 1898): 272–273.

"Experience of a Labor Agitator in Japan." *American Federationist* 5, no. 1 (March 1898): 3–4.

"Strike in Japan." *American Federationist* 5, no. 2 (April 1898): 31–32.

"Great Railway Strike in Japan." *American Federationist* 5, no. 3 (May 1898): 48–50.

"Labor Notes from Japan." *American Federationist* 5, no. 6 (August 1898): 118–119.

"Life Condition of Japanese Workers." *American Federationist* 5, no. 7 (September 1898): 133–135.

"Street Car Service in Tokyo." *American Federationist* 5, no. 8 (October 1898): 255–257.

"Japanese Farmers." *American Federationist* 5, no. 9 (November 1898): 174–175.

"Factory Legislation in Japan." *American Federationist* 5, no. 10 (December 1898): 200–201.

"Japanese Factory Legislation." *American Federationist* 5, no. 11 (January 1899): 216.

"Rōdō Kumiai Kisei Kwai." *American Federationist* 6, no. 8 (October 1899): 188–189.

INDEX

ABOUT THE AUTHOR

Stephen E. Marsland graduated from the New York State School of Industrial and Labor Relations at Cornell University, and holds an MBA from Harvard Business School. He first visited Japan as a Rotary Exchange Student in 1972. Later, he attended Keio University in Tokyo, and worked at Japan Steel Corporation in Tokyo and Kitakyushu. Marsland is the winner of numerous awards, including the Ford Foundation Scholarship for top first-year performance at Harvard. He is currently general manager at Viratec Tru Vue in Chicago.

Production Notes

This book was designed by Roger Eggers.
Composition and paging were done on the
Quadex Composing System and typesetting on
the Compugraphic 8400 by the design and
production staff of University of Hawaii Press.

The text typeface is Sabon and display typeface is Compugraphic Palatino.

Offset presswork and binding were done by
Vail-Ballou Press, Inc. Text paper is Glatfelter
Offset Vellum, basis 50.